The Lion Treasury of Saints

FOR MAJID

Text copyright © 2003 David Self
Illustrations copyright © 2003 Amanda Hall
(unless otherwise stated on p. 224)
This edition copyright © 2003 Lion Publishing

The moral rights of the author and illustrator
have been asserted

Published by
Lion Publishing plc
Mayfield House, 256 Banbury Road,
Oxford OX2 7DH, England
www.lion-publishing.co.uk
ISBN 0 7459 4471 X

First edition 2003
1 3 5 7 9 10 8 6 4 2 0

Acknowledgments
The author acknowledges the assistance he has received
from the Saint George Orthodox Information Service.
Please see p. 224 for further acknowledgments.

Typeset in 11/15 Arrus BT
Printed and bound in Singapore

The Lion
Treasury
of
SAINTS

David Self

LION
Children's Books

Contents

❧ ANDREW ❧

❧ PAUL ❧

CHRISTOPHER

NICHOLAS

🍂 HILDA OF WHITBY 🍂

🍂 FRANCIS OF ASSISI 🍂

IGNATIUS OF LOYOLA

TERESA OF CALCUTTA

MICHAEL

Introduction

WHAT IS A SAINT? The answer to that seems simple. A saint is a very good or holy person. After all, the word "saint" comes from a Latin word *sanctus* which means "holy."

But it's not as simple as that. By no means every saint was perfect. Some did things they became very ashamed of; things that were cruel or selfish. They were sinners as well as saints. So, as some people have asked, are saints simply sinners who kept on trying: trying to be good, trying to do what they believed God wanted them to do?

In some cases, that's part of it.

But the main thing about a saint is that God has given him or her a special gift, a gift of holiness. This might be the gift of loving God in a very special way or of being a good teacher or healer. It might be the gift of bravery or patience; the gift of wisdom or of being able to love those without friends or those in need. Whatever it is, we call this gift from God "grace."

So how do we decide whether a person has the gift of grace and should become known as a saint?

Not even that is simple.

Some Christians say that all true believers are saints. There is a lot of truth in this because Christians believe that every such believer has received grace from God. Other Christians, however, say the word "saint" should be given to a person only after they have died—and then only if they had lived a very good life.

For the first thousand years after the life of Jesus, there were different saints in different countries. This happened because, in each place, people told stories about the Christians they had known and respected. These much-loved Christians became known as "saints" in that district.

Then, about four or five hundred years ago, the Roman Catholic Church said that people should be remembered as saints only if they had been "canonized." Canonization involves important people in the church investigating if the person really had been very good and had done great things. If the answer is yes, the head of the Roman Catholic Church, the pope, "canonizes" the person and they are then known as "Saint." This process usually takes a long time and happens only after the death of the person being considered.

In the Eastern (or Orthodox) Church, a person is canonized by a group of local church leaders called bishops. Other churches have their own "holy heroes" or "saints."

And even in modern times, some holy people are thought of as "saintly" by ordinary people—simply because of they way they have lived their lives. One such person is Mother Teresa who was sometimes described as a saint, even before her death and even though she has not yet officially been made a saint.

So how have I chosen which "saints" (or "holy people") should appear in this book?

In the first place, I wanted to show that saints didn't all live in olden times; they weren't all men—and they lived and worked in countries all around the world. Most of all, they are people whose lives are still important to us today. They have become known as saints in many different ways but they are all saintly because, Christians believe, God has used them in special ways to do good in this world.

In the past, Christians always named a newborn baby after a saint. That saint became the baby's "patron saint," the saint who looked after him or her through their life. Many people celebrate their saint's day (or "name day") rather like an extra birthday. Countries also have their own patron saints. So too do jobs. The patron saint of England is Saint George. Bus drivers have Saint Christopher as their patron while Saint Gabriel is patron of all those who work on the telephone.

So secondly I have also included stories of popular patron saints like Christopher and George whose stories are no more than legends but who, even so, have inspired and been a comfort to people over the ages.

Thirdly, I have also included some stories of people from modern times and who have not been officially recognized by the church as saints. Maybe, one day, some of these will be named as saints.

But all of them have been respected and loved by Christians as holy people who have been given the gift of grace to do some special work in the steps of Jesus for God and for their fellow human beings. From their stories, there are valuable things to be learned; things that will help people live their lives in the way that Jesus taught. Their stories are stories that will bring people closer to God.

Each saint is remembered on a particular day of the year—though not always on the same day in all churches. Those dates are shown at the top of each story, and a fuller list is given in the calendar at the back of the book.

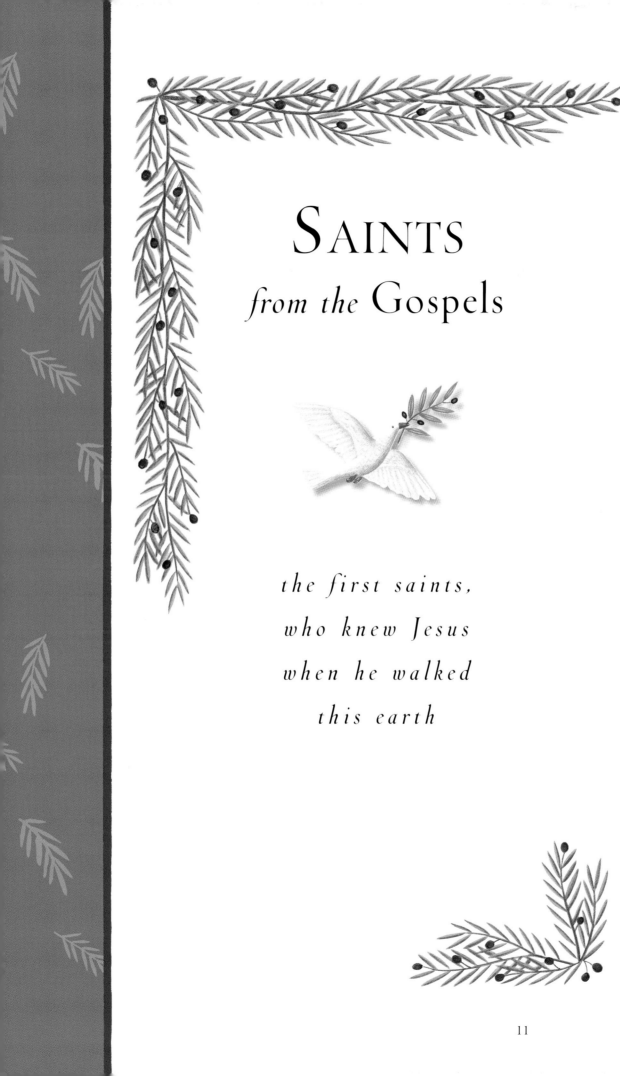

SAINTS
from the Gospels

the first saints,
who knew Jesus
when he walked
this earth

Mary

SAINT'S DAYS

Mary is remembered on
several days of the year:

2 FEBRUARY
The Presentation of
the Lord, or Mary's
Thanksgiving or
Purification after the
safe birth of Jesus

25 MARCH
The Annunciation, or
"announcing" by Gabriel
of the birth of Jesus—
nine months before his
birth at Christmas

15 AUGUST
The Assumption,
her entry into heaven
after her death

8 SEPTEMBER
Her birthday

8 DECEMBER
The Immaculate
Conception, or
the remembrance of
the belief of some
Christians that Mary
was born without sin

S HE WAS A TEENAGER. Engaged to be married to Joseph—a decent, hard-working guy. Now, as she worked in her mother's kitchen, she started daydreaming about their married life together. They would have their own house, there in Nazareth. He'd carry on his business as a carpenter. Things looked good. But then the angel turned up.

Though Mary had never seen one before, somehow she just knew this was an angel.

"Peace be with you," said the angel.

Mary was terrified.

"Don't be afraid," he said.

Easier said than done.

"The Lord God has blessed you," continued the angel, whose name was Gabriel. "You're going to become pregnant. You'll give birth to a son and you'll name him Jesus. People will say he is the Son of God. He'll be like a king and he'll reign for ever and ever."

Mary felt weak. "How can this be? Joseph and I aren't . . . we aren't married yet. I'm still a virgin."

"God's Holy Spirit will come upon you. God will be the father of your child. There's nothing God can't do."

And that is what happened. Everything that the angel had said came true. Mary became pregnant; Joseph stood by her; they got married. And when her time came, Mary gave birth to a boy. But not at home in Nazareth. It happened in Bethlehem, a faraway town. But, yes, they did name him Jesus, and later she went to the temple to make a thanksgiving for the birth of God's Son.

Like his foster father, Joseph, Jesus probably became a carpenter. He worked in Nazareth until he was about thirty. For the next three years he was to travel around the country, teaching, healing people who were ill, and doing all kinds of wonderful things.

And whatever he did, Mary was always there for him. When friends were married in a town named Cana, not far from Galilee, both Mary and Jesus were guests. Later, Mary went to Jerusalem with him for what was to be the week before his crucifixion. That week, she suffered the pain of seeing her own son after he had been beaten and tormented by the Roman soldiers. She had to watch him drag his heavy cross through the streets of Jerusalem, and she saw him hang on the cross until he died.

But when things seemed to be going so terribly, painfully wrong, she always had that secret in her heart, the message brought to her by the angel Gabriel—she had been chosen by God to be the mother of his Son. In those difficult times she could remember the words she'd said just after Gabriel had first brought her the news . . .

"My soul praises the Lord. My spirit is glad because God my Redeemer has thought of me, his lowly maid-servant. From now and for ever, all people will call me happy because of the great things God has done for me. His name is holy and his mercy is on all those who love him."

The angel Gabriel announces to Mary that she is to be the mother of Jesus.

OUR LADY

*F*rom the early days of the Christian faith, many followers of Jesus have believed that Mary remained a virgin all her life and speak of her as "Mary, ever Virgin" or the "Blessed Virgin Mary." But when Saint Mark told the story of Jesus' life and work, he mentioned a time Jesus returned home to Nazareth. The people all said, "Isn't he the carpenter, the son of Mary, and the brother of James, Joseph, Judas, and Simon? Aren't his sisters living here?" Some Christians say this means that Mary had several other children after Jesus. But the words "brother" and "sister" may simply be another way of saying "cousin."

In their prayers, some Christians (mainly Catholic and Orthodox) ask Mary to pray to God for them. They believe that because she was so close to Jesus, she can help in a special way. Many Christians think she is holy and respectfully refer to her as "Our Lady."

A lily, the symbol of purity, is often linked with the Virgin Mary.

Joseph, Joachim, Anne, Zechariah, and Elizabeth

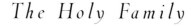

SAINTS' DAYS

19 MARCH
Joseph

1 MAY
Joseph the Worker

26 JULY
Joachim and Anne

5 NOVEMBER
Zechariah and Elizabeth

WHEN PEOPLE TALK of the "holy family" they usually mean Joseph, Mary, and Jesus. We know quite a lot about Mary, but what about Joseph and the other members of the family?

Joseph

Poor Joseph! It must have been so confusing for him. He was just about to wed Mary when he discovered she was pregnant, but he knew he wasn't the father of her baby.

He could have created a huge fuss, but he decided to leave her quietly so that there would be as little gossip as possible. Before he could do this, an angel appeared to him. "Joseph," said the angel, "don't be afraid to marry Mary. The son she is going to have has been given to her by the Holy Spirit of God. You will name him Jesus, and he will save people from their sins."

It was a lot for Joseph to take in. He was just an ordinary carpenter living in the town of Nazareth. What was all this to do with him? But soon he understood what he should do, and he did wed Mary.

When the Romans held a census to work out who had to pay taxes, Joseph took Mary to Bethlehem, which used to be his hometown. It was while they were there that Jesus was born. When Joseph realized the baby was in danger from the king, Herod, he took the family to safety in Egypt. Some time later, he took them to Nazareth.

Joseph and Mary hurry to Egypt to keep the baby Jesus safe from King Herod.

Joseph was still looking after his family when Jesus was twelve years old and the family went to Jerusalem. After that, no more is heard of him. When Jesus was being crucified, he looked down from the cross and told John, one of his disciples, to look after his mother. Many say that this shows that Joseph must have died and that Mary had become a widow.

It was a much later saint, Teresa of Avila, who encouraged Christians to remember Joseph in a special way. As late as 1933, the pope started a new festival on 1 May each year for "Joseph the Worker." This was perhaps because in Europe 1 May was becoming known as a day to remember and respect all workers.

Joachim and Anne

Mary was the mother of Jesus—but who were Jesus' grandparents? The Bible says that the name of Joseph's father was either Jacob or Heli, but there is no mention of Mary's parents.

Various stories have been told about them over the years. They are usually given the names of Joachim and Anne. Anne is often said to have been a wealthy woman, and Joachim is described as having been born in Nazareth.

Joseph was a carpenter. The tools of his trade have changed little in 2000 years.

It is also said that they had no children until they were quite old. Then, Joachim went into the desert to pray that they might have a child. Anne went to the temple and prayed for the same blessing.

An angel appeared to her and said, "Anne, the Lord God has heard your prayers and you shall indeed become pregnant and have a baby. You must name her Mary, and she will be spoken about all over the world."

An angel also appeared to Joachim and told him the good news. Nine months later, the baby was born. It is said that Joachim and Anne lived long enough to see the birth of Jesus, but that Joachim died just after seeing his grandson presented to God in the temple.

Zechariah and Elizabeth

Elizabeth was a much older relative of Mary—too old to have children. But six months before Mary became pregnant with Jesus, Elizabeth also became pregnant. At the same time, her husband, Zechariah, who was a priest, saw an angel who said the child should be named John. At that moment, Zechariah lost the power of speech.

When Elizabeth gave birth, everyone said the boy should be named Zechariah, like his father. But Elizabeth said he should be named John—and Zechariah wrote down the words "His name is John." Then, Zechariah was able to speak again. The boy grew up to be known as John the Baptist.

The entrance to the most holy part of the temple in Jerusalem. It was a rare privilege even for a priest such as Zechariah to enter.

6 JANUARY
People remember the visit
of the wise men to the
baby Jesus on the feast
of the Epiphany,
6 January.

23 JULY
The wise men are
sometimes celebrated
on this day.

*Ancient scriptures,
written on scrolls, said
that a new king would
one day be born in
Bethlehem. Scrolls
were sometimes stored
in clay jars.*

Gold, Frankincense, and Myrrh

The Wise Men

WHEN JESUS WAS BORN in Bethlehem in the land of Judea at the time that Herod was king, wise men came from the east to Jerusalem, asking, "Where is the one who is born to be king of the Jews? We have seen his star in the east and we have come to worship him."

This is how the Bible story of the wise men begins. It's easy to see why King Herod immediately became both worried and angry. If this newborn baby was to be king of the Jews, where did that leave him?

He asked his own priests to explain what these strangers meant. The priests told him that in ancient times it had been written that a new king would be born in Bethlehem. This wasn't what Herod wanted to hear. So he sent the wise men to Bethlehem to look for the newborn child. "When you've found him, bring me word. Then I can go and worship him too."

Not that he had any intention of doing that—but at least he would know where his new rival was.

So the wise men from the east left Jerusalem, still led by the same star that had guided them to Judea. When they reached the little town of Bethlehem, the star led them to where Jesus was, lying in a manger and being lovingly nursed by his mother, Mary. They unwrapped the presents they had brought the newborn child—gold, frankincense, and myrrh.

Having knelt down to worship Jesus, they left Judea to return to their own country—without going back to Herod. An angel had warned them in a dream that he meant no good to the newborn baby.

That's all the Bible says about the wise men. We don't even know how many of them there were. We've just guessed that there were three because they brought three presents. Very special presents. Gold was a sign that Jesus was a king. Frankincense is a kind of sweet-smelling gum. When it's burnt, it's a sign of holiness. So the gift of frankincense was a sign that people would one day worship Jesus. And myrrh? Well, that was a grim warning of death. For myrrh was an oil used in those days to anoint dead bodies as a kind of blessing. When mixed with wine, it also formed a painkilling drug and was sometimes given to those being crucified. The gift of myrrh was a sign that Jesus would suffer a terrible death.

A few hundred years later, Christians began to describe the wise men as kings. They certainly must have been rich and important people, and one of the psalms (the holy songs in the Bible) says, "The kings of Tarshish . . . shall offer gifts, the kings of Sheba (or, as we would now say, Arabia) and Saba (or Ethiopia, which is in Africa) shall bring gifts; all kings shall bow down before him." So the wise men became known as kings—three kings from the east (or Orient).

They also became known as "the Magi." "Magi" is the plural of the word "magus," which means a wise man or a person who is thought to see signs and meanings in the stars. The wise men are known as Magi because they saw the unusual star in the sky, which led them to Bethlehem.

There have been many attempts to explain what the star was. Some say it was a comet moving through the sky. Others say the light was caused by two stars or planets appearing to come close to each other. But in fact nowhere does the Bible say it was a bright star.

What is important about this story is that the wise men came to worship the newborn Jesus. By their journey and worship and by the gifts they brought, they showed that the birth, life, and death of Jesus would be important for people of all times, whatever their race and wherever they lived.

The wise men offer their gifts. Matthew's Gospel says that they found Mary, Joseph, and Jesus in a house, not a stable.

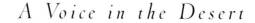

SAINT'S DAYS

24 JUNE

Most saints are remembered on the day they died, but John is remembered on his birthday. He was six months older than Jesus.

29 AUGUST

The beheading of John is remembered on this day.

John said that the one whom God was going to send was so much greater than him, he was not fit to untie his sandals.

A Voice in the Desert

John the Baptist

EVERYONE WANTED to see John—a weird man dressed in a simple tunic made out of camel's hair and tied with a leather belt round his waist. He lived in the desert, some way from Jerusalem and near the River Jordan.

As far as people could tell, he lived on honey and locusts, which are insects, a bit like grasshoppers, that are carried by the warm desert winds.

People came from all around, curious to see this man who looked as they imagined the prophets had looked in olden times. They also thought he might be the promised one, the Messiah whom God had said would one day come to save the people from all their troubles.

They didn't come just to look. They also came to listen.

"Give up your sinful ways. Be baptized and God will forgive you for all the wrongs you've done."

Many people were baptized by John. Once they'd said they were sorry for their sins, he would lead them into the River Jordan and lower them into the water for a moment as a sign that they wished their sins were washed away. But they knew this was not enough.

"What else must we do?" the people asked the man they knew as John the Baptist.

"Whoever has two shirts must give one away to a man who hasn't got one—and whoever has enough food must share it."

Some tax collectors came to be baptized. "Teacher," they asked, "what must we do?"

"Don't collect more tax than you're supposed to," John replied. That made the crowds smile because the tax collectors were famous for demanding more than they should.

Then some soldiers said, "What about us?"

"Don't make false accusations and don't take money from people by force. Be content with your pay."

All this made people wonder more and more if John was the Messiah they were waiting for. When John realized what they were saying, he immediately denied it.

"I baptize you with water but someone is coming who is much greater than I am. I'm not good enough even to undo his sandals. He will baptize you with God's Holy Spirit."

And indeed, very soon after this, Jesus came to be baptized by John. The two men had known each other when they were young because they were cousins. John now looked at Jesus and understood who he really was. He turned and spoke to the crowds. "This is the one I was talking about when I said someone was coming who'd be much greater than I am. I didn't know who it would be, but now I know."

John then turned to Jesus. "I ought to be baptized by you," he said.

"No," said Jesus. "You must baptize me because in that way we shall do what God wants." So John baptized Jesus in the River Jordan. As John lifted Jesus up out of the water, it seemed as if a light settled on Jesus, almost like a white dove coming down from the sky. Both John and Jesus believed that it was the Holy Spirit and that God was pleased with what had been done.

Ever since, John has been known as the "forerunner" of Jesus, the one who prepared the way for Jesus to begin his work on earth.

After John had baptized Jesus, he continued to preach in the desert. He also started speaking out against the local ruler, Herod Antipas (the son of Herod who had tried to kill the baby Jesus).

Herod had divorced his wife and married Herodias, who was both his niece and the wife of his half-brother Philip. John said that Herod was wrong to marry her, so Herod had John put in prison. He didn't dare have him killed because John was so popular, but Herodias wanted John dead.

She got her chance on the day of Herod's birthday. Herodias had her daughter, Salome, perform a dance for Herod. The way she did this so pleased Herod that he rashly said she could have whatever she wanted.

Salome and her mother had a whispered conversation.

"What should I ask for?" said Salome.

"The head of John the Baptist," Herodias replied.

Herod was very upset when he heard this. Even so, he sent a soldier to the prison. John was beheaded, and the soldier placed John's head on a tray and brought it back to Salome, who gave it to her mother.

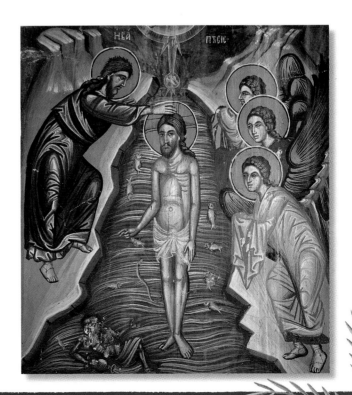

John baptized people in the River Jordan. When he baptized Jesus, a dove seemed to settle on Jesus.

SAINTS' DAYS

27 DECEMBER
John

1 MAY
Philip and James in the
Anglican Churches

3 MAY
Philip and James in the
Roman Catholic Church

29 JUNE
Simon, later named Peter

3 JULY
Thomas

25 JULY
James, son of Zebedee

24 AUGUST
Bartholomew

21 SEPTEMBER
Matthew

28 OCTOBER
Simon from Cana
and Thaddeus

30 NOVEMBER
Andrew

*Above: Two disciples
fish with nets.*

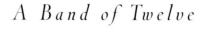

A Band of Twelve

Jesus' Disciples

"THE THING IS," said Simon, "we need a new boat."

"The thing is," said Andrew, "we can't afford a new boat."

Simon and Andrew were brothers, and they were both fishermen.

"What about James and John?" asked Simon. "They need a new boat."

James and John were also brothers and fishermen.

"If we joined up with them, we could afford a boat between us."

The four agreed and went to the local boat builder.

"I know the kind of boat you need," he said. "If you had a bit more money to spend, I'd make it all from oak. As it is, I'll also have to use some cheaper wood."

So he began building the boat, carefully making sure each piece of wood locked into the next one and hammering all the planking in place with

tough strong nails. At last, it was time to try it out.

The best time of day for catching fish was at night. So, in the late evening, they pushed their new boat onto the Sea of Galilee. They got in and rowed a little way out, then put up the sail and proudly sailed to where they thought they'd find the most fish. Then they took down the sail and threw their fishing nets into the sea.

Each net had floats sewn along the top to stop it sinking and little pieces of lead sewn along the bottom edge to make it hang down like a curtain in the water. Then, all they needed to do was wait for the fish to swim into the net. Early next morning, as it was getting light, they pulled the two ends of the net together and sailed back to the shore.

And that's what they did every night. Of course, their work wasn't over when they brought their catch ashore. They then had to sort and clean the fish and pack them in wooden barrels with salt to stop them going bad in the hot weather. Then the fish were sold and the money was divided among the four of them.

One day, when they were sorting out their nets, Jesus came to that place. He started teaching the people there about helping and loving each other and not arguing. More people came to listen and they all crowded around. He asked the four friends if he could get in their boat and if they'd row him a little way from the shore. Jesus then sat at one end of their boat and was able to talk to all the people without being jostled.

After he'd finished talking, he told the four fishermen to row farther out to the middle of the lake. "Now put out your nets," he said.

Simon wasn't eager. They'd been fishing all night and had caught very little. But Jesus convinced them, so they did what he said. They caught more fish than they'd ever caught before—even though it was daytime!

When they got back to the shore, Simon, Andrew, James, and John decided there really was something very special about this man Jesus. They made up their minds to give up being fishermen and go and travel with him from place to place, while he talked to people about looking after each other and about God's love.

We know that Simon and his brother Andrew and James and his brother John did become the first followers (or disciples) of Jesus. Many other men and women also became his followers, and from them Jesus chose twelve (including Simon, Andrew, James, and John) to be his special disciples.

But what happened to the boat? All we know is that in the year 1986, a boat just like theirs was dug out of the mud at the edge of the Sea of Galilee.

LOVE ONE ANOTHER

*J*esus told his disciples that they were not to try to be better than one another, but to find ways to serve one another. At the last meal he shared with them, he showed what that might mean by doing the work of a servant and washing their feet. This picture shows him washing the feet of Simon Peter, before sharing bread and wine with the Twelve.

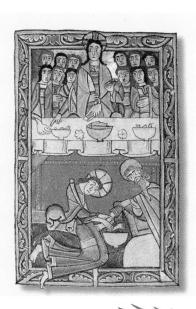

SAINT'S DAY

30 NOVEMBER

The First Disciple

Andrew

EVERYTHING SEEMED ordinary. An ordinary house near the Sea of Galilee. An ordinary family with two grown-up sons who were part of the family fishing business. But, in the end, nothing was ordinary for these brothers, Simon and Andrew.

John's Gospel tells us that Simon and Andrew were already followers of John the Baptist when they decided to leave everything and follow Jesus. This Gospel also says that Andrew met Jesus before Simon did. For this reason, Andrew is sometimes named "the first disciple."

Andrew is mentioned several times in the Gospel story. Along with his brother Simon and the brothers James and John, he seems to have been among the closest followers of Jesus.

One day, a huge crowd of people had followed Jesus out into a desert place to hear him speak. After many hours, it became clear that the people were hungry and had nothing to eat. Andrew noticed that one boy in the

Andrew played an important part in Jesus' miracle of feeding five thousand people with just two loaves and five fish. After the meal, the disciples gathered enough scraps to fill many baskets.

An ordinary house in Andrew's day, with fishing boats at the jetties beyond. Many daily activities took place in the courtyard or on the flat roof.

crowd had a basket containing five loaves and two fish. He brought him to Jesus, who blessed the food and shared it out among the thousands of people. Amazingly, everyone had enough to eat.

When Andrew and the others left their jobs as fishermen to become his disciples, Jesus said he would make them "fishers of men." After the end of Jesus' life on earth, Andrew (like the other disciples) started to travel widely, telling people all about Jesus. In this way Andrew became a "fisherman" for Jesus—"catching" people and bringing them good news.

One story suggests that Andrew visited a place named Patras in Achaia (an ancient name for the southern part of mainland Greece). There, Andrew persuaded the wife of an important Roman official named Egeas to become a Christian. Her name was Maximilla. The servant of her brother Stratocles also became a Christian.

This didn't please Egeas. He had Andrew beaten and thrown into prison. Then Egeas said that Andrew should be put to death by being crucified on the seashore.

When it came time for the crucifixion, Andrew wasn't nailed to the cross. He was simply tied to it, very tightly, by a rope.

He stayed alive for two days, preaching. More than two thousand people came to listen and many of them became Christians.

Eventually, Andrew became so weak he died. Maximilla and the servant of Stratocles came and took down his body, washed it lovingly, and buried it properly.

According to tradition, Andrew was crucified. Hundreds of years later, when people painted pictures of his last hours, they showed him tied to an X-shaped cross, known as a saltire cross. This may have been because in Greek the first letter of the word "Christ" is X (or "chi").

TO THE ENDS OF THE EARTH

*S*aint Regulus (also known as Saint Rule) lived in the fourth century and was once told in a dream to carry the remains (or relics) of Saint Andrew "to the ends of the earth." Along with a small group of friends, so the story goes, he journeyed from Greece to Scotland—a dangerous voyage in those days. They landed on the east coast of Scotland, built a church near to where they landed, and buried the relics of Saint Andrew under the church. The seaside city that now stands in that place is known as Saint Andrews.

Saint Regulus is remembered on 17 October.

The Taxman
Matthew

J UST SUPPOSE . . . for years, your family has lived in the same land. It's your country, your homeland. Then, without warning, a foreign army arrives. The soldiers are everywhere, issuing orders, seizing food and property, taking control. Your country is ruled by a foreign power.

They demand money—taxes. Taxes that have to be paid regularly to provide money for their army, for the foreign governor who's been sent to rule your country, and for a faraway emperor you've never seen.

So what would you think of the man who collects these taxes? Obviously he wouldn't be very popular. But suppose he was a local man who'd decided to work for the foreigners! Think how despised he'd be!

That's how it was in Galilee in the time of Jesus. The Romans had invaded the country and they used local Galileans to collect their taxes. They had a little booth in the marketplace to which you had to take your regular payment. And you only had the taxman's word about how much you owed. Many people were sure that these tax collectors were charging more than they should and were keeping the extra for themselves.

So unpopular were these taxmen that the local people thought they and their houses were "dirty." You never went near them if you could avoid it and you certainly didn't visit them at home.

There was one such collector in the town of Capernaum on the northwest coast of the Sea of Galilee, not far from where Andrew, Simon, James, and John had been fishermen. His name was Levi.

He'd heard about this new preacher and healer, Jesus. So he was curious when Jesus came past with his usual crowd of followers and people eager to see what he'd do and say. And when Jesus came close to Levi's tax booth, all he said was, "Follow me."

A purse of coins from the time of Jesus. Matthew was a tax collector, and people brought their coins to his booth in the marketplace.

Amazingly, that's what Levi did. He just got up, left the booth, left his valuable job and income, and followed Jesus. Plenty of the crowd thought this was extraordinary, not because Levi had given up the chance of wealth but because Jesus wanted such a person to be among his followers. But Jesus said, "I didn't come just to save good people. I came to help everyone."

Later, there was a supper at a tax collector's house. It may have been Levi's house. Several taxmen were there, and so were Jesus and his close friends. This caused a lot of gossip. "What sort of person would want to be seen with such terrible people?" "Why does Jesus want to eat in the house of a man who's betrayed his own country by working for the Romans?"

Jesus told them, "Those who are healthy don't need a doctor." By this he meant he had come to save wrongdoers, the ones most in need of his help.

Jesus gave Levi a new name to mark the start of his new life. He named him Matthew, which means "gift from God," and Matthew became one of his twelve closest followers. Matthew stayed with Jesus throughout the rest of the time that Jesus spent journeying around the country, and he was with him on his last journey to Jerusalem.

We're not sure what happened to Matthew after the Gospels say that Jesus returned to heaven. Many people believe that he journeyed far away, possibly to Ethiopia or Persia (modern-day Iran), in order to baptize people and to teach everyone he met that Jesus was with them always, until the end of time.

Saint Matthew is linked with the Gospel that bears his name, though scholars are not sure exactly who its author was.

John

Bread and grapes recall the bread and wine Jesus shared with his disciples at the Passover supper. John sat closest to Jesus at this special meal.

I WANT YOU TO GO and get everything ready for the Passover meal," said Jesus to Peter and John.

"Where do you want us to get it ready?" they asked. It was a good question.

For three years, Jesus and his disciples (including the Twelve he had specially chosen) had been going around Galilee. Now they had come to Jerusalem, to be there for the Passover festival when Jews have a special meal to remember their escape from slavery in Egypt. But although they were spending the week leading up to Passover in the city, they were staying with friends in a village named Bethany a few miles outside Jerusalem.

"As you go into the city, you'll meet a man carrying a water jar. Follow him to the house he goes into. He'll show you an upstairs room where you can get everything ready."

And that's exactly what happened. On the Thursday evening, Jesus and the twelve disciples met in that upstairs room for what was to be their last supper together. Nearest to him was John.

John, along with his brother James, was among the first of the disciples Jesus chose, and the two of them, together with Peter, seem to have been especially close to Jesus. Not only did Jesus ask John and Peter to do special jobs like finding the upper room, but he took the three of them with him on other special occasions.

Once, a man named Jairus had come to Jesus to ask him to cure his daughter who was seriously ill. By the time Jesus and his followers got to the house, they were told that the girl had died. Jesus reassured everyone that she was only sleeping.

The crowd that had gathered didn't believe him. He chose just three disciples to go with him into the girl's room where he woke her from the deep sleep she was in. Those three disciples were Peter, James—and John.

Another time, Jesus chose three disciples to go with him up a mountain where he showed himself to them in all his heavenly glory. Again the three chosen disciples were Peter, James—and John.

Of those three, there seems to have been something special about John. He was almost certainly the youngest of the Twelve (he may have been only a teenager at this time) and there is a possibility that he was a cousin of Jesus. This could explain why John is described as "the disciple Jesus loved" in the Gospel according to John.

John was incredibly loyal to Jesus. During the night following their last supper together, Jesus was arrested and put on trial before the high priest. John alone appears to have been brave enough to find his way into the court room. And, on the next day, when Jesus was hanging on the cross, the one disciple out of the Twelve who we know was there was young John. It was John whom Jesus asked to care for his mother.

After the Bible says that Jesus had returned to heaven, John and Peter worked together, spreading the message that Jesus had taught. It is said that John lived to be a very old man and that he alone of the Twelve was not killed but died naturally. Many believe he spent his last years in a place named Ephesus (in what is now Turkey). When he got too old to preach, and people still came to hear him, he would simply say, "Love one another. That is the Lord's command. If you do that, it is enough."

Jesus saw his mother standing at the foot of the cross and his friend John close by. He asked John to take care of his mother as a son should.

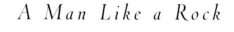

A Man Like a Rock

Simon Peter

"SO YOUR NAME'S Simon?" said Jesus.

"That's right," said Simon. "Simon bar Jonas" (which is Aramaic for "Simon, son of Jonas").

"I shall call you Kephas," said Jesus. He was speaking Aramaic and "kephas" was the word for "rock." When the Gospel story was written down, it was written in Greek. The Greek word for rock is "petra," so Simon became known as Petros or, in English, Peter.

It was a kind of nickname, as if Jesus was calling him "Rocky" because he was such a solid, dependable kind of guy.

Well, he was dependable in the end, but there was an important time when his courage seemed to fail. It was in the Garden of Gethsemane, the night before Jesus was crucified. Jesus and his twelve disciples had had their last supper together in the upper room. The disciple named Judas Iscariot, who was going to betray Jesus, had disappeared, but Jesus and the other eleven had gone to Gethsemane to be quiet.

"Stay here," he said to eight of them. Then he led Peter and James and John a little way off. "Keep watch while I pray."

"Of course," said Peter. "You can rely on me."

Jesus went on a little further alone and lay down to pray. When he came back, he found they'd fallen asleep. "Peter," he said sadly, "how is it that you couldn't keep watch even for one hour?"

This happened twice more. Each time Jesus went off to pray, Peter and the others failed to keep watch. The third time, Jesus came back to them just as the traitor Judas brought the temple guards to arrest Jesus. The disciples were completely outnumbered. Even so, Peter leaped to his feet, took out a sword he'd brought with him, and struck out at one of them—a slave named Malchus who served the high priest. In fact, Peter sliced off his ear. Immediately, Jesus stopped the fighting and healed Malchus's wound, but within minutes the guards had arrested Jesus and led him away.

Peter bravely followed, except he kept a safe distance behind.

Earlier, he had promised he would never betray Jesus: Jesus hadn't believed his promise and had said that before cockcrow the next morning, he'd have denied knowing him three times.

Jesus was led into the house of the high priest to be put on trial. Peter followed, but stayed in the courtyard. Three times that night, people

When Jesus was arrested, Peter struck out with a sword, but Jesus told him not to fight.

Judas betrayed Jesus to his enemies by greeting him with a kiss. Peter is shown on the left—he dared to stay close by, even though the other disciples all ran away.

asked if he was one of Jesus' followers or if he knew him. Three times, Peter panicked and denied knowing him. The third time he did this, he heard the cock crow.

Peter was heartbroken when he realized what he'd done.

Later that day, Jesus was crucified. John and several women followers of Jesus came to be near him as he suffered. No one knows where Peter was.

It was different the following Sunday, the first Easter Day. One of the women, Mary from Magdala, brought news to the disciples that the tomb in which Jesus' body had been buried was empty. Peter and John ran to the tomb. Not surprisingly, John (who was younger and fitter) got there first. He didn't dare go in, not knowing what he'd see.

As soon as Peter got there, he went straight in. He saw that the linen wrappings had been carefully folded. He went back to where the others were staying, amazed at what he'd seen.

It wasn't long before he understood. It wasn't long before he lost all his doubts and cowardice. It wasn't long before he was the leader of all the disciples, but that's another story (see page 40).

At the Last Supper, Jesus warned Peter that, before dawn, he would deny knowing him. When Peter heard the cock crow, he remembered Jesus' words and wept.

Simon of Cyrene and Veronica

SAINT'S DAY

Simon of Cyrene is not officially a saint and does not have a special day in his memory.

12 JULY
Veronica

The offical charge against Jesus was that he claimed to be king of the Jews. The soldiers who crucified him mocked him by forcing him to wear a crown made out of twisted thorn twigs.

IT'S JUST AN ORDINARY, narrow street like any other, but it's also one of the most special streets in all the world. It's in the northern part of the old city of Jerusalem and it's known as the Via Dolorosa, which means the "Way of Sorrows." People say it's the street along which Jesus had to carry his cross on the way to his crucifixion. It's often known as the "Way of the Cross."

In the time of Jesus, Jerusalem was ruled by the Romans, and according to Roman rule anyone who was condemned to death by crucifixion was made to walk through the city, carrying the crossbeam of the cross on which they would be crucified. (The tall, upright post would already be standing in the ground.)

What we now know as the Via Dolorosa may or may not be the exact "Way of the Cross," but it certainly starts at the Roman fortress where Jesus was put on trial before the governor, Pontius Pilate. There are fourteen special places along the route, at which Jesus may have stopped for a moment. These stopping places are sometimes described as the "stations of the cross."

The first station is the Roman fortress where Jesus was condemned to death. The second is where he was made to pick up the cross and start that final journey. The third station is where he fell for the first time, exhausted by the weight of the cross, and the fourth is a place where people believe his mother, Mary, spoke to him as he passed slowly by. By then he must have been weakened by the weight of the cross, sweating in the heat and bleeding from the flogging he'd received and from where a crown of thorns had been pressed onto his head by the soldiers.

Simon of Cyrene

Soon after this, Jesus stumbled again. The soldiers who were guarding him must have decided he was now too weak to carry the crossbeam. At a point now remembered as the fifth station of the cross, they seized a man in the crowds and made this stranger carry the cross the rest of the way to Golgotha, the place of crucifixion.

His name was Simon and he came from Cyrene in North Africa. Cyrene is now named Shahhat and is in Libya. Many Jews lived there, so Simon might have been a Jew who had come to Jerusalem for the Passover festival.

Mark explains in his Gospel that Simon was the father of Alexander and Rufus. The way Mark writes this suggests that all his readers knew who Alexander and Rufus were. So perhaps Simon and his sons all became followers of Jesus because of what happened that day.

The legend of Veronica says that, when she wiped Jesus' face with a cloth, his image remained on it.

Veronica

The sixth stop, or station, on the Way of the Cross is now marked by a small church named the Church of Saint Veronica.

A story is told that, in the time of Jesus, a middle-aged, quite wealthy lady lived in a house on this spot. As Jesus walked to his death, she came and wiped the sweat and blood from his face with a cloth.

By a miracle, says the story, his picture was printed on the cloth. Many people believe the cloth gained the power to heal people who were ill.

In a book named the Gospel of Nicodemus (which isn't part of the Bible) there is a passage that suggests this lady was the same person as "the woman with an issue of blood" (a woman who couldn't stop bleeding) whom Jesus had cured some time before. The Gospel of Nicodemus also says this person was named Bernice (or, in Greek, Berinika). We know her as Veronica.

We don't know for sure how much of this story is true, but its message of how a deed of kindness spreads goodness far and wide has encouraged Christians for many centuries.

VERNICLE

*I*n Saint Peter's Church in Rome, there is a cloth that's been kept there since the year 707. On this cloth are marks that look like the face of a man. This cloth is known as the "vernicle," a word made up of two other words—"vera," which means true, and "icon," which means image or picture. So "vernicle" means "true image."

A Rich Man

Joseph of Arimathea

JESUS DIED ON THE CROSS at about three o'clock on Friday afternoon. It was the sort of death the Romans kept for common criminals, such as the two thieves who were crucified at the same time as Jesus. And, since Jesus was being treated like a common criminal, it was likely that his body would now be thrown into a pit.

There was such a pit in the Kidron Valley, just a little way outside Jerusalem. His body might have been taken there very quickly for two reasons. One reason was that there was a Jewish law that said, "If a man has committed a crime punishable by death and he is put to death . . . you shall bury him the same day."

The other reason was that the Jewish holy day, the Sabbath, would begin at sunset, about six o'clock that evening. The Jews felt that their holy day should not be made "unclean" by leaving corpses unburied.

But all four Gospel writers say that a rich man named Joseph decided that things should turn out very differently.

He came from Arimathea, a town northwest of Jerusalem. He was a member of the Jewish council that had wanted Jesus put to death. The Gospels say that Joseph was "respected," that he was a "good and righteous" man, and also that he was "looking for the kingdom of God" and had been a follower of Jesus. So it seems he must have secretly disagreed with the other council members about having Jesus put to death.

A royal tomb from the time of Jesus. Although the tomb Joseph had was not as grand as this, it had the same kind of round stone door.

In any case, soon after three o'clock, Joseph went to Pilate to ask permission to bury the body properly. He had to do this secretly for fear of the other council members. Going inside Pilate's house was something the other council members had never done because entering a Roman house meant they became unclean. But Joseph went to Pilate and "begged" for the body. A rich, important man like Joseph humbled himself in front of the Roman governor; it shows how much it mattered to him that Jesus should be buried properly.

Then he had to wait while Pilate sent for the centurion who had carried out the crucifixion. "Is Jesus really dead?" he asked. The centurion was still much moved by what he had seen. He simply nodded. So Pilate gave permission and Joseph took the damaged body of the crucified Jesus.

It was usual for Jews to wash a body and to anoint it with oils and perfumes before burial. John tells us in his Gospel that Joseph was helped in this by another secret follower of Jesus, a man named Nicodemus. He brought a mixture of myrrh and aloe, which is a fragrant drug. Nicodemus brought a very great quantity of this mixture—dozens of jars of it.

So they anointed the body and wrapped it in a fresh new linen cloth. Then Joseph had it taken to his own tomb, which had never been used. Like the tombs of many rich Jewish families, it had been cut into a rock cliff. It would have been like a small room and probably had shelves cut into the wall. There Jesus was respectfully laid, and a huge stone was rolled across the entrance.

Two of the women followers of Jesus were watching. It was six o'clock, the sun was setting, and the day was almost over.

A legend about Joseph says that he planted his stick in the ground at a place in England called Glastonbury. It grew into a tree that bloomed at Christmas.

Joseph and Nicodemus laid Jesus in the tomb.

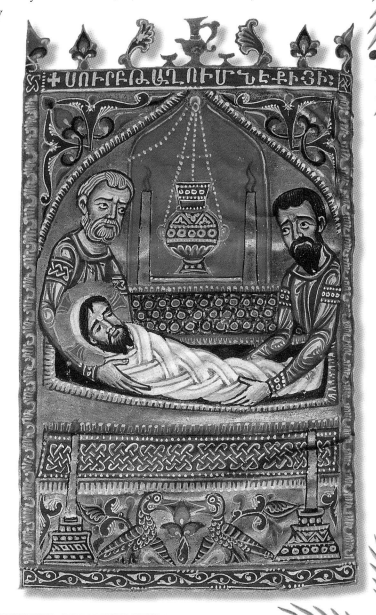

The Marys

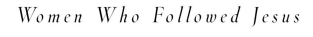

SAINTS' DAYS

22 JULY
Mary of Magdala

22 OCTOBER
Mary, the Mother of
James and John

9 APRIL
Mary, Wife of Cleophas

29 JUNE
Mary, the Mother
of John Mark

IT WAS VERY CONFUSING. They all seemed to have the name Mary. There were at least four Marys. They'd known Jesus when he was at home in Galilee. They'd heard him teach and seen him cure people who were ill. Along with his twelve disciples and several other women, they'd followed him south to Jerusalem.

They were with him when Jesus rode into the city seated on a donkey. They were still with him for much of that week. They were there at the cross when he was crucified, helpless to do anything except weep and show their love for him. Unlike some of the men who'd run away, they stayed watching so that Jesus would know he was not alone.

On the following Sunday morning, two of them went to the tomb where Jesus had been buried. They were among the first to understand that Jesus had come back to life. He had risen from the dead!

We know quite a lot about the men who followed Jesus—the twelve disciples who included Peter, James, and John. But what do we know about the women? Luke says in his Gospel: "Jesus went through towns and villages, preaching . . . and with him the Twelve and some women . . . who used their own resources to help Jesus." These women were able to see that Jesus and his closest followers did not go short of food and other things. So perhaps one or two of them were quite well off.

But who were these women? And especially who were the different women named Mary? First, of course, was Jesus' mother, Mary, who stayed with him to the very end. Then there was a group sometimes referred to as the Three Marys.

The Three Marys

This group of three women all named Mary included Mary from Magdala, sometimes known as Mary Magdalene. She was one of the closest friends of Jesus and was the first person to see Jesus after he rose from the dead on the first Easter morning.

Second was Mary, the mother of the disciples James and John. The Bible says that they were the sons of Zebedee, so she must have been Zebedee's wife. Matthew's Gospel says that she was with Mary from Magdala when Jesus first appeared on Easter morning. She is sometimes known as Saint Mary Salome but she has nothing to do with the other

Salome in the Bible who caused the death of John the Baptist.

The third of the Three Marys was Mary, the wife of Cleophas (also known as Alphaeus). She too came from Galilee. John, in his Gospel, tells us that she was there with the others, when Jesus was crucified. She is also said to be the mother of the other disciple named James (known as James the Less).

There is a very much later story (which is probably only a story) that, several years later, the Three Marys journeyed to Marseilles in France in order to tell the people there all about Jesus.

Mary, the Mother of John Mark

There is yet another Mary mentioned in the Bible: Mary, the mother of Mark who journeyed with Paul and who later wrote about Jesus in the Gospel of Mark. This Mary is mentioned in the part of the Bible known as the Acts of the Apostles, which describes what happened to the followers of Jesus after he went back to heaven.

The women who went back to Jesus' tomb on the Sunday morning were greeted by an angel.

One thing that happened was that Peter was put in prison. This was because the authorities didn't like what he'd been saying about Jesus. One night, he suddenly found the prison gates were unlocked. So what did he do? He looked for his friends! And where would they be?

There was only one place they could be. "The house of Mary, the mother of John Mark." And that's where he found them.

It was probably in an upper (or upstairs) room in her house in Jerusalem that the followers of Jesus first met in secret to pray together. Many people also say that this was the same upper room where Jesus and his twelve disciples had met to have their last supper together the night before he was crucified.

Thomas

Thomas refused to believe that the other disciples had seen Jesus alive until he had seen him and touched the marks left by the nails and the spear.

JUST AS SOME PEOPLE always get known by their nicknames, so this disciple of Jesus was always known as the Twin (although we do not know who his twin brother or sister was).

Nowadays, he is known as Thomas, but "Thomas" is simply Aramaic for "twin." Although the Bible says he had another name, Didymus, that word is simply Greek for "twin." So when the Bible speaks of "Thomas named Didymus," it's actually talking about "the twin named the Twin"!

Later, he got another nickname—Doubting Thomas.

The Sunday morning after Jesus was crucified, Jesus appeared to Mary from Magdala and one of the other Marys. That evening, Jesus appeared again. This time most of the other disciples were there. But not Thomas. When he was told about it, he didn't believe what had happened. How could anyone come back from the dead?

"Unless I see the marks of the nails in his hands," he said, "I won't believe it. Unless I put my hand on those marks and on the mark where the sword pierced his side, I won't believe."

A week later, the disciples were together again, and this time Thomas was with them. The door was locked but suddenly Jesus was standing among them. "Thomas," he said, "put your finger here and see my hands, and put your hand on my side. Stop doubting and believe!"

Thomas replied, "My Lord and my God." From then on, he did believe that Jesus had come back from the dead. Even so, it didn't stop him from getting the nickname "Doubting Thomas."

Not much else is said about him in the Bible. But there is another story about Thomas. It tells how the twelve disciples (or apostles) drew lots to decide which countries they should visit in order to tell people about Jesus. It fell to Thomas to go to India. He didn't like this idea, and it so happened that a merchant named Abban turned up at that moment, looking for a carpenter to help build a new palace for his king, Gundafor, who was king of Parthia (in what is now Iran).

Because Thomas was a carpenter, he went to Parthia. King Gundafor gave him a great deal of money to pay for the new palace and then went on his travels. When he returned, he found Thomas had given the money to the poor and had spent his time preaching and teaching people the message of Jesus. Gundafor put him in prison and threatened to put him to death.

Before that could happen, the king's brother was taken ill—so ill that everyone thought he was dying. Instead, he recovered and immediately told Gundafor not to kill Thomas. "When I was ill, I was taken to heaven by angels and I was shown a palace more wonderful than any on earth. And I was told such joys are waiting in heaven for all those who believe the Christian message."

King Gundafor was so impressed he sent a message that Thomas should be released from prison and should come to tell him about Jesus. Thomas did that, ending with the story of how he himself had doubted that Jesus had risen from the dead. He added the words Jesus had said once he did believe. "Happy are those who have not seen and yet believe."

King Gundafor and his brother both became Christians and, it is said, Thomas journeyed on to India.

About the year 1542, many centuries after all this is supposed to have happened, another Christian, Francis Xavier, went on a journey to India. He met a group of believers who had named themselves the Christians of Saint Thomas and who conducted their worship in the way the early disciples had done. So maybe the story is true, after all.

THE GOSPEL OF THOMAS

*I*n 1946, a group of Egyptian workmen discovered a number of ancient scrolls. Among them was the Gospel according to Thomas. Unlike the Gospels in the Bible, it does not tell the story of Jesus' life but lists a number of his sayings. Some are like the ones in the New Testament Gospels but it is not certain whether the others are genuine or not.

Jesus said:
"I will give you what eye has not seen and ear has not heard
"And hand has not touched and which has not come into the heart of man."

Jesus said:
"Blessed are the poor for yours is the kingdom of heaven."

Jesus said:
"I am the All…
Split wood, I am there.
Lift up the stone and you will find me there."

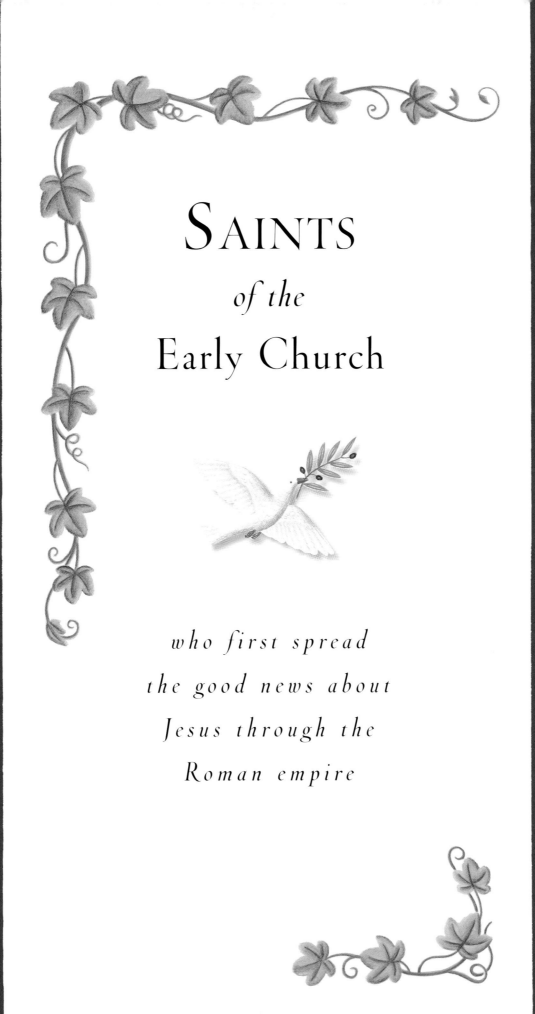

SAINTS
of the
Early Church

*who first spread
the good news about
Jesus through the
Roman empire*

Peter the Apostle

WHEN PEOPLE DIE, who lets them into heaven? Many people would answer "Saint Peter" because they picture him at the gates of heaven with a bunch of keys, deciding who deserves to be let in after their life on earth.

It's easy to see why people believe this.

One day, Jesus asked his disciples who people thought he was.

"Some say you're John the Baptist," they answered. "Others say you're one of the prophets come back from olden times."

"But who do you think I am?" said Jesus.

"You're the Son of God," said Simon.

"Good for you, Simon," said Jesus. "I tell you, you are indeed a rock and on this rock I will build my church and I will give you the keys of the kingdom of heaven." And Jesus began to call him Peter, which means "the rock."

That happened before Jesus was crucified. Later, after the crucifixion and after Jesus had risen from the dead, he gave Peter a special instruction: "Feed my sheep." Jesus said this three times. He was telling Peter to be a guardian to all his followers, to look after them just as a shepherd looks after his sheep.

And indeed, after Jesus had gone back to heaven, Peter did become the leader of the disciples. One of the first things he did was to stand up in the middle of Jerusalem and preach to a huge crowd of people from many different countries. The man who had once been afraid to admit he was a follower of

Jesus famously said to Peter that he would give him the keys to the kingdom of heaven. This saying has led to the popular view that Peter stands at heaven's gate, questioning those who wish to enter.

Jesus was now boldly standing up in the middle of the marketplace.

"Jesus, the one who was crucified, who was raised from the dead by the Lord God—he is the messenger, the redeemer God promised to send us. Now you must give up your wrongful ways, believe in him, and follow his teaching."

That day, after listening to Peter, about three thousand people became followers of Jesus.

In the years ahead, Peter did much to spread the word about Jesus. He healed people, he was sometimes put in prison, and he journeyed to many places in Palestine and Samaria, telling people wherever he went the good news about Jesus.

Later, there was some disagreement among Christians as to whether the message of Jesus was meant only for Jewish people or for all people. Peter argued very strongly that anyone could become a Christian—they didn't have be Jewish first.

It was here at Caesarea Philippi, famous for its shrines to Roman gods, that Peter declared Jesus to be the Son of God.

It is widely believed that Peter journeyed to Rome and was put in prison there, along with several other Christians. This was in the time when the emperor of Rome was Nero, a cruel man who blamed Christians for anything that went wrong in his city.

A chance came for one of the prisoners to escape. The others tried to persuade Peter that it should be him. He hesitated but at last he agreed.

When he found himself outside prison, he set out to walk away from the city of Rome. Along the road, he met a shadowy figure carrying a cross. As he got nearer, he recognized the figure. It was Jesus.

"Where are you going?" asked Peter.

"I'm coming to be crucified a second time," said the figure.

Peter was so ashamed he turned around, went back to Rome, and gave himself up. The order was given that he should be crucified, but he pleaded that he was unworthy to be crucified in the same way Jesus was and he was crucified upside down on 29 June, in the year 64, in the arena where the Romans held circuses and other entertainments.

The great Church of Saint Peter in Rome is said to be built on the spot where his body was buried. Modern excavations suggest that the tomb of Saint Peter may indeed be in this place.

DISCIPLES AND APOSTLES

*T*he word "disciple" means "follower" or "student" (it comes from a Latin word meaning "to learn"). Jesus had many disciples, but when people talk of Jesus' disciples, they often mean his twelve closest followers.

These twelve (and Saint Paul) are also known as "apostles." An apostle is a messenger or someone who is "sent out." The apostles are so called because, after Jesus had returned to heaven, they were sent out to spread his message to distant towns and other lands.

SAINT'S DAY

26 DECEMBER

Stoned to Death

Stephen

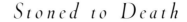

WHY DID HE SAY what he did? Why didn't he just keep quiet? He was clever, intelligent. He must have known what would happen if he spoke out. He'd be put to death by stoning. But Stephen knew that he must say what he believed was the truth.

A year or so after Jesus had risen from the dead, the Bible says that the twelve apostles had chosen seven men to be deacons. Their job was to look after any of the new followers of Jesus who were in need—such as children whose parents had died, or widows who had no one to look after them. This meant that the apostles themselves had time to concentrate on spreading the word of Jesus.

Stephen was one of those seven deacons. He was a tall, energetic young man who also found time to teach and heal many people. He was particularly successful at persuading Jews to join the followers of Jesus— a group that was beginning to be known as "the Church."

Not surprisingly, the members of the Jewish council were not pleased. They paid a number of men to tell lies about Stephen. These men agreed to say such things as, "We heard Stephen speaking against God" and "We heard him say that the temple should be torn down and everything about our religion should be changed." Having got this so-called evidence, the members of the council had Stephen arrested and brought to trial in front of the whole council.

Stephen was stoned to death. The crowd simply picked up stones that were lying on the ground and pelted him with them.

"You've heard the evidence against you," they said. "What have you got to say for yourself?"

Stephen began to speak, clearly and confidently. He told them the story of the Jewish people, of how they had been guided and helped by God at all times and how God had used a man named Moses to lead them out of Egypt when they had been slaves in that country. It was, of course, a story they all knew very well. And Stephen went on to remind them how God had sent prophets, or teachers, who had explained his will for his people.

But then Stephen reminded them how they had not always listened to the prophets and had even killed some of them. Then he said the thing that was to cause all the trouble.

"Just as you killed God's prophets in days gone by, so now you have betrayed and killed God's own Son, Jesus. You have murdered him!"

The members of the council blocked their ears. "Blasphemy!" they shouted. By blasphemy, they meant he was saying something about God that was untrue, because they did not believe that Jesus was God's Son. The punishment for blasphemy was stoning.

There and then, they seized Stephen and dragged him from the building, along the streets, and out through the city wall. The men who'd given false evidence against Stephen took off their cloaks and gave them to a young man named Saul to look after. Then they picked up stones and rocks and started pelting Stephen.

He knelt down and prayed as the stones began to hit him: "Lord Jesus, receive my spirit into heaven, and do not hold my death against these men."

Soon Stephen was lying on the ground, covered in blood, and eventually he lost consciousness. They kept on throwing stones until they were sure he was dead.

Saul, who was a Jewish rabbi, watched the execution. He thought that what they had done was a good thing. He was well educated and he knew the law. In his eyes, Stephen had committed blasphemy and so deserved to die. But Saul would later change his mind.

Stephen prayed for his executioners. The Bible says that, as he was speaking during his trial, his face shone like that of an angel.

Paul

IT WAS THE STONING of Stephen that started it. Saul had watched it happen and it made up his mind. The followers of Jesus were dangerous. They must be destroyed.

That very day he started going from house to house in Jerusalem, determined to discover all those who believed in Jesus. When he found any believers, he dragged them out of their homes and had them thrown into prison. The law was on his side too.

The Jewish authorities said that anyone who believed that Jesus was the Son of God and that he had risen from the dead was guilty of blasphemy.

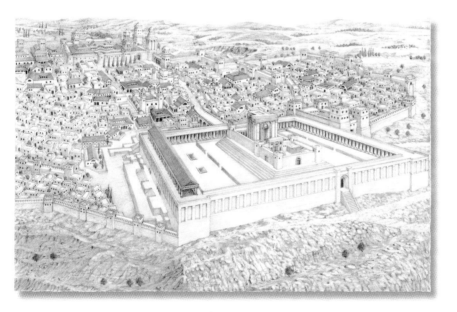

The punishment for blasphemy (as in the case of Stephen) was death.

Despite this, the Christian belief was growing stronger and spreading across the country. In particular, there was a large number of followers of Jesus in Damascus.

So Saul went to the high priest of the Jews in Jerusalem and asked for letters giving him the power to enter the synagogues in Damascus to seek out any followers of this new belief, arrest them, and bring them back to Jerusalem for trial.

The great temple in Jerusalem was a symbol of the faith that Paul so much wanted to defend. He went on a house-to-house search in the city in an attempt to find those followers of Jesus whom he thought were undermining correct belief.

Then he set off on the long and dangerous journey. Suddenly, as he was nearing the city of Damascus, lightning seemed to flash all around him and he fell to the ground. Then he heard a voice: "Saul, Saul, why do you persecute me?"

"Who are you?" Saul asked fearfully.

"I am Jesus," he heard the voice say. "I am Jesus whom you persecute. Now get up and go to Damascus. You'll be told what to do."

The men who were journeying with Saul stood there, uncertain what to do. They'd heard the voice but seen no one. It was as Saul staggered

to his feet that he realized he could see nothing. He was blind.

His companions led him by the hand the rest of the way to Damascus, to the house of a man named Judas who lived on Straight Street in the middle of the city. Saul stayed there for three days, unable to see and refusing food and drink.

At this time, a Christian in Damascus named Ananias had a vision. God spoke to him, telling him to go to Straight Street and ask for Saul at the house of Judas. But Ananias was afraid to go, for he had heard all about Saul and what he'd done in Jerusalem.

"Don't worry," said the voice of God to Ananias. "Saul's been praying. He knows you're coming."

Ananias visited Saul, put his hands on his head, and told him that Jesus had sent him so that Saul might see again and believe.

Paul's encounter with the risen Jesus began with a blinding light from heaven. This experience changed his mind about Jesus. He now believed in him as the Son of God.

And from that moment, Saul's sight returned. He was baptized as a Christian and began to preach in Damascus, praising Jesus as the Son of God.

Not surprisingly, Saul was now mistrusted by both Jews and the followers of Jesus. Eventually he had to escape from the city during the night by being lowered in a basket from the city walls.

From then on, Saul became known by his Roman name, Paul, and he started his great work of spreading the news of Jesus.

Paul

AFTER BECOMING a believer in Jesus and secretly escaping from Damascus, Paul went back to Jerusalem. The followers of Jesus in Jerusalem were highly suspicious. Wasn't this the man they knew as Saul? Saul, who had stood by, watching Stephen being stoned to death? Saul, who'd had so many of their friends thrown into prison?

At last one of them spoke up for him. This man's name was Barnabas, and he'd heard what had happened to Saul on the way to Damascus. So Saul (or Paul) stayed there, preaching the message of Jesus. This annoyed some of his old friends. Soon his life was in danger again, so he went home to Tarsus.

It's likely that he spent the next ten years teaching and carrying on his trade of tent making. Then, around the year 45, a group of Christians in Antioch (a town between Tarsus and Jerusalem) decided the message of Jesus should be spread to other countries. They chose Paul and Barnabas to do this work.

The city of Ephesus was a major town in the Roman empire when Paul visited it. The remains of an impressive colonnade leading to a large amphitheatre can still be seen.

They took a man named John Mark with them too and sailed to the island of Cyprus and then on to Asia Minor (which is now southern Turkey). Then John Mark returned to Jerusalem, but Barnabas and Paul continued their travels for another year.

Paul made two more great journeys.

His next one took him again through Asia Minor, and then, for the first time, he visited Europe, preaching in the Greek cities of Thessalonica, Athens, and Corinth.

His third journey took him back to a city named Ephesus (which he'd visited on his previous journey and where he now stayed for two years), then again to Thessalonica and Corinth, and eventually back to Jerusalem.

On these journeys, he visited old friends and made new ones. He also kept in touch with people who had become Christians. He did this by writing letters to them. For example, while he was in Corinth he wrote to the Christians in Thessalonica, and when he was in Ephesus he wrote to the Christians in Corinth.

He had many adventures on his journeys.

When Paul was on his first journey with Barnabas, he visited a place named Lystra. In the crowd there was a man who had been lame since birth. As he was listening to Paul, Paul turned to him and said, "Stand up straight!" The man stood up and started walking. He'd been healed! All the local people thought that Paul and Barnabas must be gods and tried to worship them, but Paul and Barnabas quickly told them they must worship only the God whom they believed to be the one true God.

On his second journey, while he was in a town named Philippi, Paul met a slave girl who was troubled by an evil spirit. This spirit allowed her to tell people's fortunes and in this way she earned a lot of money for her owners. Paul cured her. This infuriated her owners. They seized Paul and his companion Silas and had them thrown into prison.

While they were in prison, an earthquake destroyed all the prison doors. Instead of escaping, Paul and Silas told the prison guard about Jesus, and the guard and his family were baptized. Then Paul insisted that the Roman governor should come and apologize for having put them in prison unfairly. As soon as the governor realized Paul was a Roman citizen, he came and begged his forgiveness.

Toward the end of Paul's third journey, he returned to Troas. While he was having supper there one night, he talked and preached until midnight. A youth named Eutychus was sitting on a third-storey window ledge, looking down, and listening to what Paul said. Late in the evening, Eutychus became tired, then fell asleep and tumbled out of the window.

At first everyone thought he was dead, but Paul hugged him. "Don't worry—he's still alive," Paul said, and he carried on talking till it was dawn. Then everyone left, taking Eutychus home, greatly relieved he was all right.

This pen and writing case are from the time of Paul. Paul dictated most of his letters to someone who wrote them down. When he would take up the pen to add a personal note, he would apologize for his clumsy handwriting.

THE APOSTLE TO THE GENTILES

On all his travels, Paul preached to Jews and non-Jews (or "Gentiles") about Jesus. Like Peter, Paul felt that Gentiles who accepted Jesus as Lord didn't need to follow Jewish ways and customs, such as going to the Jewish synagogue. For this reason and because he was the first apostle to travel widely outside Palestine, he is known as the Apostle to the Gentiles.

It was Paul who began the task of making Christianity a worldwide faith.

Paul

"YOU KNOW WHO THAT IS? Paul! Used to be named Saul."
Paul was back in Jerusalem after his third great journey, and he
had gone to worship in the temple. Naturally, many local people
recognized him and started talking amongst themselves.

"He's the one who lets the heathen come into our places of worship."

"Everywhere he goes, he persuades Jews to forget about Moses and the
prophets and gets them to worship that Jesus."

This wasn't true, but within a few minutes the crowd had become an
angry mob. They turned on Paul, dragged him out of the temple, and
were trying to kill him. The commander of the Roman troops in the city
heard what was going on and quickly took some officers and soldiers
down to where the trouble was.

He couldn't work out what the argument was about, but he arrested
Paul to protect him from the mob.

Paul was kept in prison, partly for his own safety, partly because
the Romans didn't properly understand why the Jews were accusing
him. After about two years, Paul demanded (as was his right as
a Roman citizen) to be sent to Rome and tried before the emperor.

In about the year 60, Paul was sent (under arrest) by ship with
some other prisoners to Rome. His friend Luke went
with him.

It was autumn and there were strong gales
blowing. The Mediterranean Sea was rough.

Paul suggested to the captain of the ship that they
stay in port on the island of Crete and shelter there
during the worst of the winter weather, but the captain
of the ship thought he knew a safer place farther on.

Then a violent storm blew up, and it was so wet and
windy that they saw neither sun nor stars for several days.

*A grain ship from the
time of Paul. The
square-rigged sail
leaves the ship very
much at the mercy of
the direction of the
wind—as Paul and his
shipmates discovered.*

They also had to throw some of the ship's equipment
overboard to make the ship lighter and save it from sinking. "I tell you
something," said Paul helpfully, "you should have listened to what I said."

He wasn't popular.

But then he went on to comfort them, saying he'd had a dream that
not one of them would lose their lives and that he would stand trial before
the emperor in Rome.

For a fortnight, they were blown westward by the storm. Then, one daybreak, they saw land. They steered the ship toward a sandy bay, but it got stuck some way offshore on a sandbank and then began to break up under the pounding of the waves.

The sailors were all for killing Paul and the other prisoners, worrying that they would swim ashore and escape. But the army officer in charge of the prisoners stopped this and ordered all those who could swim to head for shore. The others clung onto bits of the ship as it broke up.

All 276 people on board reached the shore safely. They discovered they had landed on the island of Malta. The local people made everyone welcome. Paul healed many sick people on the island. Three months later, they sailed on another ship to Italy and then went by road to Rome.

Once in Rome, Paul was allowed to rent an ordinary house and live in it, but he was still under arrest and had a soldier to guard him. He was allowed visitors, and many Jews came to hear him teach. He also spent much of his time writing letters to Christians in places he'd visited on his earlier journeys.

This went on for two years. It's uncertain what happened then. He may have been put on trial, or he may have been allowed to undertake more travels. Some say he went back to Ephesus, others that he visited Spain. In either case, many people believe that he was finally put to death sometime between the years 64 and 67. As a Roman citizen, he would have been executed quickly rather than suffering a painful slow death by crucifixion.

Thanks to Paul, the Christian faith had reached the great city of Rome, the heart of the mighty Roman empire.

In his letters, Paul often speaks of the dramatic change in his life that began when he "saw the light" on the Damascus road.

Good Companions

Barnabas, Timothy, and Titus

SAINTS' DAYS

11 JUNE
Barnabas

26 JANUARY
Timothy

26 JANUARY
Titus

P AUL DID NOT TRAVEL alone on his journeys. He had a number of good friends who kept him company as he made his way from place to place, teaching people about Jesus.

Barnabas

It wasn't easy being followers of Jesus. In those early days, following the stoning of Stephen, everyone seemed to be against them. The Jews, the Romans . . . But there was one person they could rely on to cheer them up.

His real name was Joseph. He was a Jew, born on the island of Cyprus, who had come to Jerusalem when Jesus was still teaching and preaching. In fact, he'd become one of the close followers of Jesus. Because he was good at cheering people up, he was nicknamed "the One who Encourages." And in Hebrew or Aramaic, that's "Barnabas."

He was generous as well. Soon after Stephen was stoned to death, Barnabas sold a field he owned and handed all the money over to the apostles to help any of the followers of Jesus who were in need. He was the first person in Jerusalem to trust Saul (or Paul) after his return from Damascus.

Some time later, Barnabas went to Antioch, which was the first place where the followers of Jesus were known as Christians. The Christians there were deciding who should travel around the Mediterranean Sea to tell people about Jesus. Paul was one choice, Barnabas was the other, perhaps because he was from the island of Cyprus, where they'd go first. Young John Mark also joined them for the start of their voyage.

It was on this journey that Paul and Barnabas visited Lystra. The people thought that Barnabas was Zeus, the

king of the Greek gods, so he must have been fairly tall and impressive, perhaps quite handsome.

Barnabas faithfully accompanied Paul for the whole of that first journey. Sadly, they didn't remain good friends. Their quarrel happened when Paul was planning his second journey.

Barnabas wanted to take John Mark with them.

"No," said Paul firmly. "He only came part way on our first journey. Then he went home. He doesn't get a second chance."

Paul took a man named Silas on his second journey while Barnabas went home to Cyprus, taking John Mark with him. Some people say they were cousins or that John Mark was nephew to "Uncle Barnabas."

Timothy

On Paul's second journey, he visited Lystra again. This time, Paul met a Jewish woman named Eunice. She was married to a Greek man, and they had a grown-up son named Timothy. The whole family became Christians, and Timothy joined Paul and Silas on the rest of their journey.

Paul trusted Timothy to travel on his own to teach other Christians about Jesus. Timothy visited Thessalonica, Corinth, and Philippi, among other places. Later, Paul sent him to live in Ephesus.

Paul had visited Ephesus twice himself. There was a pagan temple there where the local people went to worship the goddess Artemis (sometimes known as Diana). When Paul persuaded many people to worship Jesus, he caused trouble among the people who sold Artemis souvenirs.

Timothy became the leader, or bishop, of the Christians in Ephesus but, it is said, was killed there in the year 97 when he (like Paul) dared to preach that it was wrong to worship the goddess Artemis.

Titus

Titus was another young friend of Paul's. He was a Gentile who had become a Christian. After Paul had visited Corinth on his second journey, he sent Titus there to be his spokesman. Later, Paul sent Titus to be leader, or bishop, of the church on the island of Crete. He lived and worked there until his death.

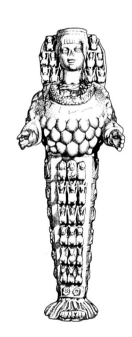

Above: *A model of the goddess Artemis, who was held in high regard by the people of Ephesus. Paul and Timothy both said it was wrong to worship her.*

Opposite: *This fifteenth century picture of Barnabas is from Cyprus—the place where Barnabas was born and which he visited with Paul.*

Two Gospel Writers

John Mark and Luke

IN THE BIBLE, THERE are four retellings of the life and sayings of Jesus. These are the four Gospels. Two of them are known as the Gospels of Mark and Luke.

John Mark

It was very embarrassing. He'd had to run through the streets with no clothes on. He only hoped no one had seen.

It had all begun earlier in the week. Two men had come to his mother's house. They'd made arrangements for a special meal to be held there, in an upstairs room. A man named Jesus and his twelve friends did have supper there. Then, very late at night, they all went out.

He'd been curious and had slipped out of bed to follow them, stupidly just wrapping a linen sheet around himself.

They went to a garden known as Gethsemane. He hid in the shadows, watching to see if anything would happen. Sometime after midnight, the high priest's guards came along with one of the men who'd had supper in the upper room. That man kissed Jesus, and then the guards arrested Jesus.

There was a scuffle, some fighting, and then Jesus' friends ran away. The guards tried to catch them, but in all the confusion, they caught John Mark. He struggled and the sheet slipped off, and he was able to dash away in the darkness. Naked.

The embarrassed young man was John Mark. Over the next few days, the friends of Jesus used John Mark's mother's upstairs room more and more, as a secret meeting place. John Mark learned about Jesus and realized just how special he was. In particular, he became a close friend of one of Jesus' disciples, the man named Peter.

In time, John Mark himself became a follower of Jesus, as did the man he thought of as Uncle Barnabas. Several years later, he set off on a long journey with Barnabas and another Christian named Paul to take the good news about Jesus to places such as Cyprus and Asia Minor.

After a while, John Mark left Barnabas and Paul and went back home to Jerusalem. This annoyed Paul very much, but years later, when Paul

Mark writing his Gospel.

was being kept under arrest in Rome, he asked Timothy to arrange for John Mark to go to Rome to help him.

About this time, Peter also went to Rome. He preached quite openly about Jesus, and the large crowds who came to listen persuaded John Mark to write down everything for Peter. It seems that John Mark did this and made copies of this "Gospel" for all who wanted. This is probably how John Mark became an evangelist, the writer of the Gospel according to Mark.

Later, John Mark went to Alexandria in Egypt to teach people about Jesus. He died there, but (it is said) hundreds of years later, his body was taken to the city of Venice in what is now Italy.

EVANGELISTS

*E*vangelists are people who teach the Christian faith to people who haven't heard about it before. The word is also used to describe the four writers of the New Testament Gospels, the books in the Bible that tell the story of Jesus' life.

It is not known for sure who actually wrote the Gospels but it is fairly certain that the one that carries the name of Mark was the first to be written and that Luke's Gospel was written by a doctor named Luke.

Luke writing his Gospel.

Luke

Not much is known about Luke except that he spoke Greek, he was a doctor, and he was a great friend of Paul. He was such a good friend that he decided to travel with Paul on his journey to Rome, and Luke stayed with him there while Paul was under house arrest.

It is evident from Luke's Gospel that he was a kind man.

He makes special mention of the many times that Jesus cared for the poor and the outcast. He also makes clear that Jesus respected women quite as much as men, even in a time when some men thought of women as "second-class" people.

While he was with Paul in Rome, it is probable that Luke also wrote the Acts of the Apostles, the book that tells the stories of the early Christians, including Paul.

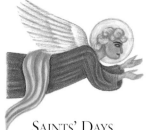

Clement and Ignatius of Antioch

SAINTS' DAYS

23 NOVEMBER
Clement

17 OCTOBER
Ignatius of Antioch

A S THE YEARS WENT BY, the people who had known Jesus and his friends personally got older and began to die. Some were put to death because of what they believed and taught.

That meant that the various groups of Christians in different places around the Mediterranean Sea needed new leaders. The title "bishop" began to be used for these leaders, so, for example, a man named Timothy became bishop of Ephesus and a man named Titus became bishop of Crete.

The first bishops were chosen by the original apostles, and in turn these bishops chose those who were to become bishops after them. Many Christians today believe that an unbroken line can be traced back from today's bishops to the apostles themselves.

Nowadays, not all churches are led by bishops. For example, in some Protestant churches, the people elect their leaders.

Peter himself is said to have been the first bishop of Rome. After he was crucified, he was followed by two other bishops and then by Bishop Clement of Rome.

Clement

In one of his letters, Paul says that one of his helpers was a man named Clement. Some thirty years later, Clement became bishop of Rome.

Clement was originally a slave and also probably a Jew, but he later became a Christian. During the ten years that he was bishop, Clement wrote (in the year 95) a "long and wonderful" letter to the Christians at Corinth. The Epistle of Clement was not included in the New Testament even though it is older than some of the books that are included.

Clement was put to death by being thrown into the sea with an anchor around his neck . . . perhaps a stone anchor like the one here.

The Christians at Corinth had been arguing among themselves about various matters, and in his epistle, Clement sent them lots of advice:

"The strong must make sure they care for the weak.
The rich must be certain to give enough to supply all the needs of the poor.
The poor must thank God for supplying their needs.
We all need each other: the great need the small; the small need the great.
In our body, the head is useless without the feet and the feet without the head.
The tiniest limbs of our body are useful and necessary to the whole."

This letter was read aloud in the churches in Corinth for many years.

It is not certain how or when Clement died, but it was probably about the year 101. There is, however, a story that suggests he was sentenced to work in slave-like conditions and was later put to death by being thrown into the sea with an anchor tied to his neck. Several hundred years after this, so the story goes, his body was recovered and was buried in Rome, where the Church of San Clemente now stands. It is said to be in the place where his home was when he was bishop of Rome.

Ignatius of Antioch

The Bible says that one day, the disciples of Jesus were arguing among themselves about which of them was the greatest. Jesus wanted to teach them not to be proud. He took a young boy and placed him in front of them. "The greatest person is the one who humbles himself and becomes like this child."

Ignatius was killed by being thrown to lions as part of the brutal entertainments that were popular in the Roman empire.

Some people believe that boy grew up to become Bishop Ignatius of Antioch, the town in Syria from where Paul and Barnabas started their first great journey. It is at least very likely that Ignatius knew (and was a disciple of) the apostle John.

Ignatius became bishop about the year 60 and was leader of the Christians in Antioch for forty years. He was then condemned to death by the Romans and sent by ship to Rome.

During that journey, he wrote seven letters to Christians in different places to encourage them to trust in Jesus.

On his journey to Rome, his ship visited Smyrna. There he met another bishop, Bishop Polycarp. Later, Ignatius was killed by being thrown to the lions in a circus arena.

SAINTS

of the

Persecuted Church

*whose love for
Jesus gave them
the courage to die
for their faith*

Polycarp

SAINT'S DAY

23 FEBRUARY
After his death in 156,
his friends vowed to
keep the anniversary of
his death "in joy and
gladness" as a reminder
of his faith. It is the
earliest mention of an
annual saint's day.

*Polycarp is often
shown as an old man,
as he was when he
was martyred; but he
had been a Christian
from the time he was
a young boy.*

I T WAS AS BIG AS a modern football ground. Rows and rows of
spectators sat on stone benches all around it, some in stands that
gave an excellent view of what was happening in the arena. But they
weren't watching a football match. It was a much more exciting game:
Christians versus lions.

First a group of terrified Christians was marched or dragged into the
middle of the arena by a guard of Roman soldiers. The soldiers made their
escape. Then a lion, which had been kept without food for several days to
make sure it was really hungry, was let out of its cage. It smelled the fear
of the prisoners. It made for them. Eager, hungry, ready to eat . . .

That was what was meant to happen to Bishop Polycarp, but it didn't
work out like that.

As a boy, Polycarp had heard about Jesus from John, one
of Jesus' disciples. He'd become a Christian, and in due time,
John had made him a bishop. That is, he became the leading
Christian in Smyrna, the town where he lived. Smyrna was in
that part of the Roman empire known as Asia Minor but which
is now known as Turkey.

At the time of Polycarp, it was against Roman law to be
a Christian, but as long as Christians kept out of everyone's
way, they were usually left alone. As a result, they often met in
secret when they wanted to pray and to share bread and wine
in remembrance of Jesus. Every so often, though, a group of
Christians would be rounded up and condemned to be thrown
to the lions.

About the year 155, the Romans in Asia Minor rioted against
the Christians there because they believed that the Christians
were bringing bad luck to the city. Polycarp, who was by then an old man
aged eighty-six, knew what would happen. So he waited patiently to be
arrested. While he was having supper one night, the soldiers arrived.
Polycarp invited them in. "You'll have to wait while I say my prayers."
They were impressed by the old man and waited. Then they took him
to the crowded local arena.

Polycarp was led in front of the Roman governor, who tried to persuade
him to give up his faith. "Just say it's all nonsense and make a sacrifice to
the Roman gods."

The crowds shouted against Polycarp, "This is the father of the Christians. He wants to destroy our gods. He says we shouldn't worship them."

The governor tried again. "Think of your age. Speak against this Jesus and I'll set you free."

"But that would be blasphemy," replied Polycarp. "That would be denying the truth. Eighty-six years have I served Jesus and he has done me no wrong. How can I blaspheme my Lord and Redeemer? I am a Christian."

The governor threatened to throw him to the lions.

"I will not deny Jesus."

The governor decided to try something else. He announced that Polycarp would be put to death by fire—he would be tied to a wooden stake and burned.

Polycarp still didn't change his mind. "You threaten me with fire which will burn for only a short time, but I know the everlasting joy of heaven that is to come. Do what you like."

The governor ordered his soldiers to put a stake in place in the arena and pile up wood around it. Polycarp was tied to the stake, and the soldiers set fire to the wood. But the flames didn't seem to harm the old man at all. Instead, they made an arc around him, leaving him untouched.

This didn't please the Roman crowds. Some began to jeer, so the governor ordered one of the soldiers to take his dagger and stab Polycarp. His body was left there in the arena. After the crowds had gone, Polycarp's friends crept back and gave his body a proper burial. Later they wrote down the story of his faith and his fight against evil so that others might "remember those who have fought before."

The Roman governor ordered Polycarp to be burned at the stake; however, the flames refused to burn him, so he was stabbed to death to please the jeering crowds.

The Hermit of Thebes
Paul the Hermit

HE WAS YOUNG. He was rich. He was well educated. He was happy. Everything should have been perfect. But he was a Christian.

His name was Paul, he was twenty years old, and his home was the once great city of Thebes, now Luxor, which stands on either side of the River Nile in Egypt. In those days, the mighty Roman empire stretched as far south as Egypt, so what the Romans said was law in Thebes. What's more, at this particular time, around the year 250, the Roman emperor was a man named Decius who disliked Christians even more than some other Roman emperors had done. He had many Christians put to death, so it was dangerous to be known to be a Christian.

Paul's parents had died when he was fifteen and left him a great deal of money. That was fine, except that Paul's brother-in-law decided he'd like Paul's money and had seen a way to get hold of it. If he told the Romans that Paul was a Christian, then Paul would be put to death and he'd inherit Paul's wealth.

As a desert hermit, Paul lived simply on dates and figs. There is a story that a raven used to bring him half a loaf of bread each day.

Luckily, Paul discovered that he was about to be betrayed and fled from the city of Thebes, out into the desert. He found a cave where he could hide. There was a stream nearby, which provided him with water, and he was able to live on the fruit of the date palms and fig trees that grew near the stream.

He even began to enjoy the life of a hermit. (A hermit is someone who moves away from normal, everyday life and lives alone in a secluded place.) Paul found he enjoyed having time to think about God and time to pray. He had all he really needed—even fresh clothes that he made from the leaves of the palm trees. So he decided to remain a hermit.

After some years, so the story goes, a raven began visiting Paul each day. On each visit, the raven brought half a loaf of bread, which it dropped near Paul's cave.

Paul continued to live in this way for many, many years. Then, one day, another Christian (who was also to become a saint) was led to Paul's cave. This man's name

This monastery dedicated to Paul the Hermit is situated in the barren wilderness in Egypt.

was Antony and he too was a devout and thoughtful Christian. But what was truly amazing about their meeting was that, on the day they met, the raven brought not half a loaf of bread but a full loaf.

The two men took a long time to start eating this meal because Paul insisted that Antony was his guest and should therefore eat first, while Antony insisted that Paul was the older and the more respected and that he should eat first. At last they agreed to start together.

The two men, who had done much thinking about what it means to be a Christian, had a lot to talk about. After some time, Paul told Antony about his home in Thebes. He also told Antony that, since he was now a very old man, he knew he was about to die. He said that he would love to be buried in a particular cloak he had once been given in Thebes.

Antony so wanted to please the old man that he set out for Thebes in search of the cloak. When he returned with it, he found Paul stretched out on the sand. Antony thought he must be praying and knelt down to pray beside him until he realized that Paul had died.

As the story goes, a pair of passing lions helped Antony to dig a grave for Paul. This may or may not be true. But Antony did keep some of Paul's palm-leaf clothes, which he wore on special occasions in memory of this most holy hermit. He himself later became known as Saint Antony the Great of Egypt.

Alexander and Gregory

SAINTS' DAYS

18 MARCH
Alexander

17 NOVEMBER
Gregory

Alexander was an old man when he, like many others, was thrown into prison for his faith. He died chained to the prison wall.

H E'D GROWN UP IN the great city of Alexandria on the northern coast of Egypt. While still a boy, he'd been deeply upset when his father was put to death for being a Christian. Even so, he too became a Christian and decided to spend his life as a teacher. His name was Origen.

While he was still a young man, he was put in charge of a Christian school in Alexandria and taught there for twenty-eight years. He made do with very little food or sleep and spent all his time studying, teaching, and writing. It is said he knew almost all of the Bible by heart and that he wrote two thousand books and other works.

Later, he had an argument with his bishop, and, in the year 231, he moved to Caesarea in Palestine and started another school there. Here he was nicknamed "the Head." He is not considered a saint but many of his pupils, including Alexander and Gregory, are considered saints.

Alexander

While Origen was still in Egypt, one of his students was a young man named Alexander. Alexander's home was in Cappadocia (in what is now northern Turkey) but he had gone to Alexandria to study with Origen. Despite all the dangers of being known to be a Christian in what was part of the Roman empire, he was never afraid to say in public that he was a Christian.

Everyone respected his courage, and in due course, he was made bishop of his homeland, Cappadocia. During his time there, he made a journey to Jerusalem to see all the places that Jesus had visited. When he arrived in the city, he was warmly welcomed by all the Christians there.

It so happened that the bishop of Jerusalem at that time was a very old man named Narcissus. In a letter, Alexander said that he was 116! Because of Narcissus's age, the Christians in the city decided they wanted Alexander to share the work with him.

When Narcissus died, in the year 222, Alexander became bishop of Jerusalem. Among many other things, he made a library of Christian books in the city. Then, around the year 250, when he himself was an old man, the Roman emperor Decius decided to round up the Christians throughout the empire. Alexander refused to deny he was Christian and was put in prison at Caesarea. He died there, chained to his prison wall.

Gregory

When Gregory was twenty, he decided he wanted to learn more about the world. He'd grown up in a district named Pontus, not far from Cappadocia (the home of Alexander), but he wasn't sure where to study.

Then a soldier arrived with a letter from his sister's husband. He was an army officer and he'd been posted to a place named Caesarea in Palestine. The letter asked Gregory to take his sister there.

When he arrived, he met Origen and first heard about Jesus. Gregory studied with Origen for five years, learning not just about Christianity, but other subjects, including astronomy and physics. He was also baptized and then returned to Pontus as a Christian teacher, or missionary.

He became bishop of Pontus around the year 238. People said that when he returned to Pontus there were only seventeen Christians there. In the course of thirty years, he converted nearly all the population, leaving only seventeen non-Christians!

Gregory was known for his learning and also for his ability to work miracles.

Every morning, people gathered at his door. He healed those who were ill, comforted those who mourned the death of a friend or relative, and gave good advice. People began to describe him as "the Wonder-Worker," and after he died, all sorts of stories were told about him. It was said that he once changed the course of a river and even moved a mountain.

Whether these stories are true or not, the real wonder that he achieved was to make the whole of Pontus into a Christian land.

The Gridiron Martyr

Lawrence

L AWRENCE WAS HEARTBROKEN. His hero, Pope Sixtus, was about to be put to death. Was there nothing he could do to save this man whom he admired and served?

Lawrence was one of the deacons of the Christian church in Rome. As deacon, Lawrence was in charge of the church's money.

The year was 258, and the emperor had tried to make Pope Sixtus worship the Roman gods. He'd refused, and that was why he'd been arrested, tortured, and was now being taken away for execution. Lawrence followed, noisily demanding to know why the pope was being murdered and his deacon left alive. Pope Sixtus warned Lawrence that he too would be put to death in three days' time.

On hearing this, Lawrence gave away everything he owned to the poor, the hungry, and the orphans and widows of the city. He even sold some of the church's gold and silver to help the needy. News of this got about, and Lawrence was seized and taken to a Roman officer known as the prefect. The prefect ordered Lawrence to produce the remaining money and any treasures the church owned (such as gold candlesticks or cups) and hand them over.

Lawrence thought quickly. "If you give me three days to organize it, I'll bring you the church's treasure."

During the next three days, he gathered together all the disabled people and beggars, together with many blind and sick people and hundreds of lepers. He led them to the prefect. "Here," said Lawrence. "These people are the true treasures of the church. You see, the church is far, far richer than your emperor."

The prefect was not amused. He ordered his men to put Lawrence to death in a slow and horrible way. They produced an iron grid and lit a fire underneath it. When the iron grid began to glow in the heat, they bound Lawrence to it with chains so that he would roast to death.

Even then, Lawrence's clever wit did not desert him. It is reported that after a while he said, "You can turn me over now. I'm done on that side."

As he neared death, he prayed that Rome would become a Christian city. This did indeed happen, but not for another hundred years.

Opposite: *When Lawrence was asked to hand over the treasures of the church, he gathered together a crowd of poor and outcast people. These, he said to the prefect, were the real treasures of the church.*

EMPIRE-WIDE PERSECUTION

*F*or much of the two hundred years following the life of Jesus, the Romans allowed Christians (and others) to worship as they wished. There were times, however, when Christians were imprisoned and executed in various parts of the empire, as happened to Peter himself in Rome and later to Ignatius of Antioch and Bishop Polycarp.

Then, in the year 249, Decius became ruler of the Roman empire. He wanted everyone to worship the old gods of Rome.

Many Christians refused. They were tortured and executed. It was at this time that Paul of Thebes fled into the desert and Alexander died in prison.

Decius was killed in battle in 251, but little changed, for the next emperor, Valerian, was equally cruel. In 257, he issued a new order: "There shall be no meetings of Christians in any place. If anyone disobeys, he shall be beheaded." He also demanded that all Christian leaders offer a sacrifice to the Roman gods.

Antony and Athanasius

SAINTS' DAYS

17 JANUARY
Antony

2 MAY
Athanasius

One of the luxuries Antony greatly missed in the desert was fine wine.

THE COUNTRY WE NOW know as Egypt was once home to two friends, both very holy men, who have inspired and encouraged many Christians by their lives and their teachings.

Antony

He was about twenty when he heard the story. The story of how Jesus had once met a rich young man who wanted to know how he might get to heaven when he died. Jesus told him to sell everything he had and give his money to the poor. "That way you will have treasure in heaven."

Antony couldn't get the story out of his mind. He himself was a very rich young man. He lived in a city named Memphis in Egypt. His parents had died and left him a huge amount of money—and a much younger sister to look after.

After thinking the matter over, he decided what he must do. He paid in advance for everything his sister would need while she was growing up. He also provided a dowry for her—the sum of money that a wife was expected to give her husband when they married.

Then Antony sold his house and all his possessions, gave all his remaining money away to the poor, and went to live in the Egyptian desert. There he found an underground cave and lived in it for twenty years. During those years, he spent his time fasting and praying. Friends helped keep him alive by occasionally bringing him loaves of bread.

While he was in the desert, he sometimes heard voices in his head and had strange visions or dreams. He believed that the devil was tempting him to give up this way of living. Why should he do without food and wine and music and all the good things of life? Sometimes the devil appeared to him in the form of a very attractive young woman and started tempting him to enjoy the company of the women of Memphis.

At the end of the twenty years, during which time he had resisted all these temptations, he decided to go to the northern Egyptian city of Alexandria.

The Romans were persecuting any Christians they found there, and Antony did all he could to help those who were sent for trial or execution. After a while, the Romans stopped attacking the Christians, and Antony decided to return to the desert.

But life there was not the same as it had been. During his time in Alexandria, Antony had become famous, and now people came out to the desert to see this holy man. Antony never turned them away but gave them any advice and help he could. Many stayed there and followed Antony's way of life, so becoming the first ever community of monks.

It was during this time that Antony visited Paul the Hermit and found Paul's cloak in Thebes.

When Antony was very old, he called two friends to him. "It won't be long before I die. I'm 105, you know. Promise me one thing."

"Of course," said his friends. "What is it?"

"Promise to bury me secretly so no one will know the place. Except you."

And that's what they did. To this day, nobody knows where his body was hidden.

When he lived in the desert, Antony struggled to resist the temptation of returning to live a comfortable life.

Athanasius

One reason so much is known about Antony is that another of his friends, Athanasius, wrote down the story of his life. His home was in Alexandria, where he became a deacon and where he was later made a bishop.

He wrote many books and letters. These writings contained "the sacred and lasting truths of Christianity." His writings were considered so important that, five hundred years after he died (when there were still no printed books), a monk once said, "If you find a book by Athanasius and have no paper on which to copy it, copy it onto your shirts."

At one time it was thought that Athanasius also wrote what is known as the Athanasian Creed, a summary of what Christians believe. It has since been proved that this was written after he died.

Valentine and Sebastian

SAINTS' DAYS

14 FEBRUARY
Valentine

20 JANUARY
Sebastian

EVERYONE HAS HEARD about Saint Valentine. He's the patron saint of lovers, and on his day people send anonymous cards or presents to the one they love.

Valentine

But who was Saint Valentine?

Well, there was a priest named Valentine who lived in Rome in the third century. He was put in prison because he helped some Christians who were going to be executed by a cruel emperor named Claudius. While Valentine was in prison, he healed the chief warder's daughter, who was blind, and the warder and all his family became Christians.

When Emperor Claudius heard this, he said that Valentine should be executed. And so, on February 14 in the year 269, Valentine was clubbed to death. Then his head was chopped off, just to make sure he was dead.

In the same year, another man named Valentine, who was the bishop of Terni (about sixty miles from Rome), was also put to death by Emperor Claudius for being a Christian.

Neither saint seems to have anything to do with young lovers. So where do the traditions come from? Some say it is because on this day of the year (in the northern hemisphere) birds pair up and start mating.

Others say the day is special for lovers because at that time of year there had been a pagan Roman festival named Lupercalia, when young men took part in a kind of lottery to find a partner. But Lupercalia has nothing to do with either Saint Valentine!

The heart is the symbol of Saint Valentine's Day, although there is no clear link between the two real Saint Valentines and romantic love.

Sebastian

Sebastian was the son of a nobleman and was born in Narbonne in France. Although he was a Christian, he joined the Roman army in the year 283. He kept his beliefs secret because he thought he could do more good as a Christian spy inside the army!

Some Christians who knew the truth about Sebastian brought a woman named Zoe to him. She had lost the power of speech. Sebastian prayed with her and she quickly recovered. As a result, many people who knew her became Christians.

About the same time, a new emperor, Emperor Diocletian, promoted Sebastian to be captain of the Praetorian Guard, a regiment that acted as the emperor's very own bodyguard. Diocletian, who hated all Christians, had no idea that his most trusted officer was leading a double life.

Some time later, the authorities discovered that Zoe and some of her friends were Christians. They were arrested and sentenced to death. Some were drowned; others were buried alive or beheaded. Diocletian believed that the Christians were a threat to the security of the empire. Even the pope had to go into hiding.

It was too much for Sebastian. He went to see the emperor, announced that he was a Christian too, and told the emperor what he thought of his cruelty. Diocletian was furious. He ordered that Sebastian be put to death in a terrible way.

Sebastian was stripped and tied to a tree. His fellow officers were then ordered to use him as a target for archery practice. Arrow after arrow was shot into his body, and Sebastian was left for dead.

A Christian widow named Irene came to rescue his body and was amazed to discover that Sebastian was still just alive. She cared for his many wounds and nursed him back to health.

As soon as he had recovered, Sebastian went and hid in a passageway he knew the emperor walked along regularly. As Diocletian approached, Sebastian stepped out and once again told him what he thought of his cruelty.

Diocletian could say nothing for a moment because he was so shocked at seeing the man he was sure had been shot to death. But as soon as he recovered, he again ordered Sebastian to be put to death. This time Sebastian was beaten to death with heavy clubs and his body was thrown into one of the city's sewers.

The emperor Diocletian ordered Sebastian to be shot with arrows. However, this torture did not kill him as expected.

SAINT'S DAY

23 APRIL

The Dragon Slayer
George

SAINT GEORGE IS ONE of the best-known saints. Yet all we know for certain is that there was a Roman centurion, or tribune, named George from Cappadocia, who became a Christian and was consequently put to death in Palestine about the year 300. Because he wasn't afraid to say he was a Christian, he was later made a saint. Although no other facts are known about George, many stories have been told about him—including the story of Saint George and the dragon.

Once upon a time, there lived a huge and terrible dragon. Its home was in a large lake near a distant city. Whenever it was hungry, it would come out of the lake and seize any sheep it could find in the area and greedily eat them up before lumbering back into the lake.

The people tried attacking the dragon, but it simply snorted fire from its giant nostrils, driving them back in terror and filling the air with its deadly polluting breath. Many of the people became ill and died from the pollution alone. Because of this, the city was always gloomy and sad.

The most famous story about Saint George is of him killing a dragon and so saving a beautiful princess.

Saints of the Persecuted Church

Finally the people went to their king and asked, "What can we do? Soon we'll all have perished because of that dragon!"

"If we sacrifice one of our daughters down by the lake each day, that would at least keep it away from the city," suggested the king. "We could draw lots to see who is to be sacrificed each day."

Sensing that the crowd wasn't too keen on this idea, the king added, "Although I've only got one daughter, she must take her chance as well." Nobody had a better idea, so they decided to follow the king's advice. Every day, a family gave up one of their daughters to be a meal for the dragon. Before long, it fell to the royal family to sacrifice their daughter, Cleodolinda.

As she was led out, the king watched her go with tears in his eyes.

She stood on the shore of the lake, sobbing bitterly. But as she did so, who should ride up on a white horse but a handsome young man dressed in a Roman officer's uniform!

"What's the matter?" he asked.

"Kind sir, whoever you are," replied Cleodolinda, "ride away from here!"

"My name is George," said the man, "and I won't leave until you tell me why you're here."

So she told him about the dragon.

Just as she finished her story, with a roar and with its usual amount of splashing, the dragon emerged from the lake.

George made the sign of the cross on himself and said the words, "In the name of the Father, and the Son, and the Holy Spirit." Then he charged on his horse at the dragon. He thrust his spear with all his strength into its throat, pinned the animal to the earth, and his horse then trampled the dragon under its feet. Once it was docile, George ordered Cleodolinda to tie the white belt she was wearing around the dragon's neck and lead it into the city, like a dog on a leash. Nervously, she did.

When they saw this extraordinary procession, the people were astonished. And afraid.

"Don't be afraid, but trust in the Lord Jesus Christ," said George, "for it was he who sent me to you to save you from the dragon."

Then he killed the dragon. The people dragged the carcass out of the city and burned it. Fifteen thousand of them became Christians.

SAINT'S DAY

25 JULY

The Protector
Christopher

CHRISTOPHER WAS A GIANT. Or maybe he was just a very big man. Whichever was the case, he was extremely proud of his size and his strength, and he had a great desire to serve the most powerful king in the world.

And that is how the legend of Saint Christopher begins. It's only a legend. But it has made him, for many Christians, a much-loved saint they can turn to in time of need.

Christopher is remembered for carrying the Christ child safely across a flooded river.

Once upon a time, so the story goes, Christopher set off to search for the most powerful king of all.

At last he found an extremely rich and powerful king and happily became his servant. Then, one day, some entertainers arrived at the king's court. They sang songs and ballads to the king and his courtiers. All went well until they sang a song about the devil. Then Christopher noticed that the king turned pale and started to tremble.

The devil must be greater than this king, thought Christopher. That's who I must serve. And off he went to find the devil.

The devil was delighted to recruit such a strong assistant, and Christopher was pleased to be serving someone he thought was more powerful than any earthly king. Then, one day, they were out riding.

As the devil rode along on his black horse, he came to a large cross that had been placed at the roadside. He took one look at it, shuddered terribly, and galloped off as fast as he could.

"Why did he do that?" said Christopher to one of the junior devils.

"Don't ask," said the junior devil.

"That's the sign of Jesus," said another.

Christopher realized that Jesus must be a greater king than the devil—so off he went in search of Jesus. Eventually, he met a holy man who told him that the best way to find Jesus was through prayer and by fasting. Christopher had never learned to pray and did not want to give up food in case it weakened his strength.

"In that case," said the holy man, "you should use the gifts God has given you." And he showed Christopher a deep and dangerous river. It crossed the route that many Christians followed when they were making a journey to the Holy Land, where Jesus had once lived. "You could use your strength to carry these pilgrims on your shoulders across the river," he suggested.

And that is what Christopher did for many years.

One night, he was woken from his sleep by a boy's voice. The child wanted to be carried across the river there and then. "But it's dark and stormy," said Christopher. "Why not wait till morning?"

But the boy insisted, so Christopher put him on his shoulders, took up his stout stick in one hand, and started to wade through the swirling river. At first it seemed easy, but then the child seemed to grow heavier and heavier, and Christopher feared he might stumble and that they might both drown. At last they reached the other side.

"You began to feel very heavy," said Christopher. "It was as if I was carrying the whole world on my shoulders."

"No wonder," said the child, "for I am Jesus, who saved the world from sin by taking the weight of all the sins of the world upon me."

"I don't believe that!" replied Christopher.

"Plant your stick in the ground. Tomorrow it will have taken root and will be bearing flowers and fruit at the same time. That will prove that you have indeed found the one you should serve."

And the next morning, the stick had become a tree bearing both flowers and fruit, and Christopher had indeed found the greatest king of all.

When Christopher planted his stick in the ground, it took root overnight and miraculously bore flowers and fruit together.

Catherine of Alexandria

SAINT'S DAY

25 NOVEMBER

S HE WAS ABOUT EIGHTEEN and her name was Catherine. She lived in the Egyptian city of Alexandria, the city that Antony the Great of Egypt had once visited and that was the home of Athanasius.

Catherine lived during the reign of the Roman emperor Maxentius and was famous throughout the city for her beauty. Despite this, she was the sort of person who liked to spend her time reading and studying. Indeed, she was just as famous for her intelligence as she was for her good looks.

Now it so happened that Emperor Maxentius made a visit to Alexandria, which was part of his empire. While he was there, he heard about Catherine's beauty and intelligence. He commanded his servants to bring her to meet him. As soon as he saw her, he decided he wanted to marry her. Immediately. But there was a problem.

Maxentius already had a wife.

Maxentius (who continued to worship the ancient Roman gods) didn't think this mattered at all. "Oh, don't worry," he said. "I'll have two wives at the same time. I'm the emperor, I can do what I like." Catherine was having none of this.

Above: *The monastery of Saint Catherine in the shadow of Mount Sinai.*

She refused his proposal, saying that as a Christian she couldn't possibly agree to such a relationship.

Maxentius then gathered together a great number of teachers and professors who also believed in the Roman gods. He told them to persuade Catherine that her Christian faith was nonsense. She listened to them for a while and then started answering their points convincingly and persuasively. The result was that, far from getting Catherine to change her mind, these wise men began to change their own minds.

Opposite: *Catherine and the wheel of torture.*

The emperor was not only angry; he was alarmed. What would happen if Rome gave up its worship of the old gods? He didn't want any of what he described as "this Christian nonsense."

So he gave orders that Catherine should be put to death in a particularly horrible way. He had a large wheel made, with sharp blades set into the outside rim. Then Catherine was to be tied around this edge, and the

PRAYING TO SAINT CATHERINE

*U*nmarried women (who wanted a husband) used to pray to Saint Catherine.

A husband, Saint Catherine,
A good one, Saint Catherine,
A handsome one, Saint Catherine,
A rich one, Saint Catherine,
And soon, Saint Catherine.

blades were intended to cut her to pieces as the wheel was rolled along.

It didn't go according to plan. When Catherine was bound to the wheel, it broke and the blades flew off in all directions, flashing in the light and wounding the soldiers who were supposed to be putting her to death. Some people say all this was caused by lightning striking the wheel. Whether that is true or not, Catherine's executioners didn't try making another wheel. They beheaded her at once.

It is said that a flight of angels then descended from heaven and carried her body to Mount Sinai, where, centuries before, God had given the Ten Commandments to Moses. Even today there is a monastery named Saint Catherine's there.

People also remember the death of Saint Catherine with the firework that is named after her, which is supposed to spin around as her wheel did.

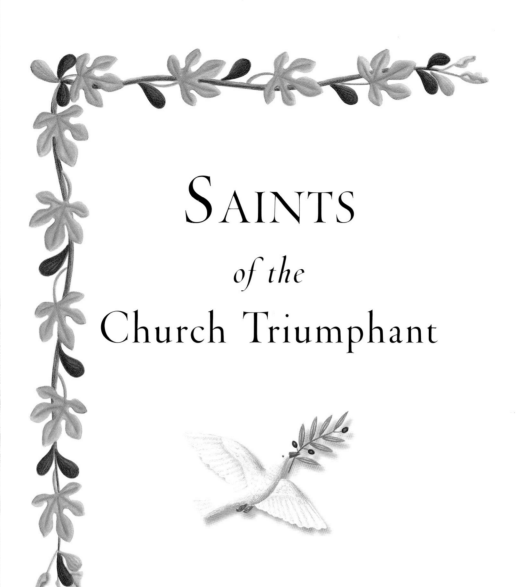

SAINTS
of the
Church Triumphant

*whose example
and teaching
helped establish
the Christian faith*

Constantine and Helena

SAINTS' DAYS

21 MAY
Constantine

18 AUGUST
Helena

IT WAS THE DAY before the battle that he saw the sign. Above the midday sun, shining in the sky, there it was—a cross. There was no mistaking it. It was the sign Christians used to remind themselves of Jesus. And circling it were the Latin words *In hoc signo vinces*, meaning "By this sign, you shall conquer." It was a vision that would change the Roman empire forever.

Constantine

The emperor Constantine believed that Jesus helped him win an important battle.

The reason Constantine was going to do battle the next day was to decide once and for all who should be ruler of the Roman empire. When his father, Constantius, had died six years earlier, he'd been proclaimed emperor. There was no doubt about that. The problem was that one of his generals, General Maxentius, had other ideas. He thought he should be emperor, and now the matter was going to be settled by a battle close to a bridge that crossed the River Tiber near Rome.

The night before the battle, Constantine had a dream. Jesus appeared to him in the dream and said that he must make the cross his own symbol and have it placed on all the imperial flags and standards.

The next morning, 28 October in the year 312, the battle began. As the army of General Maxentius began to advance across the bridge, it collapsed, flinging many of his soldiers into the river. Constantine won easily.

Helena

Constantine's mother, Helena, immediately became a Christian. She started using her wealth to help the Christian faith by building new churches. And Constantine did indeed adopt the sign he had seen in the sky to be his emblem. It was not a simple cross but what is known as the "chi-rho" symbol, after the first two letters,

X and P (chi and rho), of the Greek word *Christos* meaning "Christ." From then on, that sign was on every Roman standard.

In that same year, Constantine made it legal to be a Christian. Christians no longer had to meet in secret.

After 250 years of persecution, it was safe to be a follower of Jesus anywhere in the Roman empire.

THE GREAT PERSECUTION

*B*efore Constantine came to power, the emperor Diocletian (who had Saint Sebastian put to death) made a series of orders, or "edicts," against Christians throughout the empire. This began in the year 303.

The first edict stated that all Christian churches were to be closed and all Bibles destroyed. Then Diocletian ordered all clergy and priests to be imprisoned. This was later changed. All clergy and priests then had to be executed. With his fourth edict, in the year 304, he ordered everyone (on pain of death) to make sacrifices to the Roman gods. Many good Christians refused to do this and risked death instead.

A famous Christian historian named Eusebius wrote at the time, "So many suffered that . . . the executioners grew weary." But the edicts caused great anger, and not just among Christians. By 305, Diocletian was so unpopular that he had to resign. Constantius then became emperor in his place. Just one year later, he died, and his son Constantine became the next emperor.

Above left: *An ancient tradition says that Helena found Jesus' cross buried near the hill of Calvary.*

Left: *The chi-rho became the emblem of Constantine. It is a symbol of the Christian faith.*

The One-Eyed Farmer

Spiridion

HE SIMPLY WASN'T the sort of person you'd expect to meet at a council of bishops. He hadn't been to university. He wasn't a historian. He didn't write books. In fact, he could hardly write at all. His name was Spiridion.

But he was going to the Council of Nicea. After all, he'd had an invitation from the emperor himself.

Spiridion was a sheep farmer. He lived with his wife and children on the island of Cyprus, the island that the apostle Paul and his friends Barnabas and young John Mark had visited more than 250 years before, bringing news about the life and teaching of Jesus.

Farmer Spiros (as he was sometimes known) had grown up as a Christian. He was firm in his faith, and when, some years back, the cruel emperor Diocletian had ordered everyone to worship the old Roman gods, he'd refused. For this, he'd suffered, but not as badly as some Christians. The Romans hadn't put him to death. Instead, they'd tortured him and torn out one of his eyes.

That had been horrible enough, but he'd survived and continued in his

Spiridion journeyed on a mule, like many farmers in his day and still to this day, as this harvest scene from Cyprus shows.

Christian faith. He was so highly regarded by his fellow islanders that they had chosen him to be their local bishop. So he deserved his invitation to the Council of Nicea, along with hundreds of other bishops from all over the Roman empire.

Spiridion sailed from Cyprus to the mainland by ship. He'd brought two mules—one brown and one white—for the long journey by road to Nicea. Mules are a cross between a donkey and a horse and are not the sort of creature you'd expect a distinguished churchman to travel with. But to Spiridion they seemed to be sensible, sure-footed animals and ideal for such a journey.

On the way, he met other bishops who were also going to Nicea. Not all of them showed as much Christian love as they should have done to their fellow bishop. Indeed, one or two of them were embarrassed at being seen with a man they thought to be uneducated and, as one of them said, "a one-eyed yokel."

After a day's journey, they hit upon an idea that would rid them of his company. That night, when they were all staying at a wayside inn, they slipped into the shed where the mules were stabled and cut off their heads. That'll stop him going any further, they thought.

But early the next morning, before dawn, Spiridion was up and dressed. He went to the stable to feed and water his mules. Far from being heartbroken at what he found, Spiridion performed a remarkable miracle. He restored the heads of the two mules and brought them back to life. But, in the dark, he put the wrong head on each mule.

And that legend explains the story of how the farmer-bishop from Cyprus arrived at the Council of Nicea riding on a white mule with a brown head and leading a brown mule with a white head.

The Council of Nicea

After Emperor Constantine made it legal to be a Christian, things changed quickly. Christians were no longer persecuted by the Roman authorities, who began to help them to spread the gospel story.

Soon after he first learned about Christianity, Constantine started to worry that Christians in various parts of the empire believed different things about Jesus. "Division in the church is worse than war," he said.

To sort things out, he invited all 1,800 bishops to a meeting, or council, to sort things out. The council met in the year 325 at Nicea. Nicea (now named Iznik) was a place in what is now Turkey.

In the end, only about 250 bishops actually made the journey there. One was Bishop Eusebius, who wrote a book about Constantine. Also there was Saint Athanasius, although he was still a deacon at the time.

The Slave-Girl Saint

Nino of Georgia

THE BABY WAS ILL. So its mother did what all mothers did in those days and in that country. She wrapped her baby up warmly and then carried it around the village to see if any other mother could tell what was the matter.

As she carried her precious child from one house to another, she was met only by sad shakes of the head. No other mother had any idea what was the matter or could think of a cure.

As the mother was sorrowfully leaving the last house in the village, the people who lived there said, "You could always try the slave girl."

"What slave girl?"

"You know, Nino or whatever her name is."

The mother suddenly remembered who they were talking about. The lord of the village had recently purchased a slave girl from some distant country. At least it was worth asking her. She might know something.

So the mother carried her baby to the little hut, which offered poor protection from the winter winds but which was where the slave girl slept at night. "Look at my baby," she said to Nino. "Do you know of a cure?"

"I know of no human cure," said Nino, "but I know what I would do."

"And what's that?" asked the mother.

"I would pray to my Lord Jesus Christ, the God whom I worship."

"Anything's worth a try," the mother said.

So Nino gently took the baby and placed it on the rough hair mat that was her only blanket. Then she knelt beside the baby and prayed to Jesus to bring the child back to health.

Within hours, the baby had recovered. The news spread throughout the village, and then from one village to the next, until they heard about it in the nearest town. Eventually even the royal family heard the news.

The country in which this happened was Georgia, the mountainous land that lies between the Black Sea and the Caspian Sea. In those days, it lay just outside the Roman empire and was ruled by a king, King Mirian, who had heard nothing about the Christian religion.

Now it so happened that Queen Nana, the wife of King Mirian, had been secretly suffering from an unknown illness for some time. "Bring me the slave girl," she said. "I should like to test her powers."

But Nino refused. "I was brought here as a slave girl. I belong in a hut, not in a royal palace," she said politely, but quite firmly.

To many people's surprise, Queen Nana decided to visit Nino's hut. Nino made her lie down on the same rough mat—something the queen was not used to doing. Nino said a prayer. Shortly afterward, Queen Nana was restored to full health.

In her delight, the queen demanded to hear more about the life and teachings of Jesus. In time, she became a Christian. King Mirian, however, paid no attention to his wife's new religion. Until one autumn day when he was out hunting. Toward evening, it grew foggy and he became separated from his fellow huntsmen and servants. Soon, he was completely lost. Would he ever get back to his palace? Would he be attacked by bears or wolves?

A sudden thought occurred to him. He'd try praying to the God his wife had told him about. "Oh Jesus, if you do exist as my wife has told me, rescue me from this darkness."

Within moments,

This sixth-century church in the mountains of Georgia is a tribute to the influence of Nino in spreading the Christian faith there.

the fog lifted. King Mirian was able to find his way safely back home, and he promised from that day onward to worship only the Christian God.

He also persuaded Nino to come to the city and had her tell him all she knew about Jesus. He arranged for her to supervise the building of a church, and in due course, he sent messages to the emperor Constantine asking him to send priests to Georgia so that they might spread the gospel of Jesus throughout his country. In this way all Georgia became Christian, thanks to the faith of the slave girl Nino.

SAINT'S DAY

6 DECEMBER

Saint Nicholas as a bishop. Snowy white hair and a red robe are very much part of the Santa Claus figure he inspired.

The Original Santa Claus

Nicholas

HE WAS WISE, HE WAS KIND, and he was a bishop—the bishop of Myra in Asia Minor (or what is now Turkey). Nicholas was also rich and generous. Whenever he met a poor man, he would give him money. If the poor man tried to say thank you, Nicholas would become very shy and hurry away.

One day, as Nicholas walked around the town, he overheard three young women talking sadly about what was going to happen to them. Nicholas listened. It seemed they were so poor that nobody would marry them, even though they were very beautiful. When their father came home, he shared their sorrow. He had no work and no hope of getting any. It seemed he might have to sell his daughters into slavery so that they would survive, or they might even have to earn a living as prostitutes. Nicholas tiptoed away. That night, while they were all sleeping, Nicholas came secretly to the house and threw a round bag of gold coins in through the window. "This is the best way," he said to himself. "If I give them money in an obvious way, it may embarrass their father. Much better to do it secretly." And Nicholas went quietly on his way.

Next morning, the father was overjoyed. "Now my eldest daughter has a dowry and can get married." Soon there was a wedding and a great party.

Some time after this, Nicholas was passing the same house. The two younger daughters were still sad because nobody would marry them, and their father was again very full of sorrow. Nicholas went quietly home.

Saints of the Church Triumphant

Santa Claus

*I*n the Netherlands, Nicholas is said to visit children on his feast day and, if they have been good that year, to leave them presents. In Dutch, his name is *Sinte Klaas*.

When Dutch people settled in America in what was once New Amsterdam and is now New York, they kept up this custom. Other people in the city misheard his name and started to give him the name Santa Claus. This gave rise to all the stories about Santa Claus, or Father Christmas. Like Saint Nicholas, Santa Claus is supposed to make secret visits at night and leave presents for those who deserve them!

In some countries, children hang up stockings in the hope of receiving gifts from Santa Claus. Another tradition is to leave out an empty shoe.

That night, Nicholas came tiptoeing around again and threw a second bag of gold in through the window.

Next morning, the family was overjoyed again. "Now my second daughter can get married!" said the father. And soon there was a second wedding and a second great party.

Some days later, Nicholas was again passing the same house. The father and his youngest daughter were sitting very sorrowfully at home because there was no money for a third wedding. Nicholas went quietly home.

That night, the father didn't go to sleep. He was wondering who had been leaving such generous presents and he wanted to say thank you. Sure enough, Nicholas came tiptoeing around and was about to throw a third bag of gold in through the window when the father heard him and came to the door. Nicholas tried to run away, but the father caught him by the arm and started to thank him. Nicholas explained that he wanted to help all the daughters but he didn't want anyone to make a fuss over him. Even so, the father tried very hard to thank Nicholas properly. Nicholas replied that he must not thank him but thank God, who had given Nicholas money to use sensibly. At last, the two men gave each other a hug of friendship and then Nicholas went on his way. The third daughter was able to get married, Bishop Nicholas blessed the young couple, and there was a bigger party than ever.

Basil the Great and Gregory Nazianzen

SAINTS' DAY

2 JANUARY

THEY WERE BOTH BRAINY. Their names were Basil and Gregory, and they were both born in Caesarea, the capital of an area once known as Cappadocia but which, by this time, was known as Pontus. Both Basil and Gregory came from Christian families (Gregory's father was a bishop) and they went as students to Athens University, where they became best friends.

When he was twenty-six, Basil went home to Caesarea and earned his living as a teacher of public speaking, or what the Romans knew as oratory or rhetoric. Then, three years later, he gave up his career and set off on a long journey through Palestine and Egypt to visit Christians who were living the life of hermits in the same way that Paul of Thebes and Antony the Great had done many years before.

Eventually Basil returned to Pontus and he too began living as a hermit. But others came to join him. After some time, he was glad this had happened and that he was no longer alone. "God has made us like parts of the body," he said. "Just as one part isn't any use without the others, so we need the help of one another." He went on to say, "It is the duty of Christians to love and serve one another. How can you do that if you live alone? Who will you serve?"

Saint Basil (see also page 90).

Saints of the Church Triumphant

To help them in their daily life, Basil made up rules for himself and his new followers, rules that would stop them from wasting time or living without any purpose. In this way, they became the first Christian monks living an organized communal life in one building. In later years, such groups of monks would come to be known as orders and the places where they lived would come to be known as monasteries.

Basil himself gave up this way of life, however, and became a priest in Pontus. Nevertheless, he still believed in the monastic way of life and started several new monasteries.

In the year 370, everyone wanted him to become bishop of his hometown, Caesarea. Basil didn't feel that was right, but his friend Gregory persuaded him to accept. Once he was bishop, he worked hard and organized the building of a large hospital for the sick and the poor near the city gate. It also had a resting place for those on journeys and dwelling places for those in need. It became known as the Basiliad.

At one stage, Basil became unpopular with the local Roman authorities. They threatened to confiscate all his property, banish him, or even put him to death. Basil replied, "Such threats have no power over me. My only possessions are one ragged coat and some books. As for banishment, I'm simply journeying to heaven, and as for death, well, I am weak but it's only the first blow that will hurt me. Death will be a merciful release."

He died when he was only forty-nine, exhausted by hard work.

Basil's Rule allowed his monks only simple meals of bread and vegetables.

THE RULE OF SAINT BASIL

The rules, or Rule, that Basil wrote down said that he and the other monks must

✟ Pray regularly
✟ Help the poor and the sick
✟ Study the Bible
✟ Eat only one meal a day (of bread, water, and vegetables)
✟ Sleep only till midnight and then get up to pray

The Rule of Saint Basil is still followed by monks in the Eastern Church.

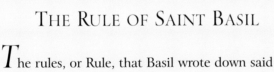

Martin of Tours

11 NOVEMBER
A spell of fine
weather in November
is known throughout
Europe as a "Saint
Martin's summer."

M ARTIN WASN'T REALLY a man; not yet. He was fifteen, strong, fit, and quite tall. Tall enough to join the Roman army, because this was in the days when the Romans ruled most of Europe.

And that was what Martin was doing in a small town in Italy not far from where he lived. Joining the army.

The army doctor examined him and all the other young men who were hoping to become soldiers. Next an officer asked them questions, making sure they were not runaway criminals or slaves who ought to be at home serving their masters.

Each of the young men had brought with him a letter from someone, recommending him as likely to be a good soldier. Martin handed over his letter. The officer read it. "Most impressive," he said. "From your father, isn't it?"

"Yes, sir," said Martin.

"Met him once. Very brave soldier. And you're going to be just like him. Excellent."

Martin took the army oath, promising to be a soldier and to be loyal to the Roman empire. He was given, as was usual, four months' pay in advance.

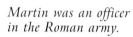

*Martin was an officer
in the Roman army.*

In fact, Martin proved to be a very good soldier. He was reliable and popular. Soon, he was promoted. He became an officer—only a junior officer but, still, an officer. Now he also wore a sword and a warm red cloak, and he no longer marched on foot with all the other soldiers as they tramped the long miles along the straight Roman roads. Martin rode on a silver-white horse.

The winter when Martin was eighteen, he and his soldiers were posted to another part of the Roman empire. They were sent to guard the town of Amiens in the north of Gaul, what's now known as France. Martin and his soldiers weren't too pleased about this. Winter in northern France can seem very damp and cold to someone who is used to the warmth of Italy and the sunny Mediterranean countries. But at least Martin had his cloak.

One raw, damp evening, Martin was riding slowly through the town, his soldiers marching behind him, when he saw a beggar. There was nothing unusual about that—there were many beggars in those days.

But Martin couldn't help noticing this man. He was wearing just a few damp, torn rags and was shivering with cold.

Martin pulled up his horse, drew his sword, and with one swift movement, cut his warm red cloak in two. He gave half to the beggar, who could hardly believe his luck. Martin's soldiers were amazed. They began to giggle. Had their officer gone mad? Ruining his cloak for a beggar? They tried not to laugh out loud. They couldn't help it. But Martin wasn't angry with them.

This detail from a medieval manuscript shows Martin cutting his cloak with a sword to give half to a beggar.

"That man was cold. I had a cloak. It was right to share it," he said.

In silence, they marched back to their barracks.

That night, Martin had a dream. He thought he saw Jesus, wearing half a Roman soldier's cloak. "Look," said Jesus in the dream, "this is the cloak that Martin has shared."

His dream made Martin determined to become a Christian. He was baptized and so became a follower of Jesus. Now he wanted to leave the army, but a war was beginning against a fierce tribe named the Goths. Martin was immediately accused of being a coward for wanting to run away from the war. When he still refused to fight, this was thought to be mutiny, so he was put in prison. Only at the end of the war was he released and allowed to leave the army and become a Christian.

SAINT'S DAY

13 SEPTEMBER

John Chrysostom. This picture and that of Basil (see page 86) are in the same church, and the pictures show the distinctive features of each saint.

Golden Mouth

John Chrysostom

A S SAINTS GO, HE wasn't a very nice man. Indeed, considering some of the things he said, it's hard to see how he ever became a saint—let alone a saint who was famous for being a good speaker.

He was very rude about women. He thought they were much more wicked than men—and that they spent their time tempting men to do wrong. He didn't like the Jews either. He even once said, "I hate the Jews."

So how did a man who said such terrible things become a saint?

The answer to that question lies in his nickname. *Chrysostom* is a Greek word meaning "golden mouth." He was given that nickname because he was such a persuasive speaker. People often pushed their way to the front of the church when he was talking so that they could be nearer to him.

John was clever. There was no doubt about that. As a young man, he started training to be a lawyer. But when he was eighteen, he decided he couldn't be a lawyer and a kind, loving Christian. So he gave up his career and became a monk. Unfortunately, the monastery he went to live in was very damp. His health suffered and John had to leave and go back home.

Home was the city of Antioch, where he became a deacon and then a priest. It was at this time that he became famous for his sermons, which were always easy to understand.

Saints of the Church Triumphant

Crowds of people packed into the churches to listen to him. They listened so hard, they forgot what was going on around them, and so the churches became popular places for pickpockets. John had to warn the people who came to listen to him to leave their purses at home or risk losing them!

He was so popular that, in the year 397, when he was fifty, the emperor of the time insisted that John became bishop of Constantinople. John wanted to stay in Antioch, but the emperor, whose name was Arcadius, was determined. John had little choice, so he went to Constantinople.

It was a city famous for its wealth and entertainments. John didn't approve. He cut down his own expenses, wearing only a shabby gown rather than expensive robes. He spent very little on food and gave all the savings to help the poor and to support a hospital. And he wasn't afraid to say what he thought. He attacked the misuse of wealth and other evils, and in doing so he made enemies, especially among the rich and famous.

One person who attracted his criticism was the emperor's wife. Her name was Eudoxia, and John disapproved of the way she lived, giving her the name "Jezebel" (the name of a wicked woman mentioned in the Bible). He spoke out against her use of makeup and the fact that she went to watch horse racing on Good Friday. John's attack didn't please Arcadius.

Arcadius arranged for John to be banished from the city and sent into exile. No sooner had this happened than an earthquake hit the city. Arcadius thought this must mean that God was angry, and he had John brought back to Constantinople. However, John was banished again a year later, this time for good.

During this time, John wrote many letters and also composed prayers, some of which are still used. He was never afraid to say what he thought. Sometimes this meant he was quite tactless and upset people, but he was always a friend of sinners. "If you have done wrong not once but twice or even a thousand times, come to me. You will be healed, through Jesus Christ," he said. And thousands of people did go to him. It is said that there were one hundred thousand Christians in Antioch when John was teaching there, and it was thanks to "Golden Mouth" that many of these people first heard about Jesus.

Make Me Good, but Not Yet

Augustine

A S HE HIMSELF ADMITTED, he'd been a naughty young man. Despite being taught about Jesus by his very holy mother, Monica, Augustine had spent his youth doing all kinds of wrong things. He was rebellious at school, and he was also idle. But he was intelligent.

He'd been born in a small village named Tagaste in what is now Algeria in northern Africa. When he was seventeen, he went to study at the nearby Carthage University, and it was here that he gave up Christianity, saying it was nonsense. He also made his girlfriend pregnant. They soon had a son, whom they named Adeodatus.

Despite all this, he did well at his studies and, in time, became a teacher. First, he started a school in Tagaste, but he soon returned to Carthage, where he taught at the university. It was at this time that he began to think again about the faith his mother had taught him. He knew that the way he was living was wrong, but he was also enjoying it. Much later in his life, he wrote down a prayer he had said at this time. It was a prayer that showed he knew he ought to be better but that also showed how much he was enjoying himself. His prayer was "O Lord God, make me good but not yet."

From Carthage, Augustine moved on to teach in Rome and later in Milan, where his mother and Adeodatus came to join him.

One day, in Milan, he was sitting in a garden. Some children were playing nearby and he heard one of them shout out the words "Take up and read." He absentmindedly picked up the nearest thing there was to read. It was a copy of Paul's letter to the Romans. He started reading the words: "Let us live honestly; not in

AUGUSTINE'S HOLY MOTHER

*A*ugustine's mother, Monica, spent a lot of her life in tears. This is why, when Spanish explorers in California found a rock from which a spring of water dribbled all the time, they named it (and the nearby town) Santa Monica.

Monica was born in Carthage in North Africa in 332 and was a devout and very holy Christian. To be fair, she had a lot to be unhappy about, mainly her son's bad ways. She told him once how worried she had been about him and how she had told a bishop about her worries. The bishop had said, "The son who caused so many tears will never be lost." Monica told this story to Augustine soon after he became a Christian, and shortly afterward she died in his arms in the year 387.

Her saint's day is on 27 August.

revelry and drunkenness, not in lust and dirtiness, not in arguing and jealousy but in the way of Jesus."

These words made him think. How had he been spending his life? Had his mother been right all along? He went to talk to the bishop of Milan, a very holy man named Ambrose (who would himself become a saint). After that, Augustine went to many of the services at which Ambrose spoke. On the evening before Easter day in the year 387, Augustine was baptized as a Christian by Ambrose. Four years later Augustine became a priest.

Some people believe that Augustine and Ambrose together wrote a famous Latin hymn of praise, which begins with the words *Te deum laudamus*, which means "We praise you, O God."

This picture shows Augustine with a crook, one of the symbols of his status as a bishop. The book is a reminder of his conversion—when he was prompted to "Take up and read."

Augustine then went back to Africa and was soon made bishop of Hippo. This oddly named seaport is now named Annaba and is in Algeria. Thanks to Augustine, the Christian church became very strong in that place.

During the thirty-five years he was bishop of Hippo, he employed men to write down his sermons as he preached them. Copies were made and sent to other bishops and to monasteries. It is from these many books and from his own life story, which is known as the *Confessions*, that we know so much about the man who had once lived quite a wicked life but who came to see that Jesus welcomes all people, including sinners, provided they are prepared to reform and live according to his sayings.

Here is a famous prayer of Saint Augustine:

Father,
I am seeking:
I am hesitant and uncertain,
but will you, O God,
watch over each step of mine
and guide me.

Simeon the Stylite

S OME CHRISTIANS give things up during the season of the year known
as Lent. For example, they may stop eating chocolate or stop
watching so much television. Or they may go to church more often
than usual. They do things like this as a small way of remembering how
Jesus gave up his life for them.

Lent is a reminder of the forty days when Jesus lived in the desert while
he prepared himself for his work of teaching and healing. For him, it was
a way of getting away from everyday life and having time to concentrate
on praying without interruption.

Some Christians have done this too, and often for more than forty days.
They have tried to live with almost none of the comforts we take for
granted (such as somewhere to sleep) and to escape from the distractions
of everyday life. One such person was Simeon the Stylite.

Simeon was the son of a shepherd, and by the age of thirteen, he was
already working as a shepherd himself. He didn't go to church much, but
one winter Sunday, when the snow meant they couldn't take the sheep
out to pasture, he did go.

That Sunday, he heard the words spoken by Jesus during the Sermon
on the Mount. "Blessed are the pure in heart. . . . Blessed are the
peacemakers. . . . Blessed are those who mourn. . . . All these people
will find blessings." Simeon asked the preacher to explain more about the
Christian faith. He did this for several hours and Simeon listened hard.

Some time later, he had a dream. He dreamed that he was digging a hole
in the ground for the construction of some sort of building. Whenever he
stopped, a voice said, "Dig deeper." At last, he had dug a foundation deep
enough for any building. And then, in his dream, he saw a tall pillar.

When he was eighteen, he became a monk in a local monastery. The
rules of the monastery did not seem strict enough to Simeon because he
felt he should give up everything to serve God. He disciplined himself by
eating even less food than the other monks and by praying more hours a
day. Gradually Simeon became certain that in order to live a really holy
life he must get away from all other people.

He left the monastery and went to live in the nearby mountains. He
survived for more than three years with little food and no shelter from the
weather. People came to see and talk with this holy man. Even in the
mountains, he wasn't alone. Then he remembered his dream.

This time he decided to follow the dream closely. He dug a hole in the ground and then built a stone pillar about ten feet (or 3 m) high with a small wooden platform on top. This platform was where Simeon now chose to live. Only the smallest quantities of food and drink were passed up to him to keep him alive, and during Lent, he survived on water alone. He spent his time praying and thinking. He became known as Simeon the Stylite because the Greek word for pillar is *stylos*.

Not surprisingly, many people came to see this strange sight. And once again Simeon found he could not concentrate on his prayers. So, after four years, he replaced his pillar with one that was twenty feet (6 m) high. The platform he now lived on was less than seven feet (2 m) across, making it difficult for him to lie down full length. It was certainly fortunate that he didn't walk in his sleep, although there was a railing around the edge of the platform.

After three more years, he was again worried by the increasing crowds of visitors, so he built a new pillar twice as high, and after another ten years, he built a fourth pillar sixty feet (18 m) high. His food and water were sent up by means of a pulley and chain. He lived in this way for another twenty years, able to pray without distractions but still able to talk to his visitors when he wished.

Simeon's pillar was so narrow that he needed a railing to stop him from falling. However, it was just big enough for him to lie down, although he could not safely stretch out. This picture shows how he must have felt on top of his pillar.

The Lion's Friend

Gerasimus

IN THE LAND WHERE JESUS once lived, there flows the River Jordan. Not far from that river is a city named Jericho, and not far from Jericho is a desert. Many, many years ago, on the edge of the desert lived a number of holy men. Unlike monks who live together, each of these men lived in his own hut, and each spent his time praying and thinking about God. They tried to keep themselves away from all the evil things in the world, and some people named them hermits. The proper name for such men is "anchorites."

One of them was named Gerasimus.

There came a day when Gerasimus decided he would go for a walk by himself in the desert in order to concentrate properly. He walked on and on, hardly looking where he was going. Then, from behind some rocks, he heard a whimpering noise.

"I suppose I'd better see what's the matter," he said to himself.

When he saw what was making the whimpering noise, he said, "Oh dear. Oh dear me. You're in pain."

He was about to go forward and help, but then he stopped as he realized the danger. It was a lion. "Oh dear," he said again. "I've never seen a lion before but I know what you are. I suppose I ought to be afraid."

The lion whimpered again and held up a paw.

Above: *The desert wilderness near Jericho.*

Right: *Gerasimus helped a wild lion by taking a thorn out of its paw, and the lion became his devoted friend.*

And Gerasimus saw that there was a large and very sharp thorn sticking in the pad of the lion's foot. Instead of running away, Gerasimus tiptoed up to the lion and very gently pulled out the thorn. Then the lion stood up. Gerasimus started to back away. "Stay," he said, wondering if the lion would understand.

But the lion still came toward him. Gerasimus considered whether to run away or stand still. He decided to turn around and walk slowly away. When he'd gone a few steps, he glanced over his shoulder. The lion was

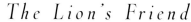

The story of the saint and the lion is often linked with Jerome rather than Gerasimus, and it is from a scene of the life of Jerome that this picture of a lion is taken.

following. It was so grateful for his help that it refused to leave him and followed him back to where he lived.

At first the other anchorites were seriously frightened, but they soon realized the lion would never hurt a friend of Gerasimus. So the lion came to live with them. Because Gerasimus had found it near the River Jordan, they named it Jordan, and Gerasimus taught it to fetch and carry things for the hermits.

Although Jordan was very friendly to them all, his special friend was always Gerasimus. This might seem like a happy ending, but in fact, the story has a rather sad ending. Not all that long after this, Gerasimus died. He was an old man by that time, at the end of his life, and he died quietly and without any pain. Jordan was lost without his special friend, and when the other hermits dug a grave and buried Gerasimus's body, Jordan lay down beside the grave and died as well.

Zosimus and Mary the Egyptian

ABOUT THE SAME TIME that Gerasimus met the lion by the River Jordan, another holy man lived in that same place. His name was Zosimus, but he was a monk, living in a monastery. Amazingly and somewhat oddly, he became a monk when he was still only a small boy, and for fifty-three years he followed the strict rules of the community, spending his time in prayer and study.

Then he decided to move to another monastery that had even stricter rules, including one special custom.

Each year during Lent (the forty days when Christians remember the time Jesus spent fasting in the desert), they would cross the nearby River Jordan and go into the desert. Each monk took a little food with him. One might take some bread soaked in water, another might take some figs or some dates. But that was all.

This picture of the desert wilderness shows how little it has to offer those who make their home among its rocks.

After crossing the Jordan, they would scatter far and wide, and if they did happen to see each other during the following weeks, they would each move off to a more distant part of the desert in order to be completely alone for Lent.

Zosimus did this. But one day, as he journeyed through the desert, he saw a strange figure in the distance. Instead of moving away, he went nearer. As he got closer, he saw it wasn't one of the other monks.

"Stop and speak to me," said Zosimus.

The figure moved away.

"Turn and show me who you are," he said.

The figure stopped moving but kept its back to him. "Forgive me," it said, "but I cannot turn and face you."

Then Zosimus realized that the figure was a white-haired woman and that she was naked.

"Throw me your cloak to cover me, so I may turn and you may give me your blessing," she said. Zosimus did so. She covered as much of her body as she could with his old tattered cloak, and then she told him her story.

She was born in Egypt and ran away from home when she was twelve. She ended up in the city of Alexandria, and there she worked as a prostitute. After seventeen years, she joined a group of pilgrims who were setting out for Jerusalem. She did this not because she wanted to worship in the place where Jesus had suffered but simply because she felt it would be a way of meeting more men.

When she arrived in Jerusalem, some strange force seemed to stop her from entering the church that had been built at the place where Jesus was laid in the tomb. She said a prayer, promising that she would give up her way of life if she was allowed to enter the church. Her wish was granted, and straightaway she realized how sinful her life had been. She thanked God in her prayers, vowed to give up her old life, and immediately left the city.

She went down to the River Jordan, crossed it, and spent the next forty-seven years living alone in the desert.

Zosimus was the first person she had met in all those years.

"What do you live on?" asked Zosimus in wonder.

"Herbs and what I can find. And my prayers. It is not by bread alone that we keep alive. Prayer gives us strength."

She made Zosimus promise to tell no one of these things until she had died. He also promised to return to the same spot on the Thursday before Easter to give her Holy Communion. That he did, bringing with him some dates and figs. She thanked him and begged him to return the following year.

When the year had passed, he went back and found only her bones, bleached white in the desert sun. But still to be seen were words she had written in the sand: "Bury the body of Mary the sinner here." And Zosimus did that, gently, praying as he did so. Then he returned to his monastery and told the other monks the story of Mary from Egypt who had given up her sinful ways in order to give herself totally to God.

A picture of Mary the Egyptian, shown in clothing that was far finer than the simple robes she would have once worn.

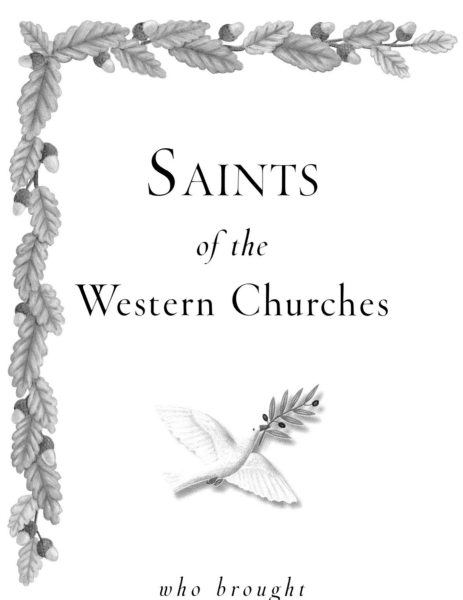

SAINTS
of the
Western Churches

who brought
holiness and wisdom
to a fearful world

Opposite: *The shamrock leaf, with its three parts, helped Patrick to explain his belief that God is three in one—God the Father, God the Son, and God the Holy Spirit.*

The Apostle of the Irish

Patrick

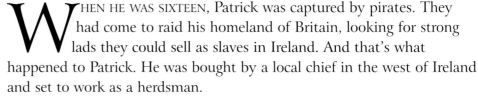

WHEN HE WAS SIXTEEN, Patrick was captured by pirates. They had come to raid his homeland of Britain, looking for strong lads they could sell as slaves in Ireland. And that's what happened to Patrick. He was bought by a local chief in the west of Ireland and set to work as a herdsman.

Ireland had never been part of the Roman empire. It had its own pagan gods, its own laws, and its own language. To young Patrick it seemed a wild and strange place. He'd been brought up as a Christian, but the faith had never meant very much to him. But now, as he looked after the animals in his care, he began to think more and more about Christianity.

In particular, he thought a lot about the belief that God is one being but at the same time also God the Father, God the Son who came to earth, and God the Spirit who is present at all times. Christians give this idea of three-in-one the name "the Trinity."

Not surprisingly, Patrick hated the hard life of slavery and eventually managed to escape. He made his way to the coast where he hoped to find a ship that would take him home to Britain. When he did find a ship, the sailors refused to take him on board. He turned miserably away but still prayed for help. As he prayed, the sailors called him back and let him on board.

It was a stormy voyage. The winds blew them off course, and when they did reach land, they had no idea where they were. Even worse, their food had run out and it seemed they might starve to death.

"You're a Christian," said one of the sailors. "Why don't you pray for food?"

Patrick did. Within minutes a herd of wild pigs came scuttling past, and the sailors were able to catch some of them. Patrick was suddenly very popular!

Over the next twenty years, Patrick lived mainly in France and studied to become a priest. Later he was made a bishop and was sent to Ireland in order to spread the word of Jesus there. He was probably chosen for this work because he spoke the Irish language.

At that time, Ireland was divided into tribal groups, each ruled by a chief—like the one who had once bought Patrick as a slave boy. One of the chiefs also had the title "high king of Ireland" and he ruled from Tara in County Meath. His name was Laoghaire, which is pronounced "Leary."

One day, as the story goes, High King Laoghaire was celebrating a pagan festival. At this festival, all the fires and lights were put out. No flame was to be seen anywhere until a burning torch was carried out of the king's palace. But this particular festival happened at the time of Easter, and Patrick lit an Easter candle in the darkness as a reminder of how Jesus rose from the dead.

The pagans were very angry and threatened Patrick with death, but he boldly explained to King Laoghaire the meaning of Easter. The king listened, and from then on Patrick was allowed to travel through Ireland, teaching about Jesus. It was dangerous work because not all the chiefs were as friendly as Laoghaire had proved to be. Patrick himself once wrote: "Daily I expect either a violent death or to be robbed and reduced to slavery."

Many other stories are told about Patrick. One tells how Patrick rid Ireland of snakes by saying a prayer, or spell, which made them all go into the sea. However, it has to be said that there were probably never any snakes in Ireland in the first place.

Much more likely to be true is the story that recalls how he used a shamrock leaf to explain the Trinity. "The Trinity is like this shamrock," he explained. "Like the leaf, it's three-in-one. It's only one leaf, but three parts make the complete leaf." And that, it's said, is why the shamrock became the emblem of Ireland.

Patrick, dressed as a bishop of a later time. Green is closely linked with Ireland.

Brigid

Brigid freely shared what she had with the poor—clothes, food, and even pots and pans.

Oᴺᴇ ᴏꜰ ᴛʜᴇ ɢᴏᴏᴅ ᴛʜɪɴɢꜱ about Brigid was that, when she was a little girl, she was very generous. She was always ready to give anything she had to other people. The problem was that she was so generous that she sometimes gave away things that weren't really hers to give.

She was the daughter of an Irish chief and one of his maids. While she was still a child, her father sold her as a slave girl to another chief. This chief set her to work in his dairy, where the milk from his cows was made into butter and cheese. One day a great number of poor people came begging for food. Brigid was so sorry for them that she gave away almost all the cheese and butter on the dairy shelves.

When she was about thirteen years old, her father brought her home to work for him. She still couldn't help giving things away if anyone was in need. Clothes, pots and pans, food—she gave them all to those who had none.

This was all very kind of her, but it wasn't long before her father decided it really couldn't go on like this. He couldn't afford to keep such a daughter any longer. So, as she had grown into a very beautiful young woman, he took her to the high king of Ireland to see if he would like to buy her as a slave.

He left Brigid in his chariot at the palace door while he went in to see if the king was prepared to buy her. The king himself came out to see her and found that she had just given away her father's sword to a man who had come by begging for food.

"But why give him my sword?" exploded her father. "It was valuable. It had jewels on the handle. What use was it to him?"

"But I'd nothing else to give him," she answered. "I had to give him something. He was so thin and hungry."

"Hm!" said the king. "She's no use to me. She's far too expensive a slave if she gives things away like this."

Brigid's father took her home again.

Sometime after this, Brigid gained her father's permission to become a nun. This she did, along with some friends of her own age. Once they were nuns, they made a special point of visiting the poor and sick, taking food to the hungry, nursing people who were ill, and teaching and helping children who had no parents. Because of this work they became the first nuns to be known as the Sisters of Mercy.

Soon after Brigid became a nun, she found a place where she felt she would like to stay for the rest of her life. It was not far from a lake, and there was a great oak tree growing there. With the help of her friends she built a hut, or cell, beneath the oak. Her friends built huts for themselves as well, not far from hers, and soon other women came to join them and to live as nuns. As time went on, this collection of huts became a proper convent. Later, a town was built there as well—a town known today as Kildare. Its name in Irish is *Kell-dura*, which means "the cell under the oak."

From this place, Brigid and her sister nuns would travel about the district, continuing their works of mercy among the poor. They also spent much time making copies of holy books and teaching those who visited that place.

Brigid had a little hut built for her in a quiet spot underneath an oak tree.

Benedict

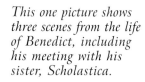

This one picture shows three scenes from the life of Benedict, including his meeting with his sister, Scholastica.

MONTE CASSINO HAS always been famous. It's a mountain (*monte* is Italian for mountain or mount) near the town of Cassino, which is southeast of Rome. First, the Romans built a temple there to their god Jupiter. Then a monk named Benedict came along and rebuilt it as a Christian monastery.

There is still a monastery on Monte Cassino, but it's not the same building. The one Benedict built in 529 was destroyed when the countryside around it was invaded fifty years later. Afterward, it was rebuilt, then destroyed three more times. On the first of these occasions, it was again wrecked by invaders. Then an earthquake did its worst. Finally it was destroyed in 1944, during World War II. The area was occupied by Nazi soldiers at the time, and the damage was done by bombs. But every time it was destroyed it was lovingly rebuilt.

Through all of this, the way of life of the monks who live there has changed very little. Just as the monks in the Eastern Church followed (and still follow) the Rule of Saint Basil, so the monks of

Monte Cassino follow the Rule that Benedict planned for them.

Basil wrote his Rule in Greek. Benedict wrote his in Latin. He began it by saying he didn't want to make it too strict or his monks would get discouraged when they failed to keep it. But he didn't want to make it too easy either.

His Rule said that his fellow monks (known as Benedictines) should meet in church several times a day to pray and to listen to Bible readings. But he said it was just as important that the monks should work. They should grow all their own food, prepare their own meals, mend the monastery when necessary, and copy books in beautiful handwriting. As he said, "To work is to pray." He also believed that "idleness is the enemy of the soul."

Unlike some monks and hermits of that time who slept little and who fasted often, Benedict said his monks should have eight hours' sleep every night and proper meals every day. He also believed that his monastery should help the people who lived in the district around it.

He also realized how difficult it was to get up for a church service in the middle of the night. "When the monks rise, let them gently encourage one another, because the sleepy ones are likely to make excuses not to get up."

It is no wonder that this strict but kind man became so popular. His Rule is still followed by Benedictine communities all around the world. His sister, Scholastica, also inspired many people to take up a monastic way of living.

THE TWIN SISTER

Scholastica (480–543) was the twin sister of Benedict, and she became a nun, living in a convent near Monte Cassino.

The rules of Benedict's and Scholastica's orders said monks couldn't enter convents and nuns couldn't enter monasteries. So they met only once a year in a house between his monastery and her convent. In the year 543, Scholastica felt her life was coming to an end. She wanted Benedict to stay the night and talk with her.

"No," he said kindly. "That would be against our Rule. A monk can't spend a night with a nun, even if they're brother and sister."

Scholastica began to pray he would stay with her. Immediately a terrible thunderstorm began. There was no question of Benedict going back that night.

"What have you done?" he asked.

"You refused my request when I asked you," she said. "When I asked God if you could stay here, he said yes."

Her saint's day is on 10 February.

David

OR LUNCH THEY ATE just bread and leeks. With salt. For lunch the next day they again ate just bread and leeks. With salt. And again the next day and the next day and the day after that . . . Always the same meal—bread and vegetables and a little salt. That was all David allowed his monks to eat.

If you were a monk who enjoyed your food, you'd have been much better off in a Benedictine monastery, for Benedict believed monks should have proper meals. David thought monks needed to live a much stricter life. So, besides making them always have the same meal, he never allowed them to drink wine or beer. He and his monks drank only water. That is how he got his nickname, David the Waterman. He is better known as David, the patron saint of Wales.

It is said that, when he was a young man, he went from his homeland to the Isle of Wight in southern England to study with a wise old teacher named Paulinus. He taught David about the Bible and helped him to understand the teachings of Jesus. When Paulinus was getting old, he started to go blind. It is said that David then touched his eyes, and once again Paulinus could see.

The cathedral of St. David's is an impressive sight along the rugged coast of west Wales.

David was made a priest, and he returned to his homeland, Wales. He built no fewer than twelve monasteries. These included one at Glastonbury in England and one at a place in the far west of Wales, which was then known as Menevia. That was where David himself settled, and Menevia is now named St. David's.

Life in David's monastery was strict, and not just with regard to food and drink. Most of the day had to be spent in silence, and no sleep was allowed between Friday evening and Sunday morning. And David did not let his monks use any oxen or horses to plough the fields. "Each monk is his own ox. He must pull the plough himself."

He himself would often pray throughout the night, rather than going to bed. He also had a very strange habit. Sometimes he would stand up to his neck in icy water, just as a test to prove he could do this without complaining!

Despite all this he was much loved by everyone who heard him preach. He must have had a wonderful voice as well, because of what happened one day when there was a huge meeting in Wales at a place named Llanddewi Brefi. Thousands of people came to hear their bishops speak, but because the crowd was so big, it was impossible for everyone to hear what was being said. First one bishop tried and then another.

But old Paulinus was in the crowd. He remembered his pupil, David. "Let David speak," he said. "You'll be able to hear him."

At first, David didn't want to. He was only a priest and not a bishop. But he prayed to God and then spoke clearly. Everyone, even those at the far edges of the crowd, could hear what he had to say.

It is said that while he was talking, a white dove perched on his shoulder. People took this as a sign that God liked what he had to say. A much stranger story says that before he started to speak, he put a handkerchief on the ground. When he stood on it, the ground under it rose up and David was soon standing high enough to be seen as well as heard by everyone.

After this, David was made not only a bishop but archbishop (or head bishop) of Wales. He became highly regarded throughout South Wales, where fifty churches bear his name. For many years, his saint's day was celebrated as a religious festival. Later it became a national festival among the Welsh, and Saint David's Day is now celebrated by Welsh people all over the world.

Above: *Bishop David, shown with a harp, the traditional musical instrument of Wales.*

Below: *The daffodil is a symbol of David and the national flower of Wales.*

9 JUNE
Columba of Iona

13 JANUARY
Kentigern

The Celtic Saints

Columba of Iona
and Kentigern

THE WORD "CELTIC" is sometimes used to describe those people who have lived in the western parts of the British Isles, such as Ireland and Scotland, over the last thousand years.

Columba of Iona

Not many saints have been responsible for the deaths of three thousand men. You certainly wouldn't suspect a saint nicknamed "the Dove."

The truth is that, although Columba (who was a Celt and an Irishman) may have been a very gentle and loving man in his middle and old age, he had quite a temper when he was young.

The trouble began with a book. In those days, before printing was invented, if you wanted a book, you had to make a copy of it by hand. The young monk Columba loved books and made hundreds of copies of holy books in his own beautiful handwriting. One time, he borrowed a book without permission and secretly made a copy of it for himself. Its owner, a man named Finnian, had got the book while visiting Rome. He claimed that because he owned the original, the copy must belong to him as well.

This led to a court case to see who had the "copy right." The high king of Ireland decided the case against Columba, saying, "To every cow, her calf. To every book, its copy. Therefore the copy you made, Columba, must be restored to Finnian."

Columba was angry. It seems that he and his followers started a war against the high king, and it was during this war that three thousand men were killed. When he realized what had happened as a result of losing his temper, Columba was deeply sorry. He decided that he must leave Ireland forever and bring to Jesus as many souls as had lost their lives in the battle.

He and twelve close friends set sail in tiny boats, eventually landing on a small island off the western coast of Scotland. We now know the island as Iona. It's less than three miles long and two miles wide, and there they

Columba's name means "the Dove." His saintly life really began after an outburst of violence, and he spent the rest of his life spreading the Christian message and the way of peace.

buried their boats and built a simple monastery. The main building was a tiny wooden church, surrounded by the small huts in which they lived.

They spent their time farming the stony soil, fishing, raising animals—and making beautiful copies of holy books. All the work stopped at regular times for services in the little church.

Once this little group of monks was settled on Iona, Columba began journeying around the mainland of Scotland, teaching the message of Jesus. His first aim was to persuade the Scottish kings and chiefs. He knew that if one of them became Christian, then the people would follow. Columba did succeed in persuading the king of Inverness to become a Christian, and from then on, his work was easier. By the time of his death, he had led many more than three thousand people to the Christian way of life.

Columba is famous for the journey he and his companions made in tiny boats across the wild seas that separate Ireland and Scotland.

Kentigern

Kentigern was also a Celt. He was a Scottish monk who lived in what was once very peaceful countryside where Glasgow now stands. He journeyed around, preaching the Christian faith, and may have met Saint Columba and also visited Saint David in Wales. A famous story told about him explains why there is a fish and a ring on the crest of the city of Glasgow.

The king of Strathclyde had given his queen a very precious ring. One day, he saw it not on her finger but on the finger of one of his knights who happened to be asleep. Not surprisingly, the king was both angry and jealous. The king gently slipped the ring from the knight's finger and flung it into the River Clyde.

He then asked his queen to show him the ring. Not knowing what to do, she asked Kentigern for his help. He told one of his monks to go fishing that night and bring back the first fish that he caught. The next day, the monk brought Kentigern the fish—it was a salmon. When it was cut open, there inside was the ring that the fish had swallowed. The queen was able to take the ring and show it to her surprised husband.

SAINTS' DAYS

3 SEPTEMBER
Gregory

26 or 27 MAY
Augustine of Canterbury

24 FEBRUARY
Ethelbert

Augustine, bishop of Canterbury.

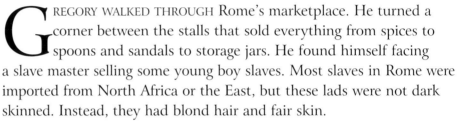

The Gospel Reaches England

Gregory, Augustine of Canterbury, and Ethelbert

❦

G REGORY WALKED THROUGH Rome's marketplace. He turned a corner between the stalls that sold everything from spices to spoons and sandals to storage jars. He found himself facing a slave master selling some young boy slaves. Most slaves in Rome were imported from North Africa or the East, but these lads were not dark skinned. Instead, they had blond hair and fair skin.

"Who are they?" asked Gregory.

"They're Angles."

"Where are they from?"

"From Deira."

"Then they must be rescued from *Dei ira*," answered Gregory, who could never resist making a pun. For, although Deira was the name of part of the island where the Angles lived, the Latin words *Dei ira* also mean "the anger of God."

And that is how Pope Gregory decided he must send someone to spread the Christian message to that part of the world, which we now know as England. The man he chose was a monk named Augustine, who set off from Rome with forty companions in the year 596.

The Romans no longer ruled Europe. Much of the North was overrun with brigands, robbers, and barbarians. On his journey through France, Augustine became fearful and went back to Rome. But Gregory wasn't going to let him give up so easily. He ordered Augustine to complete his journey north.

Augustine and his monks landed in Kent, in southeast England, in 597, again afraid. What might the pagan king of Kent do to them?

They were in for a surprise. King Ethelbert of Kent rode out to make them welcome. True, he did refuse to meet them indoors because his own pagan priests had warned him that these Romans might practice magic on him once they got indoors. But he listened to what they had to say and then gave them permission to enter his capital city, Canterbury, and to talk to people about Jesus. He also gave them somewhere to live, free of charge.

There was yet another surprise awaiting Augustine. The king's wife, Queen Bertha, was already a Christian. She was originally French and had become a Christian before marrying Ethelbert. He had allowed her to have a small Christian church in Canterbury, and that became Augustine's first base for his mission to the Angles.

Many of the Kentish people became Christian, including King Ethelbert himself, who later gave Augustine land on which (in time) was built the great Canterbury Cathedral. Augustine also followed the advice of Gregory not to destroy any pagan temples he found. Instead he blessed them for the use of Christians and put altars in them.

CANTERBURY CATHEDRAL

When Augustine established a church in Canterbury, it was part of the Catholic Church overseen by the pope in Rome. Hundreds of years later, the English king Henry VIII declared himself head of the church in England and the archbishop of Canterbury became its spiritual leader. The Anglican Church is now represented in many countries around the world, but Canterbury Cathedral remains its central focus.

The present Canterbury Cathedral is a medieval building. It was a popular place of pilgrimage after Thomas Becket was declared a saint.

THE LINDISFARNE GOSPELS

*O*ne of the main jobs of the monks of Lindisfarne was to make copies of the Bible in beautiful handwriting and to decorate them. The exquisite Lindisfarne Gospels survive and are kept at the British Museum in London.

Fire at Bamburgh

Aidan from Iona and Oswald

*E*XCELLENT, SAID OSWALD to himself, as he stood on the battlements of his fine castle. It was safely perched on an outcrop of rock, looking out over the long white sands of Bamburgh beach. But he wasn't afraid that it would be attacked. His kingdom of Northumbria (in the north of England) was at peace now, after he'd won that last battle.

Yes, everything was fine, thought Oswald. Except he had one slight worry—a promise he'd made and not yet kept.

The morning before that last battle, he'd made a Christian cross out of wood, called all his soldiers together and made them kneel before it. Oswald had then prayed aloud, asking God to defend his soldiers and guide them in the fighting. He'd promised that if he could drive the enemy from his kingdom and bring peace to Northumbria, he would do all he could to teach his people about Jesus and the Christian religion, something they knew nothing about.

As it turned out, his soldiers quickly drove the enemy onto marshy ground where they were easily defeated. Oswald then named the battle area Heavensfield and went back to Bamburgh, where he was now wondering how to keep his promise.

He himself had heard about Christianity when he was a boy and his father had sent him north to an island named Iona. He'd been taught by the Christian monks there. And as he remembered his time at Iona, the answer became obvious. He'd send a messenger asking for a monk to come to Northumbria to teach his people.

The monk who came from Iona was named Aidan. Oswald wanted him to live comfortably in Bamburgh Castle but Aidan politely said no.

"I'd like to live on an island like Iona, a place apart where I can be quiet and pray and read, but not so far away that I can't reach the mainland and the people of your land."

"I have the perfect place," replied Oswald. "We know it as Lindisfarne. You can see it from here. Six miles by boat, more if you insist on walking."

"You can walk to this island?" asked Aidan.

The king laughed. "It's only an island at high tide. When the tide goes out, you can walk across the sand to reach it."

Aidan settled on what came to be known as Holy Island. Other monks came and they built a church and places to sleep and eat. They built a guest house and a hospital—and they kept bees. From the bees' wax they made candles, and from their honey they made a drink known as mead. Aidan also spent time going around Northumbria teaching the people about Jesus, and King Oswald often went with him. In time, Aidan became bishop of Northumbria.

All was well until the fierce army of King Penda, a cruel and pagan king, came north from the land of Mercia, attacking towns and villages and stealing from the people. Oswald locked himself inside his castle.

Outside, close to the south gate, Penda's men built a huge bonfire. They stole thatch and wood from all the houses round about and set fire to it. Soon the gatehouse was on fire. Soon the castle itself would be on fire. Soon Oswald would be captured or burned to death.

Across the bay on Lindisfarne, Aidan and another monk whose name was James watched. Then they felt a south wind that made the fire burn all the more fiercely.

"If only the wind would change," said James, "and the fire would blow back on Penda's men."

"I think it might be right to pray," said Aidan. And he did.

"The wind's dropping," said Brother James.

"It's not!" said Aidan firmly. "It's changing direction!" And it was. The fire now blew back toward Penda's men. Soon they were fleeing, and Bamburgh Castle and King Oswald were saved—saved by the powerful prayers of the monk named Aidan.

This window depicts Bishop Aidan. In real life, he lived simply and without wealth or special comforts.

Hilda advised the villagers nearby how to deal with a troublesome flock of wild geese.

The Organizer and the Poet

Hilda of Whitby and Caedmon

THE ABBEY OF WHITBY was once a hub of the Christian church. Here many people learned and taught about the Christian faith. The kindly, wise and efficient Hilda was the chief reason for its importance.

Hilda

Everybody felt safe with Hilda. When she was around, people knew things wouldn't go wrong. She was fair. She was kind, and she was patient. As Saint Bede wrote sometime later, "No wonder everyone thought of her as 'mother.'"

Saint Aidan needed someone to do a particular job. "She's the obvious person to take it on," he said.

"But she's a woman," said one of his Lindisfarne monks, who was set in his ways. "You can't have a woman in charge of this."

"This" was something special. It was a "double monastery." Half of this monastery, like the one on Iona and the one Aidan had started at Lindisfarne, was for monks. The other half was for nuns.

It was at Hartlepool in northeast England, and the monk who'd been running it was not very efficient. Aidan needed a good organizer.

"It should be the best person for the job," said Aidan. "And that's Hilda."

So that's how Hilda came to be in charge of Hartlepool Abbey. Seven years later, the problems at the abbey had been sorted out, and it was time for Hilda to move on. She went to Whitby, a little further south on the Yorkshire coast, to start another double monastery for monks and nuns there.

Hilda was famous for her good advice. She told someone who had a plague of snakes how to get rid of them. She advised some villagers what to do when their crops were being eaten by a flock of wild geese. Even kings and princes came for her help when they had problems.

In the year 664, a great conference, or synod, of church leaders was to be held. "Whitby is the obvious place to have it," everyone said. "Hilda will see everything goes all right."

The churches in Britain were divided. On the one side were the churches in the west of England, in Wales and Ireland and Scotland—sometimes known as the Celtic churches. They had first heard about Christianity from people like Patrick, David, and Columba. On the other side were the churches in southern England who had first heard about Christianity from Augustine of Canterbury.

Various things divided them. They argued about when Easter Sunday should be each year. The Celtic monks thought the Benedictine monks in southern England lived in too much comfort. The Synod of Whitby was being held to sort everything out.

After much argument, they agreed to follow the ways of Canterbury—mainly because they were also the ways of Christians all over Europe, Africa, and Asia.

Hilda had been on the side of the Celtic Christians, but once matters had been decided by the synod, Hilda made sure that all its decisions were carried out.

Caedmon

Caedmon wasn't a monk. He was a farmworker who helped in the stables that were part of the great Whitby Abbey.

Every feast day, as soon as the singing and storytelling started after the evening meal, Caedmon crept away. He didn't know any stories, and he certainly wasn't able to sing. Everyone laughed at his tuneless voice.

One night, as Caedmon lay sleeping, he heard a voice.

"Caedmon, sing to me."

"I can't sing. That's why I left the feast."

"But sing to me," said the voice.

"What shall I sing?" asked Caedmon.

"Sing of creation."

And in his dream, Caedmon did sing.

To his delight, when he woke the next morning, he remembered the song. The other workers heard about it and took him to Abbess Hilda. She asked him to make up more songs and poems. Recognizing how beautiful they were, she decided he'd been given a gift from God.

Cuthbert

SAINT'S DAY

20 MARCH
(or 4 SEPTEMBER)

When Cuthbert spoke to the birds that were eating a crop of barley, they flew away.

CUTHBERT NEVER FORGOT the moment. It happened when he was quite young, about nine. He and a group of other children were playing in the middle of the village. Without any warning, one of the other boys came up to him and said the oddest thing: "Bishop Cuthbert, why do you play with children when God has marked you out to teach grown-ups?"

It was one of those things that stayed in the back of his mind until he was sixteen. By then, he was earning his living as a shepherd, guarding sheep on the hills of Northumbria in northeast England. One night, as he was keeping watch, he suddenly saw a pathway of light appear in the sky. A number of angels seemed to be passing upward on it. Somehow he knew that they were carrying up to heaven the soul of someone who had just died.

Wanting to share this strange sight, he woke the other shepherds. "Rubbish," they laughed.

"It was just a shooting star," added one. "Or maybe an owl or falcon."

Cuthbert wasn't put off. He set off down the hill to a cluster of huts not far away. This was the home of a group of monks who had come to live and work in this place from their monastery on Lindisfarne, also known as Holy Island.

They didn't laugh at his story. They knew such a sight must have a meaning, and while they were wondering what it might be, a messenger arrived from Lindisfarne. He brought sad news. The previous night, just at the time when Cuthbert had seen the light in the sky, Brother Aidan had died.

It all seemed to make sense to Cuthbert. The boy's remark to him when he was younger, the vision in the sky just as Aidan died . . . Surely God was calling him to be a monk?

Cuthbert did indeed become a monk, but he didn't remain in a monastery. He spent much of his time journeying around Northumbria, meeting many of the people Aidan had met and reminding them of the teachings of Jesus. Having grown up in that area, Cuthbert had the advantage of speaking the local language.

Some years later, another saint, Saint Bede, described Cuthbert's journeys: "He made a point of searching out those steep, rugged places in the hills that other preachers dreaded to visit because of their poverty and squalor."

Once he was on a journey with a young lad for company. It was a long walk to the next village and they'd run out of food.

"We're going to die of hunger," said the boy.

"Those who serve God will never be hungry. See, up there." Cuthbert pointed to a bird of prey in the sky. At that moment, the bird swooped down to the nearby river, snatched a fish from the water and landed on the bank to eat it.

"Run and get what God has sent."

The boy did so and came back with a large fish.

"Cut it in two and put half back on the riverbank for the bird. We'll cook the other half."

Cuthbert loved birds and animals, and they loved him.

One time, as a way of trying to make himself more humble, he walked into the icy North Sea up to his armpits and stood there, praying. A number of seals swam up and nuzzled up to him as though to keep him warm.

It is said that birds and animals respected Cuthbert. There is a story of how seals tried to keep him warm in the icy sea.

Another time, when some birds were eating the monastery's crop of barley, Cuthbert spoke to them: "Why are you eating crops you didn't grow? If God has given you permission, so be it. If not, be off with you." The birds flew away.

After some years, Cuthbert became a hermit on an island named Inner Farne. It's one of twenty tiny rocky islands not far from Lindisfarne and Bamburgh. There he lived on a stone bed, meeting occasional visitors, and surrounded by his special friends—the seals and seabirds. He was particularly fond of the eider ducks, which are even now sometimes called Cuthbert's ducks.

A tiny chapel still stands on Inner Farne, on the island where Cuthbert lived and died.

Willibrord

SAINT'S DAY

7 NOVEMBER

IT COULD HAVE BEEN a total disaster. Twelve monks sailing across the North Sea in a flimsy boat, hoping to preach Jesus' message of love and peace to the warlike tribes of northern Europe—people to whom Christianity meant nothing at all.

Their leader had the unusual name of Willibrord, and he felt they should go first to Friesland (which is now the northern part of the Netherlands).

What must they have been expecting? Instant death? Imprisonment? Certainly something very different from the peaceful lives they'd lived on Iona and Lindisfarne. Probably the last thing they expected was Prince Pepin.

"Welcome," he said. "You're just the sort of men I need."

"We are?" they asked, somewhat doubtfully.

"Yes," said Pepin. "I've heard about monks."

"You do know we're Christians, not pagans?" asked Willibrord.

"But you know about farming and cultivating the soil."

"Of course."

Recently, and after much fighting, Prince Pepin had driven a pagan warlord named Rodbod out of Friesland. Now he needed someone to teach his people how to use the battlefields for pasture and how to grow crops. Willibrord and his monks did this and, with the agreement of Pepin, they also taught the people about Jesus.

So successful were they that all Friesland became peaceful and prosperous. Pepin was delighted. He decided Willibrord must become the bishop of his land, and so he sent him to Rome to be made a bishop by the pope. This did happen— except that the pope of those days couldn't say Willibrord's name and named him Bishop Clement instead.

With Friesland now a Christian country, Willibrord decided he should turn his attention to nearby Denmark. This time it was a disaster. In those days, none of the Danes wanted to hear about the Christian faith. Eventually Willibrord and his companions gave up and sailed back to Friesland.

During the voyage, a great storm blew up, but their ship found shelter on the tiny island of Heligoland. This island was supposed to be sacred to two pagan gods whose names were Forseti and Nanna. The few people who lived there believed that no animal on that island could be killed, and that any water taken from the well must be drunk in silence.

But Willibrord, his monks, and the sailors were famished after days at sea. They needed food. So Willibrord ordered one of his men to kill a cow, and while they were doing that, he went to the well, took water from it, and baptized three of the sailors who wanted to become Christians. Naturally, he said the prayers of baptism as he did this.

The local people were terrified. "You've broken both rules! What will the gods do to us?" they asked.

"Nothing," said Willibrord.

"They will, they will," said one of them. "And our king will be furious with you."

"It's lucky for us he's on the island now," added another.

"What's his name?" said Willibrord.

"Rodbod," came the reply.

Rodbod decided to kill Willibrord, but Willibrord spoke up boldly to him. "It's nonsense to worship these pagan gods. See, they did nothing when I killed the cow and used the water. I, Willibrord, bishop of Friesland, ask you to worship the one true God."

When Rodbod heard who Willibrord was, he changed his mind. Secretly, he was embarrassed to have lost a battle against Prince Pepin and didn't want to annoy him by harming his bishop. So he arranged for Willibrord and his men to travel safely back to Friesland.

Rodbod never became a Christian, but many years later, his grandson not only became a Christian but also became a bishop. Meanwhile, Willibrord returned to Friesland and spent many more years spreading the gospel throughout that area.

THREE STEPS FORWARD, TWO STEPS BACK

*W*illibrord died in the Abbey of Echternach, in Luxembourg, and was buried in its church. Since then, Echternach has been a place of pilgrimage.

Every year, on the Tuesday after Pentecost, pilgrims to Echternach perform a curious dance in which they form up in a long procession. Traditionally taking three steps forward, then two steps back, this procession makes its way through the town, into the church, around Willibrord's tomb and then out of the church.

In the Middle Ages, it was thought that remembering Saint Willibrord in this way would cure all sorts of illnesses and guard against the plague.

Opposite: *This picture from an altar panel shows Bishop Willibrord with Saint Joseph.*

Bede

Bede is famous as the monk who wrote the first history of the English church.

DEATH IS NEVER A HAPPY event. But it's hard to imagine a happier or more peaceful death than that of Bede. He was both a monk and a priest and he'd spent almost all his life in a Benedictine monastery at a place called Jarrow in northeast England. Now he was an old man, tired and weak.

He had been taken seriously ill a fortnight before Easter Sunday but continued his work of translating John's Gospel from Greek into Anglo-Saxon, or Early English, the language then spoken in much of England. In those days, of course, all books were handwritten, using quill pens dipped in ink.

When he was younger, Bede used to write his own books. Now he dictated what he wanted to say to an assistant, or scribe, a young monk named Wilbert.

On the Tuesday before Ascension Day (the day that recalls how Jesus ended his work on earth), Bede became weaker and knew he was close to death. All that night he lay awake, but at dawn he insisted that the work of translation and dictation should carry on. There was still one chapter to be translated. "Take your pen and sharpen it, and then write fast," said Bede to Wilbert. Lying on his narrow bed, Bede continued dictating slowly with Wilbert writing down what he said until it was three o'clock in the afternoon.

Bede then said, "There are some things of value in my chest, such as peppercorns, napkins, and incense. Run quickly and get them and bring the other priests of the monastery to me that I may distribute among them the gifts that God has bestowed on me."

When this was done, he asked the priests to pray for him. "You shall see my face no more in this life. My soul longs to see Christ my king in heaven in all his beauty." They promised to do this but, as they did so, their eyes were full of tears.

When evening came, Wilbert noticed that one sentence of the passage they were translating was unfinished. "Write it," said Bede.

Wilbert wrote down the words Bede dictated. "Master, now it's finished," he said.

Bede lay down on the floor of his little room, saying, "You have spoken truthfully. It is well finished." They had reached chapter six of John's Gospel, which describes Jesus feeding five thousand people in the wilderness.

Bede was happy. "Raise my old head in your arms, Brother Wilbert, that I may look once more at the happy, holy place where I used to pray, and so that sitting up, I may call on my Father God." And so, sitting on the floor of his little cell, he sang the words, "Glory be to the Father, and to the Son, and to the Holy Spirit." As he chanted the last word, he breathed his last breath and died.

But what had he done with his life? He was born in the year 673. At the age of seven, he'd been sent away to a monastery to be educated by monks. By the time he was ten, he was living in this monastery at Jarrow. He spent the rest of his life there, never going further north than Lindisfarne, never going further south than York. He wrote, "I have devoted my energies to the study of the Bible . . . singing the daily services in church. Study, teaching, and writing have always been my delight."

A page from a translation of Bede's history. The translation is more than a thousand years old.

As a boy, he learned to read and write in Latin and Greek, and he wrote one of the greatest history books ever written. It tells the story of the English church from the times of the Romans up to his own lifetime. Because he wrote this first English language history book, he is often known as the father of English history.

Soon after his death in 735 he was given the title "the Venerable Bede." The title "Venerable" means "worthy" and is given to people who are likely to be made saints in the future. Amazingly, the church did not officially make this holy man a saint until 1899.

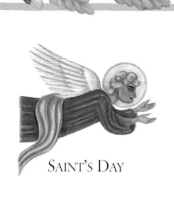

Thor's Oak
Boniface

I T WAS A HUGE TREE. A great sturdy oak, growing near the town of Geismar in what was later to be known as East Germany. It stood near the top of Mount Gudenberg and it was sacred to the great Norse god of thunder, Thor.

That, at least, was what the local people said. So, naturally enough, when this Englishman turned up and said he was going to cut the tree down, they were horrified. What would Thor do to such a man? Strike him dead with lightning seemed the most likely answer. They were also not a little terrified for themselves. Surely Thor would punish them for allowing anyone to damage, never mind destroy, his precious oak tree?

In the end, a huge crowd decided it was worth that risk. They'd climb Mount Gudenberg and watch the Englishman get struck by lightning.

The Englishman's name was Boniface, and he was both a monk and a priest. He'd come to what was then a pagan land to teach its people the Christian message of love and hope, and he'd spent two years learning their language in order to be able to do this.

Now he wanted to prove that the old Norse gods such as Thor had no power over a Christian believer. More than that, he wanted to prove that the Norse gods weren't even real.

So he climbed the hill to the so-called "Thor's Oak" with a few fellow monks and a large axe. The local people followed. They felt safe—and certain that Thor would know who was damaging his oak. He would surely strike Boniface dead for this terrible insult to him and his tree.

Boniface gripped the axe and took a mighty swing. The blade sank into the trunk of the tree. Boniface wrenched it free and took another swipe. Again the blade sank into the wood.

By now there was a rustling in its upper branches. A wind was getting up. The crowd all had the same thought. Thor's getting angry.

Boniface and his monks dealt a few more blows to the tree. Now its upper branches were shaking violently.

Boniface is famous for cutting down an oak that was the symbol of a pagan god.

124

Saints of the Western Churches

Then, with a mighty creak and a groan, the tree shuddered and began to fall. As its upper branches toppled to the ground, they broke and splintered.

The locals were positive that Thor had shown his power. Boniface must be dead under the weight of the trunk. But then he stepped smiling out of the pile of broken branches and shook some twigs out of his monk's habit.

"So what have you to say now?" he asked. "Where was Thor? I told you he wasn't real."

The people had to admit that Thor appeared to have no power over a Christian. Some immediately decided to become Christians. Over the days and weeks that followed, more and more followed their example. Soon much of the area was Christian.

As for the tree, Boniface chopped and sawed it up and used the wood to build a small wooden church on that very spot, naming the church Saint Peter's.

Boniface baptized people who wanted to become Christians.

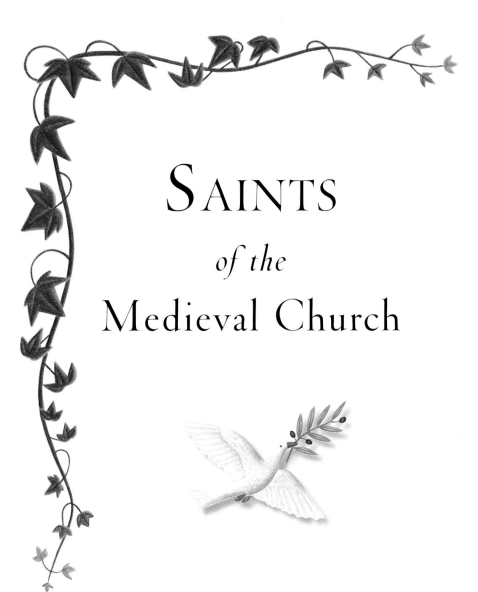

SAINTS
of the
Medievel Church

*who would not
let their faith
be conformed to
the world*

A Question of Language
Cyril and Methodius

"IT'S ALL VERY FLATTERING," said Cyril.

"To be invited by the prince, you mean?" replied his elder brother, Methodius.

"Exactly. Very flattering. But . . ." Cyril sounded depressed.

"But? . . ."

"Well, it's not exactly an easy job, is it?"

Prince Rotislav had invited the two brothers to his land of Moravia in the middle of Europe in order to bring the message of Christianity to his people. Being a pair of intelligent men, they'd had the wit first to learn the local Slavonic language in order to teach the people about Jesus, but now they'd come up against a serious problem.

Having journeyed there along the rocky mountain roads and been well received, they wanted to share the Bible with their new friends. However, in those days, the Bible was always written in Latin or Greek and the Moravians spoke only the Slavonic language.

"So we've two choices, my dear Cyril," said Methodius. "Either we teach everyone in the country to read and understand Latin or Greek—"

"That's what I meant about it not being an easy job."

"Or we translate the Bible into the Slavonic language."

"All of it?"

The two brothers agreed to translate at least the New Testament from Greek into the Slavonic language of Moravia. It was only then that the next problem dawned on them.

"Have you ever seen any of their language written down?" asked Cyril.

"Erm . . ." Methodius thought for a moment. "Well, actually, no."

At that time, the Slavonic language was only a spoken one. So, before they could begin their task, they had to invent a Slavonic alphabet. They did this by basing it on the Greek alphabet but also borrowing some Hebrew letters for sounds that didn't exist in Greek.

What's more, they began holding church services (including the Holy Communion service or Mass) in the local language, so that all the people would understand what was being said.

Yet another problem then emerged. Prince Rotislav had invited the two brothers to come to his country from the Eastern Church, which had the great city of Constantinople at its heart, but there were already other Christian missionaries working in Moravia who had come from Germany.

Like Boniface, who had brought Christianity to Germany, they used the Latin language.

Arguments started up about which language should be used for Christian services.

Who else should settle such an argument in those days but the leader of the church, the pope? The two brothers went to see him in Rome.

Pope Adrian II was so impressed by the work being done by Cyril and Methodius that he said they could continue to use the local language and also that both men should be made bishops. Sadly, before this could happen, Cyril died and was buried in Rome. However, the pope made Methodius not only a bishop but also archbishop of the whole area.

Methodius returned to Moravia to find that the Western Christians had become much more powerful while he had been away. Perhaps because he had the support of the pope, many of the Western Christians working there were jealous of him. Soon after his return, they had him arrested and put in prison for two years. When the pope eventually heard about it all, he arranged for Methodius to be released.

Before Methodius died, he finished translating the whole Bible into the Slavonic language. However, the next bishop insisted on the use of Latin. So too did the next pope, and from then until the twentieth century, services in the Roman Catholic Church throughout the world were held in Latin.

Cyril and Methodius shown with writing materials—the tools of their work as Bible translators.

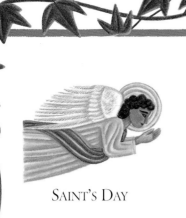

Vladimir the Great

❦

ONE THING WAS CERTAIN about Prince Vladimir. He wasn't a Christian. He had five wives, ten sons, and two daughters. He also enjoyed a good battle. When civil war broke out between different parts of what we now know as Russia, Vladimir was soon waging war against his brother, capturing cities, slaying other princes, and finally making himself ruler of Kiev and all Russia.

He had many statues and shrines built in Kiev, to remember pagan gods with strange names: Dazhdbog, Simorgl, Mokosh, Stribog, and others.

But then he began to get interested in other religions. "Tell me, what do Muslims do?" he asked.

"They don't eat pork or drink alcohol," said one of his advisers.

"Drinking is the joy of Russia," he answered. "I couldn't become a Muslim. What about Jews? Where do they come from?"

It was explained to the prince that the Jews no longer had a homeland but were scattered across Europe.

"I don't want that to happen to our people," said Prince Vladimir. "That leaves the Christians. What about them?"

His advisers then explained to him that there were Christians who came from Germany and the West, who had their headquarters in Rome. Then there were Christians who came from Greece and the East, who had their headquarters in Constantinople.

"Send messengers to those countries," ordered Prince Vladimir, "so we may learn more about how they worship their God."

In time, the messengers returned.

"We've been to the West," they reported. "Their churches are plain. Their services are holy but serious. But when we went to Constantinople, we were taken to their great church of Saint Sophia. We didn't know whether we were in heaven or on earth. On earth, nowhere is there such beauty."

At that same time, an argument arose between Vladimir and the city of Kherson in the Crimea, which belonged to Emperor Basil of Constantinople. Vladimir set off with his army to sort the matter out. After a long siege, he finally made the city surrender. He then sent messengers to Emperor Basil at Constantinople, asking if he could marry Basil's sister Anna. He also threatened to do to Constantinople what he'd done to Kherson if Basil said no.

Emperor Basil simply replied that a Christian like Anna could not marry a pagan.

"But I've already learned about Christianity," replied Vladimir. "I'm ready to be baptized."

Hearing this, Basil agreed to send his sister with a number of priests to Kherson. As they were on their way there, Vladimir developed a great pain in his eyes. When Anna arrived, she said he must be baptized at once if he wished to regain his sight.

"The Christian God is indeed great if he can cure me," said the Prince.

The priests therefore baptized Vladimir, and his sight recovered. He then married Princess Anna and gave up his pagan wives. He also gave back the city of Kherson to Emperor Basil and returned to Kiev.

As soon as he had returned, he ordered the statues of the pagan gods to be thrown down, chopped to pieces, and some of them burned. One was dragged through the mud and thrown into the river. All this proved to his people the helplessness of the old gods, so when the people were told to follow Vladimir's example and become Christians, they did.

Vladimir built many churches and monasteries and gave up his warlike career. In this way he became the first Christian ruler of Russia and became known for his enthusiasm in spreading the Christian faith.

VLADIMIR'S SONS

*V*ladimir had two sons by his wife Anne, Boris and Gleb (also known as Romanus and David, which were their baptismal names). They too are remembered as saints because of the way they died. They were murdered in the same year that their father Vladimir died, when they were attacked and refused to defend themselves. They believed it was un-Christian to use violence even in self-defence. Their saints' day is on 24 July.

Stephen of Hungary

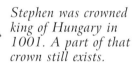

Stephen was crowned king of Hungary in 1001. A part of that crown still exists.

EVEN FOR THOSE DAYS, they were a fierce and warlike people. They came from the distant east and settled in the land where the River Danube curves its way through what we now know as Hungary.

These invaders were known as Magyars and they lived in groups, or tribes, each ruled by a duke. They seemed strange and frightening to the people who already lived in that area. Indeed, the French word for Magyar is "ogre," a word that has come to mean any evil or terrifying person.

Gradually, however, the Magyar tribes settled along the banks of the Danube. Then, in the year 985, one of their dukes, the duke of Geza, was baptized as a Christian. So too was his ten-year-old son, Vaik.

Some people say the duke only became Christian to please the people who lived nearby. Young Vaik was different. When he was baptized, he took a Christian name, Stephen, or in his own language, Istvan. And, as he grew up, being a Christian became more and more important to him.

In 997, when the Duke of Geza died, Stephen became duke in his father's place. Even though he was a Christian, he wasn't any less warlike. But he didn't fight the next-door countries. He did battle with the other Magyar dukes until he had persuaded the Magyars to be one people and one nation. This country became known as Hungary.

When he'd achieved this, he sent a messenger to the pope in Rome, asking that Hungary be recognized as a proper country and that he should be its first Christian king.

The pope agreed. He sent official letters to Stephen's castle confirming this. These letters were read out loud and, as a mark of respect, Stephen stood to listen to them. Some time later, in the year 1001, Stephen was solemnly crowned king of Hungary with a crown sent to him as a gift from the pope.

Together with his wife, Gisela, Stephen worked hard to teach his people about Jesus. Nowadays, his methods can seem cruel. He severely punished anyone who did not follow Christian ways. He forbade marriages between Christians and non-Christians, and he introduced heavy taxes. But he was a fair man and he treated the poor with justice. He gave them money, sometimes doing so in disguise. He built many monasteries and churches. Most of all, he made Hungary into a settled and united nation.

THE AMERICAN LINK

*E*meric (also known as Americus, Henry, or Imre) was Stephen's only son and was born in 1007. Stephen planned that Emeric would be king of Hungary after him and arranged for several wise monks, such as Gérard from Venice, to be his teachers. Sadly, Emeric was killed in a hunting accident when he was only twenty-four, in the year 1031.

Four hundred years later, an Italian was named Amerigo after Emeric (or Americus). Amerigo Vespucci (that was his full name) grew up to be an explorer who made several voyages to the lands that had then been recently discovered by Christopher Columbus. He gave his Christian name to these newly discovered lands, so America indirectly owes its name to young Prince Emeric of Hungary. His saint's day is on 4 November.

The Odd Couple

Margaret of Scotland

I N THE YEAR 1066, William the Conqueror invaded England, won the Battle of Hastings, and became king. It became clear that the English court was no longer a safe place for the young Princess Margaret.

She was just twenty-two. With her mother, she'd been brought to England ten years earlier and had grown up in the court of the kindly King Edward, known as Edward the Confessor because of his holiness. But he had died, his son had been killed, and the new King William didn't want anyone around who'd been connected with that family.

So, before he could harm the princess, her mother decided they must escape. But where should they go? France was out of the question: William ruled there as well. The answer seemed to be Scotland.

They went by sea. It wasn't good weather but at last they arrived safely. King Malcolm of Scotland welcomed them. After all, he knew what it was like to be a royal refugee. Some years earlier, he'd had to flee for his life when his own father, King Duncan, had been murdered by a man named Macbeth.

But he not only welcomed the beautiful princess, he fell in love with her, and they were married three years later.

Now it has to be said they were an odd couple. She was quiet, holy, prayerful, kind, and generous. He was different. To be blunt, he was noisy, rough, rude, and fond of war. And his palace where they lived at Dunfermline was grim, bleak, and cold.

Margaret set about changing her husband, his palace, and the country. She helped him control his temper. She brought bright hangings and tapestries to the castle—and she brought books. In particular, she had a beautiful illustrated copy of the Gospels. But she never managed to teach Malcolm to read. She did however persuade him that books were important and he would kiss the Bible to show he respected it.

Gradually, she made the court more beautiful and refined. The courtiers began to join her at her prayers. Every day, she opened the palace doors to the sick and the poor and personally gave food to those in need. Twenty-four people lived entirely at her expense, and when she journeyed

The abbey at Dunfermline. Hundreds of years before it was built, Margaret played an important part in making the town a place where Christianity was respected.

Margaret's Protector

*E*dward, the son of Ethelred the Unready, was born
in 1004 and became king of England in 1042. He was
too gentle a person to be a strong king in those rough-and-ready days,
but he was popular. He ended a heavy tax known as the Danegeld and
spent time meeting his people and touching those who were ill. His
touch seemed to cure many who were ill.

He wanted to make a pilgrimage to Rome, but his advisers warned
that it was unwise as a rival might try to become king while he was
away. Instead, Edward rebuilt an abbey church to the west of London.
It became known as West Minster, to distinguish it from Saint Paul's
Cathedral, which lay to the east in the city of London. After his death
in January 1066, he was buried in his new Westminster Abbey, where
his body still lies.

His son Harold became king but was killed at the Battle of
Hastings soon afterward in the year 1066. Edward's saint's day
is on 13 October.

*Margaret of Scotland
shared her wealth
with the poor.*

around Scotland, she carried money to give to those who
were hungry. If she ran out of money, she used Malcolm's.
He learned not to notice when this happened.

But all was not well between Scotland and England.
The two countries began fighting each other, and
during this war, Malcolm was killed. So too was
their eldest son.

At the same time, Margaret had become
ill. When a younger son returned from
the battle, she asked him how they
were. So as not to worry her, he said
they were well.

She replied, "I know how it is."
Four days later, she prayed to God:
"Let me be free." Then she died.

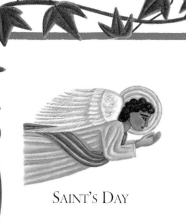

Hide Your Husbands, Hide Your Sons

Bernard of Clairvaux

I{T WAS CHRISTMAS.} Bernard was only eight, and he was trying to stay awake so that he could go to the midnight service. In the end, he did fall asleep and dreamed that he was in Bethlehem at the very first Christmas. Not just that, he dreamed that Mary let him kiss the baby Jesus. From then on, he became very religious.

Bernard's father was a wealthy nobleman, and Bernard's two elder brothers, Guido and Gérard, grew up to become soldiers. Not so Bernard. He wasn't strong, but he was exceptionally intelligent. He was sent away to school and became very learned. It wasn't a surprise when he was twenty-two that he decided to become a monk.

His mother had died by this time so Bernard went to her brother, his Uncle Gaudry (himself a nobleman and a soldier), and asked what he thought about his plan.

"Great idea," said Gaudry, somewhat to Bernard's surprise.

Bernard's cousins didn't agree. "You're rich. Why give it all up to live like a ploughman?"

"I still think it's a good idea," said Gaudry. "And I think I might follow his example."

To the family's utter dismay, the two of them set off to join a monastery at a place named Cîteaux. But first, Bernard had a chat with his younger brother, sixteen-year-old Bartholomew. He too decided to join them.

Encouraged by this, Bernard then visited the army camp to see his elder brother Guido and yet another brother, Andrew. Andrew refused point blank to become a monk. At first, Guido said no too.

"I'm married. I've got a wife and children. I can't leave them."

"Oh don't worry about that," said Bernard. "Your wife'll say it's all right. Eventually."

And eventually she did let Guido go.

That left Gérard.

"But I'm doing so well in the army. I shall soon be promoted."

"I doubt it," said Bernard.

A few days later, Gérard was captured and put in prison.

Meanwhile it was time for Bernard to go to Cîteaux. He went to say goodbye to a schoolfriend named Hugh of Macon. A day later, Hugh decided to join Bernard. So did another friend named Geoffrey.

It was no wonder that by now wives and mothers were saying, "Look out, it's Bernard. Hide your husbands, hide your sons. Otherwise he'll take them off to be monks."

In the end, thirty-two of them went to Cîteaux, including Gérard, who'd managed to escape from prison.

Cîteaux was a Cistercian monastery and much stricter than a Benedictine one. That was why Bernard chose it. "My weak character needs strong medicine," he explained.

Cistercian monks were known as "white friars" because they wore plain, undyed habits. Benedictines, who dyed theirs black, were known as "black friars."

At first, the abbey of Cîteaux had little food for Bernard and its new monks. "How much money do we need?" asked Bernard.

"Eleven pounds," said the monk in charge of the food and drink.

Bernard prayed about it. Shortly afterward, a woman brought the monks a present of twelve pounds as a way of saying "thank you" to God for her husband's recovery from an illness.

Two years after arriving at Cîteaux, Bernard was asked to build a new monastery. The place he chose was in a valley in the part of France known as Champagne. Because it attracted so many holy men, the valley became known as "the valley of light" or, in French, Clairvaux.

Bernard of Clairvaux. This picture of him within a manuscript shows his tunic to be dark, but in fact he would have worn a tunic of undyed cloth that would have been creamy white.

Bernard became famous throughout Europe. He wasn't afraid to tell kings when he thought they were doing wrong. And when there was an argument about which of two men should be pope, it was Bernard who persuaded everyone who should be chosen. Bernard was, after all, very good at persuading people to do what he wanted. That was why he was nicknamed "Doctor Mellifluous," or "the honey-sweet teacher."

Thomas Becket

L IKE SO MANY THINGS, it began with a quarrel. Several quarrels in fact—all of them between King Henry II of England and Thomas Becket, who was archbishop of Canterbury. Once, they'd been friends. But sadly they fell out.

At the start of this story, Henry was the most powerful king in Europe. Thomas Becket was the son of a rich merchant. He'd done very well for himself, getting better and better jobs (both in England and Rome) until he got the best job of all. The king made him royal chancellor of England, responsible for seeing that everything the king ordered was carried out.

So Thomas was powerful. He lived in his own palace, which was nearly as luxurious and as well furnished as the king's. He enjoyed good food, fine clothes—and hunting.

Meanwhile, Henry had a problem. He was having trouble getting the leaders of the church, the bishops, to do what he wanted, because they didn't like being bossed around by King Henry. They felt that not even the king should tell the church what to do.

Henry didn't like that.

Then he had an idea. He made his friend Thomas archbishop of Canterbury. That meant that he would be in charge of all the bishops. They would have to do what Thomas said. And of course, as Thomas was a friend of Henry, that would mean the king would get his own way.

Thomas was made archbishop. He also gave up living in luxury and lived very simply. What mattered most to him now was the church. He took its part against the king. So it was little wonder that they soon

This portion of a window in Canterbury Cathedral is one of many recalling the story of Thomas Becket, its famous martyr.

argued so seriously that Thomas had to leave England for his own safety. He went to live in Rome in the year 1164.

Six years later, when Thomas and Henry were both in France, they met and made up their quarrel. Thomas returned to Canterbury. Everyone treated him as a hero. The people cheered as he made his way into the city. Again Thomas became the champion of the church, and soon the king's temper flared up again.

One December day while he was still in France, he lost patience well and truly. "Who will free me from this turbulent priest?" he shouted.

Four of the king's knights heard what the king said. They decided he could mean only one thing. The four of them looked at each other and nodded. And so those knights, Sir William de Tracy, Reginald FitzUrse, Richard le Breton, and Hugh de Morville, rode north as fast as they could and took a ship across the Channel. Some people say that Henry realized what had happened and sent messengers after them to stop them. If he did, they failed to catch up with the four knights.

Four days after Christmas, the knights arrived in Canterbury and met Thomas. An argument took place. Thomas went into the cathedral to pray at one of the altars there. The priests of the cathedral wanted to bar and lock the doors. Thomas said no, the church of God should not be locked. Then, just as it was getting dark, the knights made their way into the cathedral and there, in a holy part of the cathedral, with their great heavy swords, they struck down Thomas and killed him.

Thomas was brutally murdered while he went about his work as a priest.

Christians all over Europe were horrified when they heard what had happened and soon people started to call him Saint Thomas Becket. It wasn't long before people started making journeys to Canterbury to pray where Saint Thomas was buried.

In the end, King Henry realized how much he was to blame. He too visited Canterbury, walking barefoot to show how sorry he was. But Thomas was dead and nothing could alter that. Henry knelt to pray at the grave of the man who, once upon a time, had been his best friend.

Francis of Assisi

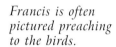

Francis is often pictured preaching to the birds.

PETER BERNARDONE was furious. Really fuming with anger. It was all to do with his boy, Francis (who was really no longer a boy but a young man).

Peter Bernardone was a very rich merchant who lived in the Italian town of Assisi and bought and sold silk linen and other expensive cloths. He wanted his son to enjoy the same sort of life as the other wealthy young noblemen of the town. That way, he thought, the family would be both respected and feared by the ordinary people.

At first, Francis had enjoyed going to parties, spending money, and staying out late. His father was satisfied. But then, Francis was ill for a while. As he got better, he started to spend more time on his own, praying. Whenever he could, he gave his money and food to people who were poor and needy. He no longer wore his fine, expensive clothes.

One day, he was praying in a church named Saint Damian's, just outside Assisi. The church was rather old and almost in ruins. As Francis prayed in front of a large crucifix (a cross with a statue of Jesus on it), the statue seemed to speak: "Francis, repair my church."

At that time, Peter Bernardone was away on business. So Francis went back home, took some of his father's goods, and sold them. Then he took the money to the priest at Saint Damian's to pay for the repairs. When Peter Bernardone returned home and found out what had happened, he almost exploded with anger. He grabbed hold of his son, led him off to see the bishop, and told him the whole story.

The bishop listened. Then, turning to Francis, he said gently, "Francis, the church cannot take what does not belong to it. You must give back to your father what is his."

So Francis took the money and gave it back to his father. Then he started tearing off all his clothes and throwing them at him. "Now I owe you nothing, Father! I've got nothing of yours," he said, taking off the very last of them. "You're no longer my father, and I've no father but my Father in heaven."

Peter Bernardone took his money and stormed out. Someone put an old workman's tunic around Francis. His new life had begun. From that day, Francis lived very simply, owning nothing, eating only the food he could beg, and wearing a rough brown cloak, or tunic. Other young men (many of them rich) gave up everything and joined him. They became known as Franciscans.

Francis became especially famous for his love for animals and birds. This became clear when Francis was outdoors one day, teaching a group of people about God.

"What God wants us to do is—" said Francis.

"We can't hear you!" interrupted the people.

It was true. They couldn't. Francis was standing on a little hill, talking to the people. The reason they couldn't hear him was because a large number of swallows were building nests nearby and chirping very loudly.

"My dear sister swallows," said Francis, "listen to the word of God and be quiet till I've finished."

To everyone's amazement, the swallows all settled on the edges of buildings and in trees and were silent.

"Thank you," said Francis. "As I was saying, what God wants us to do is to love each other. Be kind to each other. We are all brothers and sisters—even the animals and birds. That is why I call the swallows 'sisters.'"

The swallows kept silent until he had finished teaching. Then, once again, they began to sing.

Francis was famous in his own day, and a church in his memory was built shortly after his death—though Francis did not want such attention. This near-contemporary painting is believed to show a true likeness of the man.

The First Christmas Crib

Francis of Assisi

IT WAS JUST BEFORE CHRISTMAS in the year 1223. Francis decided to show the people who lived around a place named Grecchio exactly what it had been like for Jesus to be born in a stable. "Friar John," he said to one of his older followers. "I want to talk to you about Christmas."

"Why, you are going to spend it with us, aren't you? Here at Grecchio?" asked the old man, afraid that Francis might be leaving them.

"Yes, yes. Yes, I shall spend Christmas here," said Francis. "This is a good place." It was too. High up in the mountains, sheltered by the trees that grew on the hillside, near the ancient city of Rieti in central Italy.

Friar John was one of the many men who had given up everything in order to live the simple life that Francis had chosen after he left his father's home. More and more of them followed Francis and they became known as Franciscans, after their leader. They moved from place to place, in a group, helping the poor, comforting those who were ill or dying, and greeting everyone with the words, "The peace of God be with you."

Although their life was a little like that of monks, they were properly called "friars," or brothers, like Friar John.

When their number became too great for them all to stay in one group, Francis wrote down a "Rule" for their way of life. The friars were to promise to live in poverty and to have no possessions; they could not marry nor have any kind of love life, and they were to be obedient at all times. This Rule was later approved by the head of the church, the pope. Present-day followers of Saint Francis are still known as friars and still live by the same Rule.

Despite this strict Rule, Franciscans have always been cheerful. Francis thought it was wrong to be gloomy and encouraged his followers to smile and laugh whenever possible. Friar John was soon smiling again when he realized Francis was going to spend Christmas at Grecchio.

"I've been thinking, Friar John, about the very first Christmas. I want all the people from the villages down in the valley to understand what it was like. John, I want you to arrange something for me."

Together they made a plan. On Christmas Eve, Francis asked all the people from the villages around to come to Grecchio, bringing a lighted torch or candle. From all along the valley they came, wondering what they would see. They soon found out. There, at the entrance to the cave, Friar John had placed a manger—the kind of wooden trough that holds hay for

animals to eat. Beside it were a man and a woman looking into the manger where a little bundle of clothes represented a baby. There were other men there dressed up as shepherds, together with a real ox and an ass.

"But that's just how it must have been in Bethlehem," the people said. "When Jesus was born."

Francis was pleased. "Yes. That's how it was. He was born in a simple stable among brother and sister animals. Let's sing and give thanks to God for sending Jesus to us that very first Christmas."

And that is what Christians have done at Christmas ever since.

Francis is famous for having set up a real-life reconstruction of the story of Jesus' birth and the visit of the shepherds. His example is followed to this day, not least in the thousands and thousands of nativity plays performed each year.

Clare and Antony of Padua

THE WORK OF FRANCIS was continued by two of his close friends. Like him, they dedicated themselves to living with few possessions, out of respect for the teaching of Jesus.

Clare

They searched the whole house. She was nowhere to be seen. Clare was missing. Clare, the beautiful eighteen-year-old eldest daughter of the wealthy Count Offreduccio, could not be found. She had just eloped; run off to get married without telling anyone.

It was the evening of Palm Sunday in the year 1212. That morning, she had gone with all the family to the Palm Sunday morning service in their parish church in Assisi. Francis of Assisi had been the preacher as he had been throughout Lent.

Clare and Francis had first met five years earlier in the ruins of the church of Saint Damian's, where he'd first felt called to follow Jesus. He'd just given up all his wealth to live a life of simple poverty and he'd begun by repairing the church. She'd met him regularly after that, and she too had decided she wanted to serve Jesus through poverty.

There was only one person with whom Clare had shared her dream of joining Francis in his new way of life. That was her younger sister, Agnes. Yet Clare had not told even her exactly when she planned to elope to "marry" poverty. In her mind, she knew it must be at the start of Holy Week, which of course began with Palm Sunday.

So that evening, Clare had dressed herself in one of her finest dresses and crept out of the house. She made her way out of the town and through a wood to a secret meeting place where she was met by Francis and some of his new friars. There she exchanged her gown for a simple

A group of "poor Clares"—the order of nuns established by Francis's friend Clare.

habit tied with rope, her dainty shoes for a pair of sandals. Francis cut off her long, golden hair, and she covered her head with a veil.

The Franciscans had no convent, or nunnery, so they took Clare to a nearby Benedictine convent. Her father tried to drag her away, but she clung to the altar of its church. When she showed him that she had had her hair cut off, he gave up. Shortly afterward, Agnes joined her.

When Francis finished repairing Saint Damian's church, it became their home. For forty years, Clare lived there with her followers. They never ate meat, they did without shoes and socks, and they had no personal property. This order of nuns, a sister order to the Franciscans, are even now known as the Poor Clares.

Antony of Padua

Antony of Padua was born in Portugal. He was short and chubby, but had a voice that seemed to carry for miles. He lived quietly as a priest until he decided to visit Morocco to spread the gospel there, but soon after arriving, he became ill and had to return to Portugal. His ship, however, was caught in a violent storm and blown toward Sicily, where Antony remained for some time. Later, he went to Italy and lived as a hermit.

Here Antony is shown by the sea shore. Antony is often remembered for having preached a sermon to the fish of the sea—rather as Francis preached to the birds.

He said little about himself and nobody knew much about him. One day, a number of Franciscan friars arrived for a service. No one had been chosen to preach. All the friars refused, saying they had not prepared a talk. They then asked Antony whom they thought was just a country priest and not very good at speaking.

Antony spoke so wisely and with such learning that Francis himself appointed him to become a teacher to the Franciscan friars. He rapidly became a very famous and respected preacher but died when he was only thirty-six.

One day, a young monk borrowed Saint Antony's prayer book without permission but returned it quickly because he thought he had seen a devil and this sight had made him feel guilty. For this reason, Antony has always been associated with things that have been lost, and some Christians pray to him to help them find lost objects.

The Dumb Ox

Thomas Aquinas

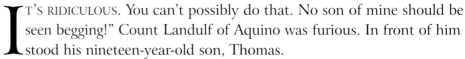

I T'S RIDICULOUS. You can't possibly do that. No son of mine should be seen begging!" Count Landulf of Aquino was furious. In front of him stood his nineteen-year-old son, Thomas.

"Father, I am going to join the Dominicans."

"You are going to join the Benedictines. I say so."

There was no doubt that Thomas (named Aquinas, after his father's hometown, Aquino) was going to be a monk. The argument was about which order of monks he should join. Count Landulf was, frankly, a bit of a snob (as well as a very rich banker). He wanted his son to live in a respectable Benedictine monastery. The Dominicans didn't live in monasteries but went around teaching, helping those they met, and living on what people gave them.

"To think," spluttered Count Landulf, "to think that a son of mine should live like a common beggar."

Thomas had already tried to join the Dominicans in nearby Naples. As soon as his mother had heard about this, she'd hurried off to Naples to make him change his mind. By then Thomas had gone to Rome. She'd followed after him, but by the time she got there, he'd moved on to Bologna. Eventually, his two elder brothers (who were soldiers) had managed to find him and bring him back to Aquino.

Since Thomas refused to change his mind, his father now decided to lock him up in a room in the castle. "He'll soon do what I say," he said.

Thomas didn't. Not even when his brothers played a trick on him, hoping to prove he wasn't as holy as he seemed to be. They paid a woman to go up to his room to tempt him. Thomas simply drove the woman away, refusing to have anything to do with her.

After fifteen months, the family realized there was no way of changing his mind and he was allowed to go to Cologne, in present-day Germany, and to Paris to continue his studies. He was quite well built, and in class he said so little that the other students nicknamed him "the Dumb Ox."

One day, Thomas' papers fell from his desk to the floor. Another student helped pick them up and noticed what Thomas had been writing.

"Look," he said, showing them round the class. "Our Thomas has understood everything we've been discussing after all."

The teacher realized how intelligent Thomas was. He said, "One day that Dumb Ox will bellow so loudly he will shake the world."

Thomas did—partly because he himself became a famous university lecturer, but most of all, because of the many books he wrote. Even those who disagree with some of his ideas respect his wisdom and his certainty that God is a loving father and that people can make themselves better by following his wishes.

He spent much of his fairly short life in Paris where his advice was sought by many, including the French king Louis IX.

In the year 1272, Thomas went back to Naples. On Saint Nicholas' Day, he led a service in church. During the service, he saw a vision that moved him very deeply. "The end of my work has come," he announced. He wrote no more and died in March 1274.

Thomas Aquinas is remembered for the way he strengthened the church by writing wise books that explained the Christian faith.

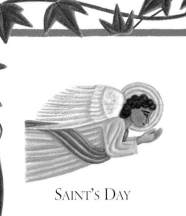

The Boy Who Couldn't Read

Sergius of Radonezh

B ARTHOLOMEW DREADED the other boys finding out his secret. He dreaded them knowing he couldn't read. He often prayed privately to God about it: "O Lord, help me to understand books."

His parents had once been rich, but they'd lost their money when they'd had to leave their home because of a war. Now they lived and worked as poor farmers near a place named Radonezh in the Russian countryside.

One day, Bartholomew was sent out into the nearby fields to look for a young horse that had strayed. In the fields, he met an old man. They started talking and the old man asked him what he was looking for. Bartholomew told him that, beside finding the horse, he wished most of all to be able to read and write.

He took the old man back home to his parents for a little soup, and then they all went to the local chapel. The old man told Bartholomew to read aloud from the book of psalms.

"But I don't know how," said Bartholomew.

"Read the word of God with confidence," replied the old man.

Bartholomew began to read, at first with a few stumbles but then more easily. He beamed with pleasure! He no longer had an embarrassing secret. He also knew what he wanted to do with his life.

Over the next five years, Bartholomew cared for his parents in their old age, a task he was happy to do. But by the time he was twenty, they had died and he was free to carry out his plan.

Together with one of his brothers, Stephen, he went deep into the nearby forest. They built a small church, which they named after the Holy Trinity, and also a hut where they could live as holy men. But Stephen hated the cold and the lack of food. He was also afraid of the wild animals in the forest, so he returned to Radonezh. Bartholomew continued to live there alone. After three years, he officially became a monk and from then on was given the name Sergius.

Like many monks, Sergius got on well with animals. One bear in particular would visit him. Sergius used to place a small slice of bread on a log and the bear would come and take it without harming Sergius. Sometimes he had no bread, and both of them would go hungry. Other times Sergius would give his only slice to the bear, being unwilling to disappoint him.

After two years, more monks came to live with Sergius. Although he had gone to the forest to be alone, he never turned anyone away. Each monk built his own hut, or cell, and they all met together to pray in the chapel. Eventually, Sergius was persuaded to become a priest, and at the same time, the group of monks formally became a monastery. Sergius shared in the work of baking bread, cooking, and making candles, as well as making shoes and clothing for the other monks.

One day, Dimitri, prince of Moscow, came to see Sergius. A vast foreign tribe, known as the Tartars, had raised a huge army and was near Moscow. Prince Dimitri was unsure whether to fight or simply surrender. Sergius didn't want to say either way but finally blessed the prince. "Go forward and fear not; God will help you," he said.

Dimitri's forces were on one side of the River Don. Should he cross it and fight, or wait? Again, he couldn't make up his mind until a message came from Sergius: "Be in no doubt, go forward with faith. God will be on your side." At the battle, Dimitri was victorious.

In 1378, Sergius was asked to become patriarch, or bishop, of Moscow. He refused, saying, "Since my youth, I've never worn gold." He cared quietly for his monastery for another fourteen years and then died peacefully.

Although this icon is richly decorated, it faithfully depicts Sergius as a hermit, who in his lifetime refused to wear gold.

Lady Julian of Norwich

SAINT'S DAY

Julian is not officially a saint
but is remembered on 8 May.

I T WAS ALL GOING WRONG. First there had been the plague—a terrible illness that had swept across most of Europe, killing thousands of people. Some people gave it the name the Black Death; most hardly dared speak of it. They just mouthed the words by which everyone knew it: "the Death."

The first outbreak had happened in Britain at the end of the year 1348. It happened again twenty years later. It was worst in the towns and cities because there people lived close together. The streets were narrow and filthy and without proper drains. No wonder infection spread quickly.

In the city of Norwich in the east of England "the Death" killed at least one person in three, perhaps one in two. That meant at least ten thousand people died. In fact, so many died there weren't enough people left to bury the bodies.

When the plague was over, there weren't enough men left to plough the fields or gather in the crops. So food became scarce and expensive. The poorest people suffered most.

And as if all this wasn't bad enough news, England was at war, fighting the French. Then, in 1372, Spain joined in with France against England. There was a huge sea battle and the English were defeated. Many English sailors were taken prisoner and an English treasure ship was sunk. Back home, there was another poor harvest. It was a miserable winter. It was all going very wrong.

But then came spring and Easter. Would everything get better? Would all be well?

Not for one woman who lived in Norwich. A fortnight after Easter, she was taken ill. She was so ill by Wednesday evening that everyone thought she was going to die.

Then, early the next Sunday morning (8 May), her parish priest visited her, bringing a crucifix, a cross with a small statue of Jesus on it. "Look at it," he said. "Be strong." At first, she was too weak to move even her eyes. Then she managed to look at the figure of Jesus on the cross. For a moment, the room seemed to go dark and she thought she really was at the moment of her death, but then she was no longer in pain! During the next twelve hours or so, she saw many wonderful things in her mind— but as clearly as if they were quite real.

Lady Julian's comforting words were given during harsh times, when a disease spread by rats killed thousands of people.

The Lady Julian (as we now know her) got better. Later, she wrote down the many things that she had seen when she was ill.

Just one of many sights that came to Julian was what she described as "a little thing, the size of a hazelnut and round, like a ball." It was on the palm of her hand. She looked at it and wondered.

"What is it?"

Then an answer came to her. "It stands for everything that has been made and everything that will be made."

It was so small, so fragile, she wondered how it did not break into pieces.

More words came to her.

"It exists because God loves it."

And from the sight of that "little thing" (we know no more about it), Julian understood three things:

God has made everything.

God loves everything.

God looks after everything.

Julian felt that God was telling her that, yes, things do go wrong in the world. There is illness, war, famine. It can't be helped. That is the way the world must be, but because God loves us, in the end all will be well. As she wrote in her book:

Lady Julian's writing was inspired by the things that came into her mind as she looked at a crucifix.

"In those words, I saw one of God's great secrets. And when we share that secret, we shall understand why he had to allow bad things in the world . . . Until then, we must remember, all shall be well, and all shall be well, and all manner of thing shall be well."

A Woman in a Man's World

Catherine of Siena

SAINT'S DAY

29 APRIL

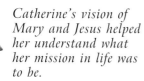

Catherine's vision of Mary and Jesus helped her understand what her mission in life was to be.

CATHERINE WAS ONLY six when she had her first vision. In her mind, she saw him quite clearly. She knew he was Jesus, even though he was dressed not like a carpenter's son but in the fine robes usually worn by a pope. And she was equally certain that the two men with him were Saints John and Paul.

Catherine's father was a wealthy man who owned a business that dyed wool. Her mother was a quick-tempered woman whose own father had been a poet. They had twenty-five children who all lived upstairs above their father's business in the town of Siena in northern Italy.

Like Clare of Assisi, Catherine was determined to become a nun even though her parents wanted her to marry. She got her own way by cutting off her own hair to prove she was serious. As a punishment, her mother fired the family's servant and made Catherine dress as a maid and do all the household jobs.

Catherine obeyed without ever complaining until her father decided she should be allowed to become a nun.

Instead of living with other nuns, Catherine spent all her time in one room in her parents' home, eating hardly anything and often seeing more visions. Sometimes these were of Jesus. Other times they were more like nightmares in which she felt the devil was coming to get her.

After three years, she had a special vision.

Saints of the Medieval Church

This time she seemed to see not only Jesus but also Mary, his mother. From this vision, she learned her life was not to be spent alone in prayer but in helping other people.

In those days, all Europe was being swept by the plague known as the Black Death. It was highly infectious, but Catherine had no hesitation in working among its victims.

When a priest who was in charge of a hospital caught the illness and was thought to be close to death, she went bustling into his room. "Get up, Father," she said. "Have something to eat. There's work to be done. It's no time for you to be lying in bed."

The priest was so surprised he got up—and discovered he was no longer ill.

Catherine bustled around the city. She worked as a nurse. She dug graves for those who died of the plague and then buried them properly herself. She also continued to see visions, and then (in the year 1375) she began to dictate letters to anyone she thought needed her advice. She sent letters to kings, princes, and dukes all over Italy.

At this time, Italy was divided into a number of small but powerful and quarrelsome city-states. In particular, the city of Florence was a serious enemy of the city of Rome. There was another problem too. For the last seventy-five years, whoever was pope had been living at Avignon in France, rather than in Rome. Catherine thought that the pope should be in Rome, because that was where the popes had always lived and because she believed it would bring peace to Italy.

So she wrote to the pope of that time, Gregory IX, explaining what he ought to do. Then she went to Avignon in order to tell him so in person. She failed to get him to make peace with Florence, but she did at least persuade him to return to Rome.

The next pope sent Catherine to Florence where she lived in considerable danger for her life. But thanks to her determination and the respect everyone had for this holy woman, she finally established peace between Florence and Rome.

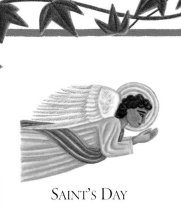

Voices

Joan of Arc

JOAN WAS AN ORDINARY French country girl, about thirteen years old. She was at home, in the garden, when the local church bell began to ring. It was then she first heard the voices. They seemed to come from a blaze of light. At first she was frightened, but then she became convinced they were angel voices. One was the archangel Michael. He seemed to be saying she must become a soldier and help the dauphin win the war against the English.

"Dauphin" was the title given to the eldest son of the king of France. At this time, the old king had died but his son, Charles, had not yet been crowned. He was still called the dauphin and, it has to be said, he hadn't much idea how to defeat the English. Years before, they'd invaded northern France and were ruling it as if it was their own country.

Back in the village of Domremy, whenever the church bell rang, young Joan heard her voices. Again and again Saint Michael seemed to speak to her. So too did other voices whom she believed to be Saint Catherine and Saint Margaret.

But what could a farmer's daughter do about winning a war? So she did nothing. Time passed. But the voices didn't stop. She told her priest and some friends about them. Some believed her; most didn't. But she became more and more convinced she must do something.

At last she got an opportunity. She was away from home, staying with an aunt. One day, she managed to slip away and see the local nobleman, Robert de Baudricourt.

"My name's Joan," she told him. "I come from the village of Domremy and I've been told to save France from the English, so please will you give me some soldier's clothing and a horse, and help me get to the king?"

"Who sent you?" he asked.

"The king of heaven," replied Joan.

"Why on earth should I believe you?"

"Because our army is about to be defeated again."

Soon after, news came of that defeat.

Robert de Baudricourt was impressed. He arranged for Joan to go to the dauphin. It wouldn't be an easy journey for the countryside was full of robbers and rough soldiers. So Joan had her hair cut short. She wore a young man's tunic and was given two soldiers to act as her guardians.

The dauphin was staying at a castle at a place named Chinon. He'd arranged a trick to discover what sort of person Joan was. A crowd of courtiers gathered in a room lit only by candles. One of the noblemen pretended to be the dauphin while Charles hid among the crowd. Joan went straight to the real dauphin and started to persuade him she could rescue the city of Orleans. It was being besieged by the English, and part of the French army was trapped inside its walls.

Joan's prayers helped the French army to cross a river and rescue the besieged town of Orleans.

The dauphin agreed she could try. She was given a suit of white soldier's clothing, some soldiers, servants, and a banner on which was written "For Jesus and Mary." When they reached Orleans, she met the commander of the part of the French army that wasn't trapped in the city.

This gruff commander, whose name was Dunois, explained how the English army was surrounding the city on three sides. On the fourth side was a river. So how could the French soldiers be rescued from the city?

"Simple," said Joan. "We get boats, cross the river and save them."

"I've got boats," said Dunois. "And rafts. But the wind's blowing the wrong way. See? They can't get across."

"Is that all? We just need the wind to change direction," said Joan. "I'll go to church and pray about it."

When she got back, the wind had indeed changed. The boats crossed the river, and the two parts of the French army were able to link up and save Orleans.

Under her leadership, the French had more victories against the English. At last it was time for the dauphin to be crowned king of France. The coronation took place in the cathedral at a place named Rheims. Joan herself was there, standing just behind the throne and dressed in her soldier's clothing.

Plenty of people questioned why a peasant girl should stand in such an important spot, but nobody dared to object. After all, without her leadership, there would have been no victories and no coronation.

Burned at the Stake

Joan of Arc

UNDER THE LEADERSHIP of Joan, the Maid from Domremy, the French had many victories against the English. Even so, the English army still occupied part of France, including Paris. It was in the month of May, while leading a small band of soldiers near that city, that she was spotted by a force of troops belonging to the duke of Burgundy, who was on the side of the English. A Burgundian archer managed to shoot her horse and she fell to the ground and was captured. She was immediately taken to the duke of Burgundy himself who eventually sold her to the English. She was kept in various prisons despite making several brave attempts to escape. King Charles of France, however, did little to rescue her. By Christmas, she was a prisoner in the castle of Rouen in northern France.

The English found it difficult to understand how such a young woman could have helped the French army to be so successful. They decided that it could mean only one thing—she was a witch and on the side of the devil. The punishment for witchcraft was death by burning.

It was agreed that Joan should be put on trial and her judge was to be Bishop Pierre Cauchon. He was French, but on the side of the English (like the duke of Burgundy). He was a cold man, bad-tempered, and full of envy and hatred.

She never stood a chance. The truth was, Bishop Cauchon and the English had agreed secretly before the trial that even if she was found innocent, she would be taken to England and executed.

The trial lasted many, many days. Joan firmly refused to answer what she thought were their questions. She told one official she'd pull his ears if he made a mistake in what he said. And she told Bishop Cauchon he'd be in great danger if he judged her wrongly. But still the questions came.

"Whose were these voices?" "Were they not devil voices?" "How do you know?"

Then they tried to persuade her she had been wrong and that the voices had tricked her. For a moment, she thought that if she said she had been wrong she might be set free. Yes, she would agree with them! But, almost at once, she realized this would not mean freedom. They would never set her free! So she went back to her original story, which she really believed was the truth.

"They were the voices of the saints," she said again.

"Guilty," they all said.

English soldiers took her to the crowded marketplace, there in the French town of Rouen. She was taken up onto a platform and tied to a post. Wood was piled up round her feet. An English solder made her a cross out of two pieces of wood. She asked him to hold it up so she could see it. They set light to the fire. The flames flickered and then burned strongly.

One of those watching was the English king's secretary, a man named John Tessart. As she died, he said, "We've burned a saint."

Her ashes were thrown into the River Seine in case people came to worship at her grave and treat her as a saint.

Joan of Arc was burnt at the stake by the English, on the charge that she had been listening to devil voices.

SAINTS
of the
Renaissance
and the
Missionary Church

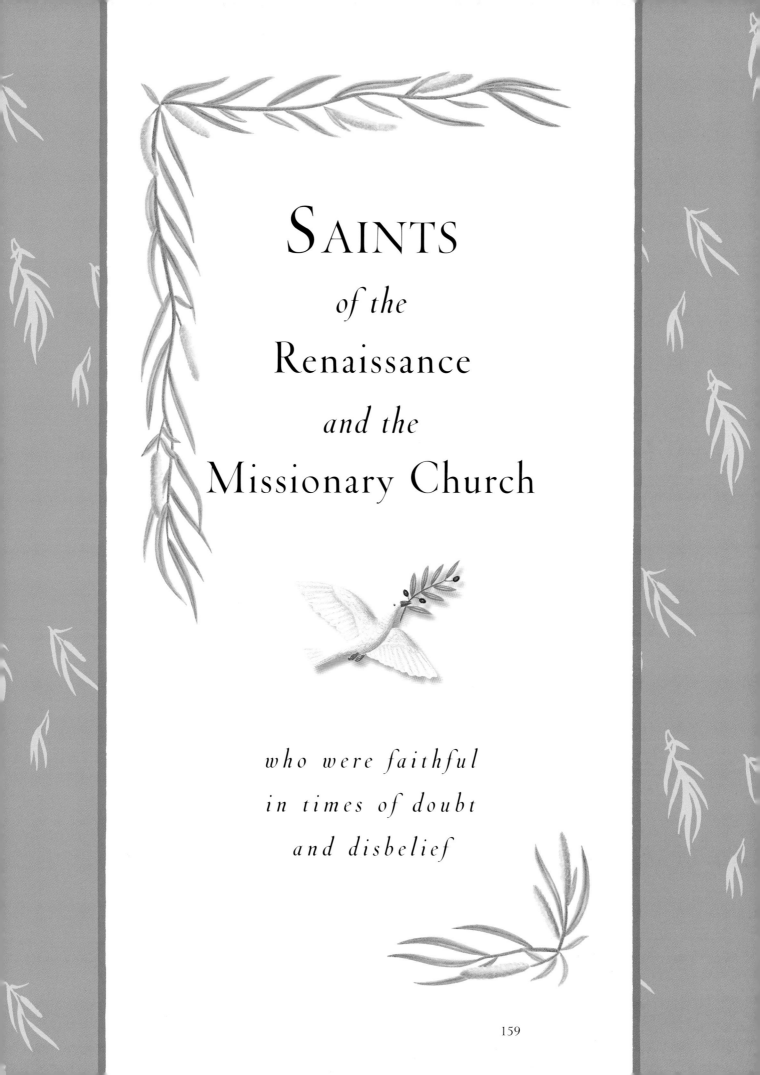

*who were faithful
in times of doubt
and disbelief*

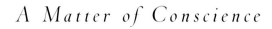

A Matter of Conscience

Thomas More

A MARTYR'S PRAYER

*H*ere is a prayer by
Thomas More:

*Good Lord, give me the grace to spend
my life, that when the day of my death
shall come, though I feel pain in my
body, I may feel comfort in my soul;
and with faithful hope of thy mercy,
with due love toward thee, and charity
toward the world, I may, through grace,
depart into thy glory.*

"B UT IT'S EASY. You just say what he wants you to say." Margaret, a young woman in her twenties, pleaded with her resolute father, Thomas More.

"Margaret, my dear, it's not easy," he replied.

Thomas More had been a writer and a lawyer. He'd been a member of parliament and a judge (and was famous for being a very fair judge). King Henry VIII had chosen him as one of his advisers, and had then made him lord chancellor. Thomas was not only popular; he had become very powerful. But within a few years, he'd resigned as lord chancellor and there was every chance he would be sent to prison or even executed— just because he would not say a few words to please the king. So how did this all come about?

King Henry very much wanted to have a son who would be king when he died. He had a daughter named Mary but no sons, and now the doctors said his wife, Queen Catherine, could not have any more children. So Henry claimed he had never been properly married to her and divorced her.

Henry then married another woman named Anne Boleyn. The pope, who (in those days) was the head of the whole church, said this was wrong. So too did Thomas More. It was then he resigned as lord chancellor because he believed that the king was doing wrong. He also refused to go to see Anne crowned queen. All this made Henry very angry, but Thomas was still popular with the ordinary people.

Two years later, the pope still said Anne Boleyn was not truly Henry's wife so Henry persuaded parliament to make a law saying that, in England, he himself and not the pope was head of the church, and that Anne was his legal wife and that her children (and not Mary's) should rule after him. What was more, Henry wanted all the important people in the country to swear by the Holy Bible that all this was true and right.

Thomas More allowed himself to be executed rather than betray his sense of right and wrong.

So, of course, Thomas was asked to swear this holy oath. When he said he wouldn't, the king became angrier still.

What's more, he didn't want someone as popular as Thomas standing up against him—so he wanted Thomas "out of the way." Which was why Margaret was now trying to persuade her father to say the oath.

"It's easy," she said to her father. "It's just a few words. Say anything if it'll save you."

"But it's very wrong to say what's not true is true," her father insisted.

Nothing she could say would persuade him to take the oath. Some time later, he was locked up in a cold, dark, damp cell in the Tower of London. Friends came to see him. They too tried to get him to change his mind: "If you swear the oath, you can go free." Thomas kept silent.

A year after being put in prison, Thomas was charged with being a traitor to the king and the country—what's known as "treason." The punishment for treason was execution. He still refused to take the oath. He was taken to court and found guilty. Later he was beheaded. His head was stuck on a post on London Bridge.

He could have saved himself. He didn't. It was a matter of conscience and Thomas More kept true to his conscience.

SAINT'S DAY

31 JULY

I Could Be As Saintly

Ignatius of Loyola

I̲T ALL BEGAN WITH the cannonball. That was the turning point for Ignatius. He was a soldier, fighting for Spain against the French. That was how he came to be wounded by the cannonball. It hit him in the legs, tearing open his left calf and breaking his right shin. He was captured by the French, but they allowed him to be carried home on a stretcher to Loyola, where his father was a nobleman.

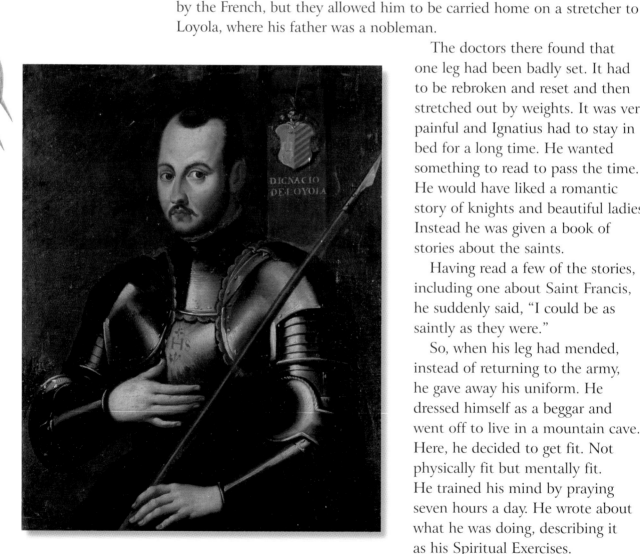

The doctors there found that one leg had been badly set. It had to be rebroken and reset and then stretched out by weights. It was very painful and Ignatius had to stay in bed for a long time. He wanted something to read to pass the time. He would have liked a romantic story of knights and beautiful ladies. Instead he was given a book of stories about the saints.

Having read a few of the stories, including one about Saint Francis, he suddenly said, "I could be as saintly as they were."

So, when his leg had mended, instead of returning to the army, he gave away his uniform. He dressed himself as a beggar and went off to live in a mountain cave. Here, he decided to get fit. Not physically fit but mentally fit. He trained his mind by praying seven hours a day. He wrote about what he was doing, describing it as his Spiritual Exercises.

Ignatius was once a Spanish soldier, but after he was wounded, he became a soldier for Christ.

He next decided he needed more education, so at the age of thirty-three, he went back to school in Barcelona and sat in a class of eleven-year-olds to learn Latin. He then journeyed to Rome and Jerusalem. He next set about serious study in Spanish universities and in Paris.

THE NORTH AMERICAN MARTYRS
OF THE SOCIETY OF JESUS

*I*gnatius started the Society of Jesus in the year 1534. The pope gave it his approval in 1540, and within the next hundred years the Jesuits had started five hundred schools and several universities. Members of the Society also journeyed as missionaries to many distant countries.

Several French Jesuits made the voyage to Canada with the aim of persuading the Native Indians to become Christians. One of the first was John de Brebeuf (1593–1649). He had been born in Normandy in northern France and, after becoming a Jesuit, went to Quebec (in what was then called New France) in 1615. With much difficulty, he learned the language of the Huron Indians. He worked among them from 1633. He was joined by another French Jesuit, Gabriel Lalemant in 1648.

The next spring, the two men were captured during an attack by Iroquois Indians on the Hurons. The Iroquois tomahawked John de Brebeuf and Gabriel Lalemant and then burned them to death. In all, eight Jesuit priests were killed between 1642 and 1649.

It was John de Brebeuf who named the present-day version of the Indian game lacrosse because the stick reminded him of the staff or crozier (in French: *la crosse*) carried by a bishop.

The saints' day of the Jesuit Martyrs of North America is on 19 October.

Saint John de Brebeuf.

Here he was joined by six other students. They jointly made vows of poverty, chastity, and obedience. They also agreed to follow the Spiritual Exercises that Ignatius had written down and promised to carry out whatever jobs the pope might ask them to do. They felt they were to become an army or society, with Ignatius as its general, fighting for Jesus.

The pope (Paul III) liked the idea and so began the Society of Jesus. Since 1544, its members have been known as Jesuits. Sometimes they have been accused of being too strict, but ever since the days of Ignatius, they have thought of themselves as Christ's soldiers.

Francis Xavier

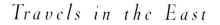

I T WAS A GHASTLY VOYAGE. For one thing, it took them thirteen months to sail from Portugal round the southern tip of Africa to India. There was a complete mixture of people on board the small sailing ship—slaves, soldiers, and merchants. Then there was an outbreak of the illness known as scurvy, and Francis had to turn his tiny cabin into a hospital.

While he was at sea, he remembered one day seven years earlier. He was then a student in Paris where he had met a fellow Spanish student, Ignatius of Loyola. Ignatius had asked him a question from the Bible: "What profit is it if you gain the whole world but lose your own soul?" That was when Francis had given up everything to become one of the first seven members of the Society of Jesus. And that was why he was now sailing east to India.

The ship set sail in April 1541. They landed at Goa on the west coast of India in May 1542, and that was where Francis made his new headquarters. There were some Christians there already: Europeans who'd come to trade. Francis was horrified at how cruelly they treated the local people and how wickedly they lived their own lives.

He began his work among these Europeans (they were mainly Portuguese), but also preached to the local people. He would walk round the streets, ringing a little bell to call children to him. Then he would sit under an umbrella to guard against the sun and tell them Bible stories in their own language.

Francis was always very practical. He helped people in hospital and prison. He was also a kind man, often close to tears at the suffering he saw in the crowded streets. It was no wonder he became popular with the poorest people, sharing in their troubles by eating only rice and water and by sleeping only four hours a day.

Some time after his arrival there, he journeyed along the coast to visit other Portuguese settlements. To his complete surprise, he found a group of Indian people who still worshipped Jesus in the way that had been used by the earliest Christians. These people were known as the Christians of Saint Thomas. They believed their faith had been brought to them centuries earlier by the same Thomas who had touched Jesus after he rose from the dead.

During the next few years, Francis made a trip to the Malay Peninsula and spent four months in a city called Malacca. While he was there, he met a Japanese man and heard stories about Japan, which no European had previously ever dared to visit.

Francis returned to India, determined to take the Christian message to Japan. He did this in 1549 with just five Christian helpers.

On his arrival, he spent a year learning the language. He then started to travel around the country. He was greeted in a variety of ways. In some towns, the local ruler made him welcome. In several, he was given permission to preach. In one, he was allowed to turn a disused Buddhist temple into a church. In other places, he was less popular and was quickly turned away. Nevertheless, Francis (the first European to reach Japan) made at least two thousand converts to Christianity before he returned to India three years later. His work in Japan was continued by other missionaries until 1597, when the Japanese authorities turned against them, fearing they were the beginning of a European invasion.

Francis on one of his many travels.

Meanwhile, Francis decided he would next go to China. He set off with five other Jesuits and an interpreter. As foreigners were not then allowed into China, they landed secretly on an island called Sancian. Here Francis developed a fever and died in early December 1552, aged just forty-six.

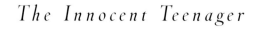

SAINT'S DAY

13 NOVEMBER

T HE WHOLE FAMILY used to laugh about young Stanislaus. If anyone said anything the slightest bit rude, they all immediately said, "Oh don't say that in front of Stanislaus—he'll probably faint."

It has to be said that the young boy did blush very easily. He was embarrassed by rude words or rude stories, and he spent a great deal of time praying.

His father, John Kostka, was both a nobleman and a senator in Poland, while his mother, Margaret, was the sister of a duke. There were seven children, of whom Stanislaus was the second. His older brother, Paul, was a rather nasty bully.

The two boys were taught at home by a tutor who was strict but not always fair. For example, if Paul played a practical joke on Stanislaus, he would only laugh.

When Stanislaus was thirteen, the two brothers were sent to Vienna in Austria to attend a new Jesuit school. The tutor went along to look after them both. Stanislaus soon became popular with the other students because he was always cheerful, and he was soon noticed by the priests who taught in the school because he was careful to say his prayers and he was so well behaved. But Stanislaus's goodness only made Paul want to tease him all the more.

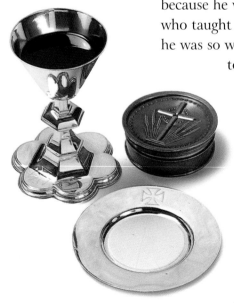

The Kostka family were, like most Polish people, Roman Catholics. So too were most Austrians. But in Vienna there were also many followers of Martin Luther—Protestants known as Lutherans. The story of Stanislaus is also a story about the sad divisions that were growing between Protestant and Catholic Christians.

Paul thought of a joke to play on Stanislaus, to tease him for being so religious. With the help of their tutor, he arranged for Stanislaus to live in the house of a Lutheran family. After a while, Stanislaus became ill.

His Lutheran landlord wouldn't let a Catholic priest enter the house, so Stanislaus couldn't receive Holy Communion. But then something strange seemed to happen. Two angels appeared in his room, bringing him the bread and wine of Holy Communion.

The bread and wine of Holy Communion in silver vessels.

Stanislaus's holy way of behaving continued to annoy Paul. He began to behave violently toward his younger brother, and Stanislaus finally lost patience. He didn't fight back. But one night after he had again suffered the harsh words and blows of his brother, he turned to Paul and said quietly, "Your rough treatment will end in my going away never to return, and then you'll have to explain it all to our father and mother."

Paul's reply was to swear very rudely.

Stanislaus had already thought of joining the Society of Jesus and becoming a Jesuit priest. He'd even spoken about it to his teachers in Vienna. They'd discouraged him, fearing what a rich Polish nobleman would say when he heard his son was going to become a poor priest. Stanislaus understood this, and when he'd had enough of being bullied by Paul, he decided to go to the general of the Society at Rome.

Rome was 350 miles away. Stanislaus knew he would have to travel on foot, without a guide or any food or money other than what might be given him by friendly people along the way.

On the morning when he was going to start his journey, he left a message for Paul and his tutor to say he wouldn't be back for dinner that day. Then he set off, swapping his fine coat and shirt for a beggar's tunic. He hoped that would stop people he might meet from asking him questions.

Stanislaus once saw angels bringing him the bread and wine of Holy Communion.

That evening, Paul and the tutor realized Stanislaus had run away. The tutor knew John Kostka would be very angry, so they set off to follow him. Even though they hired horses in the hope of catching him up, they failed to find him. The tutor admitted that they had taken the wrong route.

Stanislaus eventually reached Rome and joined the Society of Jesus. Ten months later, he developed a high fever. He'd never been strong, and after a few days, he died peacefully and full of faith.

21 OCTOBER
and 25 MARCH
Margaret Clitherow

25 OCTOBER
The Forty Martyrs are
collectively remembered
in the Catholic church
on this day

*The memorial to
Margaret Clitherow
inside her house in
York.*

Pressed to Death
Margaret Clitherow

JOHN CLITHEROW WAS a butcher. His shop was in a tiny narrow street known as the Shambles, in the middle of York in the north of England. The street's still there, and on a hot day, it's easy to imagine how awful the smell must have been in Elizabethan times.

Sheep, cows, and pigs would be brought to the shop's front door. There, on the step, they'd be killed and then carved up, ready to hang in the butcher's shop. John Clitherow's young wife, Margaret, helped with the business. She was liked by the customers and by the people around. They brought her their problems and worries. Despite her youth, she always gave calm, good, practical advice.

But they also knew her secret.

Upstairs, high above the shop, was a secret room. Here, Margaret hid any Roman Catholic priests who were trying to avoid being caught by the authorities. And here, Margaret's Roman Catholic friends could meet secretly to share Mass.

At this time, the Church of England was the official church of the whole country. It had been made illegal to protect a Roman Catholic priest, and it was forbidden to take part in a Roman Catholic church service. Many people were being put to death for breaking these new laws. But that didn't stop Margaret who, despite the laws, was Roman Catholic.

Early in 1586, a young Flemish boy was staying with the Clitherow family. One day, the local authorities seized him in the street and frightened him into telling them all about the secret room and what went on there. Margaret was arrested.

On 14 March, she was put on trial before two judges: Judge Clinch and Judge Rhodes. The charge against her was that she "had hidden priests and heard Mass."

"How do you plead?" asked Judge Clinch.

"I have done no wrong," she answered. "I need no trial."

"But you know the law?"

"Yes."

"And if you refuse to plead, you will be judged guilty and pressed to death."

Margaret refused to argue her case since the officials would make her own small children be witnesses against her. She did not want them to have the worry of lying in court nor the agony of accusing their own mother.

"My death will be on no one's conscience except on yours," she told the judges.

Judge Clinch stopped the trial for the night. He hoped she'd change her mind the next day. She didn't.

This infuriated Judge Rhodes.

"You're nothing but a wicked, stubborn woman," he shouted angrily.

And so she was condemned to be pressed to death on 25 March.

She was taken from the prison and laid on the ground. A sharp stone was placed under her back and her arms were stretched out in the form of a cross and bound to two posts. Then a door was placed on her. Heavier and heavier weights were placed on the door until she was crushed to death. Her last words during an agony of fifteen minutes, were "Jesus! Jesus! Jesus! Have mercy on me!"

THE REFORMATION IN ENGLAND

At the time of the Reformation, England did not become a Lutheran country as did many other countries in northern Europe. Instead, it had its own national church, the Church of England, which had begun when Henry VIII was king.

When his daughter, Elizabeth I, became queen, Roman Catholics were persecuted and many (like Margaret Clitherow) were put to death.

Saints of the Reformation are remembered in the Anglican Church on 31 October.

SAINT'S DAY

23 (or 30) AUGUST

I Don't Want to Be Pretty

Rose of Lima

Rose made herself a crown of prickly roses, not to look more beautiful but to punish herself.

S HE WAS A BEAUTIFUL baby and, later, a beautiful child. Everyone said so. And because her cheeks were such a pretty pink, they all named her Rose—which was a lot easier to remember than her real name: Isabel de Flores y del Oliva.

She was born in Lima, Peru, and her family had fallen on hard times. They had originally come from Spain and had become rich by mining in the Andes Mountains in South America. But the mines had failed, and now the family lived in poverty in Lima.

In those days, most young women got married as soon as they were old enough, and everyone was sure that beautiful Rose would marry. Her parents secretly hoped that she'd marry a rich young man who could help look after the whole family.

But Rose didn't like being pretty. She hated it. She hated people noticing her and admiring her. And she didn't want to be married. One day, when she was worried that her beauty might make some young man fall in love with her, she rubbed her face with pepper until it was red and blistered. And because everyone called her Rose, she decided to wear a crown of roses. But she made it out of very prickly ones and pushed it down hard on her head so that the thorns stuck into her scalp and made it bleed.

So why did Rose behave so very oddly?

In her mind, it was simple. She wanted everyone to love and praise Jesus and no one else—certainly not her. She also wanted to give up her whole life to serve him. So, although she loved her parents and wanted to obey them, she refused to get married. One thing she did do to please them, however, was needlework. She was extremely good at sewing and took on jobs that helped support the family.

Then she read a book about Saint Catherine of Siena. She decided she wanted to copy her way of life.

She did this in a strange way too. She got her brother to help her build a garden shed. She called this her grotto, and from then on, she lived in it all the time. She spent her time praying and started going without food three times a week.

Rose believed that many people cared very little about Jesus. She also believed she could make up for their thoughtlessness and carelessness by suffering pain and hardship. So she found ways of deliberately hurting herself. She wore gloves full of nettles. She slept on a pile of bricks. She made her hands rough. And then she cut off all her hair.

It's not surprising that many people thought she was mad. Many of them tried to persuade her to live normally. Others just laughed at her. But Rose did many worthwhile things. She helped the people of Lima who were ill or suffering, especially the poor, the Native Indians, and the many slaves that the Spanish kept there in those days.

Then, one day, she made an announcement. She said that the city of Lima had been saved from an earthquake because of her prayers. Immediately, she became popular throughout the city. No one thought she was mad any more, but no one seemed to ask whether there would have been an earthquake if she hadn't been praying.

For fourteen years, she continued living a life of deliberate hardship. It was no wonder that it made her body ill and that she died at the early age of thirty-one.

Rose was good at needlework and took on sewing jobs to help earn money for her family. However, her main concern was to help the needy.

Seraphim of Sarov

IN THE DARK PINE FORESTS south of Moscow, there lived a hermit—a monk who had chosen to live all alone. His name was Seraphim and his only home was a simple wooden shack. He lived there even in the bitter, snowy winters. He grew vegetables for food, he kept some bees, and he studied the Bible.

He wanted to live in complete silence. "Silence," he said, "brings a person closer to God." One day the silence was broken.

As he was chopping wood for his small fire, three robbers came along. Although he was strong and was holding an axe, Seraphim did not try to defend himself. He simply put his axe on the ground, crossed his arms on his chest, and waited.

They began to hit him over the head with the handle of his own axe and stopped beating him only when they thought he was dead. Eventually, Seraphim recovered enough to drag himself to the nearby monastery where he had once lived.

Later, the robbers were caught and put on trial. Seraphim asked the judge to treat them kindly, even though, as a result of this beating, he walked with a bad stoop.

When he was older, Seraphim began to receive visitors—especially those who needed his help. One such person was a nun named Matrona.

Many people in Russia were afraid of the bears in the woods, but Seraphim was so gentle and understanding that he made friends with a bear and fed it by hand.

She was finding it hard to live as a nun and her faith was weak. Seraphim told her to visit him in his forest.

On the day he suggested, she set out, walking into the dark forest. As she went further in among the trees, she got more and more afraid. Just as she thought she'd never find him, she suddenly saw him. He was sitting on an old tree stump. She smiled with relief—until she realized what the great dark shape was that lay at his feet. It was a bear.

"Batiouchka!" she cried—which is a Russian word meaning something like "dear old man" or "little grandpa."

When he heard her shouting, Seraphim tapped the bear gently and motioned it to go away. As if it understood exactly what he meant, it heaved itself up onto its four paws and lumbered off among the trees.

"Don't be frightened," said Seraphim.

"But it could kill us . . . Eat us . . ." she said, her voice full of terror.

He beckoned her to join him, and after saying a prayer, told her to sit on the tree stump. Then he sat down beside her just as the bear returned from the woods. It came to them and quietly settled down at their feet.

Seraphim took some bread from a little satchel he wore over one shoulder and began feeding it to the bear. When Matrona had calmed down, he gave her some bread for the bear.

"Go on," he said. "It won't eat your hand."

Nervously, she took the bread and held it out to the bear. Gently it snuffled it out of her hand—and at that moment, she felt a great calmness come over her. All her worries had disappeared, and she felt incredibly peaceful.

"You see?" said Seraphim. "Just as Gerasimus had his lion, so I have a bear at my service."

"Can I tell people about this?" asked Matrona.

"After I'm dead, you can," he replied.

After this, Matrona happily remained a nun, and many years later, she told her friends about what had happened. From that time on, the hunting of bears in the forests of Sarov was forbidden as a sign of respect for Seraphim.

SAINT'S DAY

4 JANUARY

The Nun from Wall Street

Elizabeth Ann Seton

E LIZABETH WAS ALWAYS being invited to parties. No wonder. She was a very popular young lady. She enjoyed riding her horse. She was musical. She spoke French—just the sort of things that fashionable young ladies in New York were expected to be good at. What's more, she was very beautiful with her dark brown eyes and long dark hair.

It was not surprising that young William Seton fell head over heels in love with her. When she fell adoringly in love with him too, they were married and seemed certain to live happily ever after.

Their married life began well enough in a grand house on Wall Street. William worked hard at his family's shipping business. Elizabeth was occupied with babies. First came Anna Maria, then young William was born, followed by Richard, Rebecca, and Catherine. But worries came too.

William was no longer as healthy as he had been. To make matters worse, his father died, and the shipping business began doing badly. William was terrified that they might lose all their money and end up in prison.

Two years later, some of his fears came true. They went bankrupt and many of their possessions had to be sold. Then, in the year 1803, their doctor said William might get better if he got plenty of sea air by going on a long voyage. Elizabeth sold her remaining possessions (some silver, vases, and a few pictures) in order to pay the fares for herself, William, and Anna Maria. The other children, William, Richard, Rebecca, and Catherine, were left with William's sister, Rebecca.

The young Elizabeth Seton was a noted beauty in New York society.

They sailed across the Atlantic Ocean to Italy to stay with some friends they had there. The voyage was very enjoyable, but disaster was waiting for them when they arrived at the port of Livorno in Italy. Because there had been an outbreak in New York of an illness known as yellow fever, they were not allowed to leave the port in case they were infectious. Instead, they were put in a stone tower just outside Livorno and kept apart from all other people.

For forty days, the family suffered. Elizabeth looked after her husband, who was now coughing up blood; she tried to amuse Anna Maria with stories and games; and she held little prayer services.

Eventually, they were free to join their friends, but William died soon afterward in Pisa at the age of thirty-seven.

While waiting to return to America, Elizabeth went to church with her Italian friends. They were Roman Catholics. Elizabeth liked the services, even though they were not what she was used to. She had grown up in the Anglican (or Episcopalian) Church.

Back in New York, she realized she had to earn a living to support her children. She did this by becoming a teacher. At the same time, she became a Roman Catholic, despite the opposition of family and friends. Then she was asked to start a girls' school. Other young women joined her in this work, and eventually they formed a religious community, the first in the United States.

Elizabeth was a wealthy young woman who had expected to marry a handsome man, be a loving wife, have a number of happy children, and live in style. Instead, she had to face illness, the loss of her husband, and poverty. With each new problem, she found that God gave her strength and courage to cope.

THE PURPOSE OF OUR DAILY WORK

*E*lizabeth Ann Seton wrote these words:

What was the first rule of our dear Savior's life? You know it was to do his Father's will.

Well, then, the first purpose of our daily work is to do the will of God; secondly, to do it in the manner he wills; and thirdly, to do it because it is his will.

We know certainly that our God calls us to a holy life. We know that he gives us every grace, every abundant grace; and though we are so weak of ourselves, this grace is able to carry us through every obstacle and difficulty.

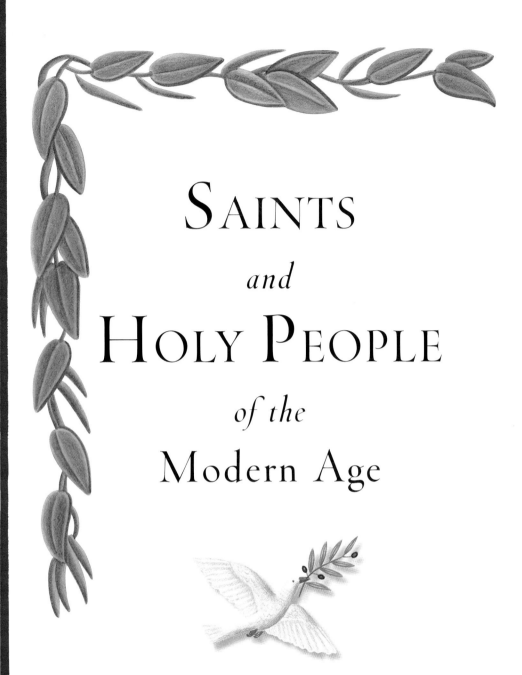

SAINTS
and
HOLY PEOPLE
of the
Modern Age

*shining for God
in times of darkness*

The Man with a Dream

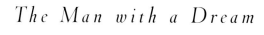

John Bosco

John Bosco was not afraid of upsetting people in authority over him if it would help him to do good.

EARLY ONE DECEMBER DAY in 1841, a young priest was about to take a service in a church in the Italian city of Turin. From the back of the church, he heard the rough voice of the church's caretaker, or sexton.

"What are you doing here if you don't want to come to Mass?"

The priest heard a timid boy's voice reply, "It's cold outside."

"That doesn't mean you can come in. Get out, and be quick about it!"

The priest, whose name was John Bosco, called to the sexton, "Joseph, what are you doing? Call him back."

With a few bad-tempered mutterings, Joseph went outside and eventually persuaded the nervous boy to come back. Shivering, the boy stood in front of John Bosco. "Stay for Mass," the priest said gently, "and we can talk later."

The youth's name was Bartollomea (or Bartholomew) Garelli. He was sixteen, an orphan, and he was helping a bricklayer in return for a few coins a day.

"Where do you live, Bartollomea?"

"In an attic."

"Alone?"

"With some other guys."

"Can you read and write?"

The boy shook his head. "I don't know anything," he said.

He had been a farm boy and had never been to school. His parents had both died, and he'd come to the city looking for work. John Bosco knew there were thousands of boys like this one in Turin. The lucky ones (like Bartollomea) had somewhere to sleep. The others slept in doorways.

"Bart, would you like to learn to read if I were to teach you?"

"I suppose so."

"When you come, bring your friends."

This had been John Bosco's dream for a long time. He wanted to help, feed, and teach the street boys of Turin. By February, twenty boys were coming to his classes. By March, thirty. Two years later, there would be four hundred. Meanwhile, it was hard to find suitable meeting places.

They tried meeting in a public park where they could play and talk and then go to a service in a nearby church. Local people complained about the noise and called the police, saying that John Bosco was creating a disturbance. Then people started saying, "Don Bosco must be mad." ("Don" was a title often given to priests.)

"Why don't you cut down the number of boys?" asked another priest named Don Borel. "Limit yourself to twenty or so of the best behaved ones."

"Don Borel, you speak of twenty boys when I see thousands. I dream of a huge school with beautiful buildings, large courtyards, a magnificent church. I picture classrooms; training shops where the boys can learn a trade. I even see some of them becoming priests themselves."

Word then spread that Don Bosco was indeed going mad. He would be taken away for a few weeks' rest in a mental asylum.

Two priests went in their horse-drawn carriage to his house.

"Join us for a ride, Don Bosco," one of them said.

"Willingly," Don Bosco replied. "But first," he went on, "I have a plan I should like to discuss with you." And he began to tell them his dream of starting an order (a bit like the "orders" in which monks lived) for the boys.

John Bosco dreamed of a time when monks would travel by modern forms of transport in order to go about the world doing good.

"Let's talk about this while we're riding around the city," said one of the priests craftily.

"Of course," Don Bosco replied.

"Get into the carriage then," they said.

"You first, please. You're more important than I am," he replied. No sooner were they seated in the coach than he slammed the door shut and called to the driver. "To the asylum, at once! These two gentlemen are expected there!"

Later, John Bosco's mother came to Turin to help him run a boarding house to shelter some of the boys. Gradually, dormitories were found where the rest could live safely. The city authorities recognized the good work John Bosco was doing and helped him to continue his work.

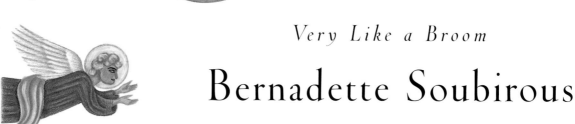

Very Like a Broom

Bernadette Soubirous

When Bernadette first saw the Lady, her sister tried to awaken her from her trance by throwing pebbles at her.

IT ALL BEGAN ONE DAMP February afternoon. Bernadette, her younger sister Toinette, and a school friend named Jeanne were walking beside a shallow river, looking for firewood. They were near a small cave, or grotto, formed out of rocks and boulders.

Seeing some fallen branches on the other side of the river, Toinette and Jeanne took their shoes off and waded through the icy water. Bernadette hesitated. She had a cold and she didn't want to bring on one of her asthma attacks. Then the wind started blowing through the bushes near her. A soft light appeared—and then Bernadette saw the Lady.

When the other two girls returned, they found Bernadette looking terribly pale. Rather cruelly, Toinette threw pebbles at her. Bernadette seemed to wake up and then raced off home.

Later, Bernadette told Toinette about what she'd seen, and Toinette told their mother. Next day, Jeanne told everyone at school what had happened. The teachers told Bernadette to keep quiet or everyone would laugh at her.

During the following weeks, Bernadette claimed that she saw the Lady seventeen more times. Sometimes she took other children or grown-ups to the grotto, but they never saw the Lady. They heard Bernadette talking as if someone else were there, and they became certain that Bernadette was seeing and hearing something special.

After several appearances, the Lady spoke to Bernadette. It was a warning that she would never be happy in this world, but she would be happy in heaven.

The people of the nearby town of Lourdes weren't sure what to make of it all. They began flocking to the grotto in crowds. Some were disbelieving and said that Bernadette was a silly young girl or even mad. The local priest and doctor talked to her and examined her. So too did the police. But her story never altered. Perhaps she was telling the truth, after all, they thought.

One Saturday, the Lady appeared to Bernadette and told her to kiss the muddy ground near the river. At once a spring of water appeared. It's still flowing today.

On the same day, the Lady also told Bernadette that the priests must build a chapel or church at that place.

News of what was happening appeared in the newspapers. People began to come to Lourdes to see Bernadette, and more particularly to visit the spot where the Lady had appeared. It became impossible for Bernadette to live a normal life, and she hated the way that some of these people said she had made her story up.

After one of the last occasions that Bernadette saw the Lady, she came to understand that the Lady was Mary, the mother of Jesus. In due course, the church authorities agreed that Mary had actually appeared to young Bernadette.

Bernadette meanwhile just wanted to escape from all the visitors so she went to live in a convent. By now, she was very ill with severe asthma.

In 1876, a great church was built near the spot where Bernadette had seen Mary, but Bernadette did not attend the ceremony when the church was opened. "If only I could go to see and not be seen by the crowds," she said.

When she was very ill, one of the nuns in the convent asked her about having once been famous but now being hidden away. Bernadette replied that she felt very like a broom. "Our Lady used me and now I am put back in the corner."

Bernadette is revered in a shrine at Lourdes, although she never wanted to be famous.

LOURDES

*L*ourdes is in southwest France, near the Spanish border. Its spring now produces 27,000 (British) gallons of water a week (or roughly 13 l a minute). Every year, three million pilgrims and tourists from all over the world go to bathe in its waters, to pray, or to seek healing from various illnesses. A committee of doctors investigates reports of healings that are claimed to be miracles.

Tamate Meets the Cannibals

James Chalmers

SAINTS' DAYS

James Chalmers and
Oliver Tomkins were killed
in 1901 and are not
officially saints, but they
are remembered by some
churches on 8 April and
by others, along with other
Saints and Martyrs of
Australia and the Pacific,
on 20 September.

EVERY WEEK, YOUNG James Chalmers went to a Sunday school class at his local church. One week, the clergyman read out a letter from a Christian teacher who had journeyed to Fiji in the Pacific Ocean. When he'd finished, he looked around the room and said, "I wonder if any boy here this afternoon will become a missionary, and take the gospel to cannibals like these?"

James decided he would do exactly that.

Ten years later, in 1866, he started his work and sailed first to Australia. He and his wife were trying to reach Rarotonga, a tiny island in the South Pacific. After many delays, they managed to persuade a famous pirate named Bully Hayes to take them there on his ship.

The ship couldn't get close to the shore so one of the locals waded out to carry them to land. This man (who spoke a little English) wanted to know their name.

"Chalmers," said James.

Trying to imitate a word that he'd never heard before, the man repeated it as "Tamate." Tamate became Chalmers's name for the next thirty-five years.

He found that this beautiful island was already Christian. So, he spent his time getting used to the climate, learning the local language, and building schools for the local children. He also wanted to find local people to become Christian teachers. He wrote: "As long as the native churches have foreign pastors . . . they will remain weak and dependent."

At the same time, he was pleading with the London Missionary Society to send him to places that hadn't yet

THE MISSIONARY MOVEMENT

In the early days of the Christian Church, the apostles spread the teachings of Jesus across the Roman empire. They often met danger and even death while doing this. It was some time before the gospel reached other countries such as Poland and Russia.

After the Reformation, the Jesuits began to spread the gospel to countries in the Far East and in the Americas.

By the 1800s, the Protestant Churches had started sending missionaries to places that had still never heard of Jesus. Many of these missionaries did much good, but sometimes their work got confused with attempts by European countries to conquer these places.

heard the Christian message. He finally received instructions to move on to the island of New Guinea.

New Guinea lies across the sea from the northern tip of Australia. Although the local people were cannibals, Tamate got on well with many of them.

But one day, he was surrounded by a group of angry local people, who were wearing war paint and waving sticks. One had a huge stone club. Tamate looked at him calmly and asked him what he wanted.

"Tomahawks, knives, iron, beads," the man answered. "And if you do not give them to us, you will be killed."

Tamate said he didn't give presents to armed people. Again the man repeated his demand. And again Tamate refused.

The local people eventually moved away. Tamate spent the night nervously. The following day, the man (without his war paint) returned and apologized. Tamate then gave him presents and so gained the trust and friendship of the local people.

He continued this work of making friends and winning respect for Christianity for many years. Then, in 1901, he sailed with a group of younger helpers, including a man named Oliver Tomkins, to a small island called Goaribari.

When their ship anchored near the island, it was surrounded by native boats. Tamate said he'd go ashore the next day. He and Tomkins did as they had promised. Time went by. The captain of the ship became alarmed when he saw a number of war canoes approaching. He sailed away to report what was happening. Later, British investigators discovered that Tamate and Tomkins had been clubbed, beheaded, boiled, and eaten.

James Chalmers and the author Robert Louis Stevenson dressed in the rather formal clothes of British explorers among the flower-decked people of New Guinea.

Thérèse of Lisieux

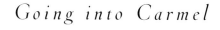

Thérèse changed from being a spoiled child to a humble and obedient nun.

THÉRÈSE'S MOTHER DIED when Thérèse was quite young. She grew up with her father and her four older sisters. Marie, the oldest of the sisters, became a sort of mother to the family—except to little Thérèse. She thought of her next-oldest sister, Pauline, as her mother.

"You're my mother now," she said.

Pauline took special care of Thérèse, and perhaps because Thérèse was the youngest and often ill, they all rather spoilt her. When things didn't go as she wanted, Thérèse would burst into tears. Sometimes she would do this quite deliberately, just to get her own way.

When Thérèse was eight, Pauline decided to become a nun and live in a Carmelite convent in Lisieux, not far from where the family lived in northern France. Carmelite nuns believe that, by staying in "Carmel" (as they call their convents), they can help people by praying for them. They hardly ever leave the convent and are allowed very few visitors. Thérèse was incredibly miserable about "losing" Pauline.

But Thérèse slowly got used to life without her. Then, when she was thirteen, her oldest sister Marie said that she too was "going into Carmel." There were more tears. Lots more tears.

But that Christmas, things changed. Thérèse made another decision—like her elder sisters, she too would enter Carmel.

At first there were problems. People said she was too young to enter Carmel. But that autumn, her father took her on a visit to Rome. She was allowed to see the pope. When she was kneeling before him, even though she wasn't supposed to say anything, Thérèse spoke up. "Holy father," she said, "allow me to enter Carmel."

The pope seemed unsure what to say to this young girl. At last he said, "If it be God's will."

So, at the age of fifteen, Thérèse entered Carmel. The doors closed behind her. I'm here for good! she thought. And she was happy.

Even though she was near her older sisters again, not everything was easy. Whenever Thérèse took her turn at doing the housework or weeding the garden, one of the older Carmelite nuns would always criticize her.

Gradually, Thérèse learned not to answer back. One of the first times she managed this was when someone had left a little jar by a window and it had got broken. One of the other nuns supposed it had been Thérèse's fault. "You mustn't be so untidy. You must be much more careful!" the nun said.

Thérèse nearly said it wasn't her fault, but just stopped herself. "I'm sorry," was all she said.

After five years, Thérèse's sister, Pauline, became prioress, or leader, of the nuns. One evening, she and Marie were talking with Thérèse about when they were children. Pauline told Thérèse to write down her memories. At first, Thérèse didn't want to, but she obediently agreed to do so. She had little spare time, so it took her more than a year. When she'd finished it, she gave it to Pauline.

Pauline showed it to Marie. Both sisters were impressed, but they felt that Thérèse should write more about her "little way"; that is, her way of pleasing God by doing little things for other people and putting up with things without complaining.

But by now, Thérèse was seriously ill with tuberculosis. In those days, there was no cure for this illness. Even so, Marie encouraged Thérèse to finish writing her story. Although Thérèse was in great pain, she did so, completing it two months before she died.

Thérèse learned to accept humble tasks such as weeding the garden.

THE LITTLE WAY

*H*er book, describing her "little way" of serving God, was published after her death. Since then, it has sold millions of copies all around the world and has inspired Christians. It shows how anyone can serve God by doing everyday things in a spirit of love and kindness. The edited version of the book was called *The Little Way*. But when the full text became available in 1958, the book was called *The Autobiography of a Saint*.

We Need a Patriarch

Tikhon of Moscow and All Russia

I T WAS A FRIGHTENING and terrible time to be living in Russia. The country was at war against Germany. Thousands, even millions, of Russian soldiers were being killed across the country. Many people had no work. Most had little food.

Then came the revolution. A group of people known as Bolsheviks began to seize power. First, they forced the emperor (or tsar) to leave his royal palace at St. Petersburg. That was in March 1917.

Tikhon was made a patriarch at a cathedral inside the Kremlin.

In November, there was a second revolution. The Bolsheviks now took complete control of St. Petersburg. There was fighting on the streets of Moscow. People feared what might happen next.

At this time, the Russian church was run by a group, or council, of bishops and other people. At a meeting, one of them stood up. "We no longer have a tsar, no father of our country. We need a patriarch."

"Patriarch" is a name or title usually given to a much-loved head of a family.

Because the council felt the church needed to be strong against the Bolsheviks, they chose Bishop Tikhon to be patriarch of Moscow and all Russia. This wise and very humble man was loved by all the people and they showed their love by coming to the ceremony at which he was made patriarch in a cathedral inside the Kremlin in Moscow. This would be one of the last church services to be held there for many years.

This was because the Bolsheviks (or Communists, as they were becoming known) now decided that the church was their enemy. They said religion was no better than a drug that fooled the people. They closed thousands of church buildings. They said people were no longer considered properly married if they got married in a church. Priests were imprisoned and some were killed. Atheism (the idea that there is no God) had to be taught in all schools.

Patriarch Tikhon spoke out. "You have replaced the love of Jesus with hatred. You cause bloodshed, violence, and destruction!"

As much as they hated him, the Communists did not dare do anything to Tikhon because he was so popular. Eventually, however, they did arrest him. It is thought that they then told him that the church was almost dead. After some time, he signed a piece of paper that said he was no longer an enemy of the Communist state and that he regretted what he had said in the past. Then he was set free—but the Communists still kept a very close eye on all that he said and did.

We don't know if he was tricked into writing that paper or if he actually did sign it. He may have signed it only so that he'd be set free and would be able to keep safe what was left of the church. We do know that he once wrote, "Let my name be ruined as long as the church benefits by it."

During the following months, Patriarch Tikhon struggled to keep the church alive, but he was now very tired. He died as peacefully as he had tried to live his life.

REMEMBERING TIKHON

From 1917 onward, the Communists made it difficult for Russians to be members of the Christian Church. It was only in 1988 that President Gorbachev announced that "mistakes have been made in such matters as religion." This was the start of a new period of freedom and openness or *glasnost*.

A new council of the church met in 1989 and Tikhon was named a saint. A ceremony to mark this took place in the cathedral in the Kremlin, the first service to be held there for seventy years. It was also almost one thousand years from the time Christianity came to Russia.

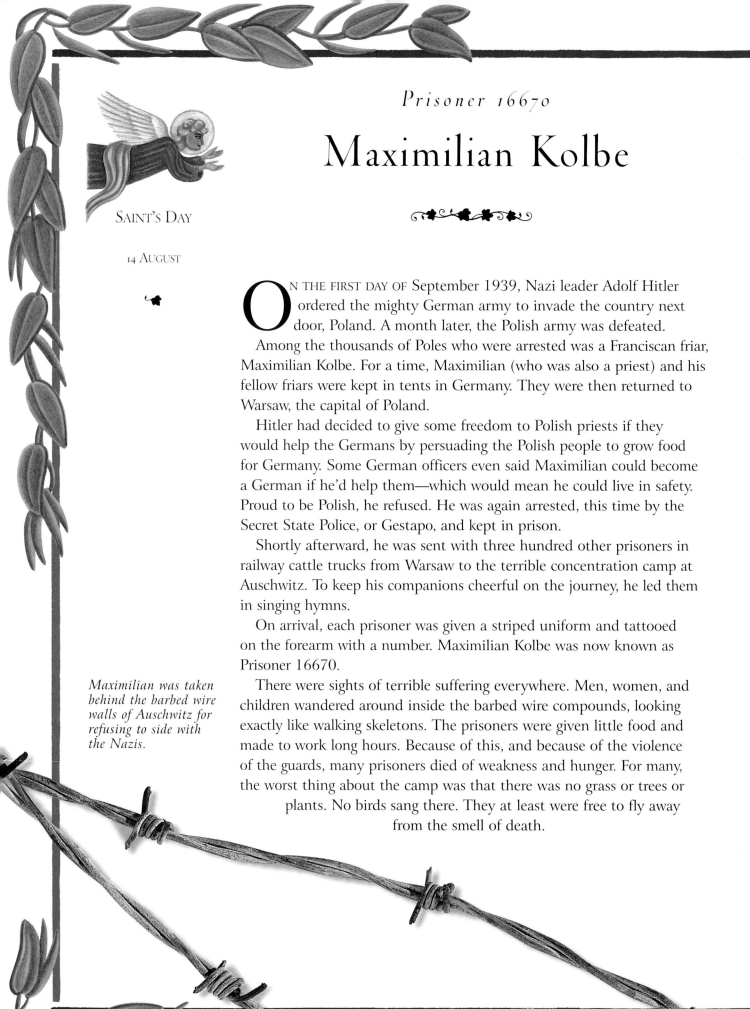

Prisoner 16670

Maximilian Kolbe

O N THE FIRST DAY OF September 1939, Nazi leader Adolf Hitler ordered the mighty German army to invade the country next door, Poland. A month later, the Polish army was defeated.

Among the thousands of Poles who were arrested was a Franciscan friar, Maximilian Kolbe. For a time, Maximilian (who was also a priest) and his fellow friars were kept in tents in Germany. They were then returned to Warsaw, the capital of Poland.

Hitler had decided to give some freedom to Polish priests if they would help the Germans by persuading the Polish people to grow food for Germany. Some German officers even said Maximilian could become a German if he'd help them—which would mean he could live in safety. Proud to be Polish, he refused. He was again arrested, this time by the Secret State Police, or Gestapo, and kept in prison.

Shortly afterward, he was sent with three hundred other prisoners in railway cattle trucks from Warsaw to the terrible concentration camp at Auschwitz. To keep his companions cheerful on the journey, he led them in singing hymns.

On arrival, each prisoner was given a striped uniform and tattooed on the forearm with a number. Maximilian Kolbe was now known as Prisoner 16670.

Maximilian was taken behind the barbed wire walls of Auschwitz for refusing to side with the Nazis.

There were sights of terrible suffering everywhere. Men, women, and children wandered around inside the barbed wire compounds, looking exactly like walking skeletons. The prisoners were given little food and made to work long hours. Because of this, and because of the violence of the guards, many prisoners died of weakness and hunger. For many, the worst thing about the camp was that there was no grass or trees or plants. No birds sang there. They at least were free to fly away from the smell of death.

Then, one day in August 1941, one of Maximilian's fellow prisoners in Block 14 was reported missing after the usual evening roll call. Somehow, he had managed to escape. The next day, all the prisoners were brought to the parade ground and were forced to stand for hours in the hot sunshine. Many fainted. Some died where they fell.

Then the camp commander announced that ten men from Block 14 must die because someone had escaped. He went along the ranks selecting his victims. The silence was unbroken until one of those chosen, a Polish soldier named Franciszek Gajowniczek, cried out, "What'll happen to my wife and children?"

When he heard this, Maximilian quietly stepped out of line, took off his cap and stood in front of the commander. The commander was, for a moment, speechless. Then he yelled, "What does that Polish pig want?"

Forty-seven-year-old Maximilian replied, "I'm a Catholic priest. I'm old. I'm ready to take that man's place because he's got a wife and children."

The commander hesitated. Why should anyone, he wondered, make such an offer? But then he waved Gajowniczek back into his place and told Maximilian to join the other nine he had already chosen. They were taken to Block 13, the starvation bunker.

No clothing, no food, and no water was allowed. Anyone who asked for them was kicked to the ground. Slowly, one by one, the men starved to death. Five remained, half alive. Of these, Maximilian was the only one still conscious.

Soon, the Germans needed Block 13 for a new batch of victims. A doctor was ordered to execute Prisoner 16670 and his last few companions by injecting them with a deadly poison. Maximilian said a brief prayer before holding out his left arm to receive the lethal dose.

Franciszek Gajowniczek survived Auschwitz and lived for more than forty years.

Maximilian was only forty-seven when he declared himself an old man, ready to die for a younger man.

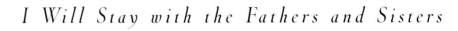

Lucian Tapiedi

SAINTS' DAYS

The Papua New Guinea
Martyrs are remembered
on 2 September; Saints
and Martyrs of Australia
and the Pacific are
sometimes remembered
on 20 September.

O N THE HUGE ISLAND of New Guinea in the Pacific Ocean, there is a row of graves. Two of them are the graves of Australian Christians, May Hayman and Mavis Parkinson. The third is Lucian Tapiedi's grave.

After Greenland, New Guinea is the largest island in the world. It's a mountainous place, and between its mountains are miles of mosquito-infested swamps. It also has vast rain forests. These may look beautiful on television but they are places where diseases spread easily, plants are poisonous, and travel is difficult.

Christian missionaries began working on the island in the 1860s—one of the first being James Chalmers, known to the local people as Tamate. He found that many of the local people were friendly—but not all of them. Over the following years, more and more of the people became Christians. Then came World War II. By then, the island was divided into three separate countries. There was Dutch New Guinea in the west (now part of Indonesia), the Australian Territory of New Guinea, and Papua, which also belonged to Australia.

At first, the war seemed far away. Then, in December 1941, Japanese forces decided to bomb the American fleet at Pearl Harbor. In the same month, Japan, which was already at war with China, invaded Malaya. The war in the Pacific was getting closer. The Christian missionaries who lived in New Guinea feared that Japan would soon invade their island. Should they stay or should they try to get home to Australia or Europe?

The nursing sister May Hayman, who was murdered for being a Christian.

The anglican bishop of New Guinea, Philip Strong, wrote a letter to all the missionaries and clergy. "We must try to carry on our work," he wrote. "God expects this of us. The church at home, which sent us out, will surely expect it of us. The people whom we serve expect it of us. We could never hold up our faces again if, for our own safety, we all forsook Jesus and fled."

They stayed.

The Japanese invaded in July 1942.

They first landed at a place called Garara. Three Christians who had been working there fled inland, toward the mountains. Their names were

May Hayman, Mavis Parkinson, and James Benson. They soon met some other Australians who were in hiding. But it wasn't long before the Japanese found them. When they did find them, May Hayman and Mavis Parkinson were murdered.

Meanwhile, about thirty miles inland, in northern Papua, a second group of missionaries (including some priests and nuns) was also trying to avoid being captured by the Japanese.

With them was a young Papuan teacher named Lucian Tapiedi. He was a local man and could easily have pretended to the Japanese that he had nothing to do with these Christians. Instead, he simply said, "I will stay with the Fathers and Sisters."

This group of ten Christians started on a journey, unsure of where they were going but determined to avoid the Japanese. After some time, they came to a village inhabited by the Orokaiva people, who weren't all Christians. In order to please the Japanese, the Orokaiva decided to betray the Christians.

A memorial to the Papua New Guinea Martyrs shows the martyrs in native dress.

One of them, a man named Hivijapa, killed Lucian beside a stream. The remainder of the group died soon afterward. Six of them were beheaded by the Japanese on Buna beach, near Garara.

Altogether, more than three hundred Christians lost their lives in New Guinea during the invasion and occupation of the island by the Japanese forces.

Hivijapa later became a Christian. He took the name Hivijapa Lucian and built a church dedicated to the memory of Lucian Tapiedi at Embi.

Corrie ten Boom

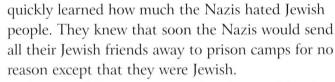

The man had two large bulldogs. Because Corrie and Betsie had never seen him without them, they nicknamed him "the Bulldog." Then, one day, they saw him without his dogs. Corrie went up to him in the street.

"Please, where are your dogs? Are they all right?" The man looked sad.

"They are . . . they are dead," he said slowly. "I put the 'medicine' in their bowl myself. Then I stroked them to sleep."

"But why did you kill them?" asked Corrie.

"Ladies, I'm a Jew. You know what the Nazis are like. Soon they'll put me in prison, or worse. Then who'd look after my dogs?"

This happened in Holland during World War II. The Germans had invaded the country, and Corrie and her sister Betsie ten Boom had quickly learned how much the Nazis hated Jewish people. They knew that soon the Nazis would send all their Jewish friends away to prison camps for no reason except that they were Jewish.

Corrie and Betsie were watchmakers and lived in a house above their shop. They got a friend to make a secret room for them on the top floor of their home. This friend built a false wall that divided Corrie's bedroom in half. The friend painted the wall and made it dirty, so it looked as if it had always been there. You could get into this hiding place behind this wall through a secret panel. It was small but it was a place where their friends could hide if the Nazis ever came to search the house.

The hole in the wall shows how the hiding place was hidden in an upstairs room. The wall was built so it would not sound hollow.

One night, the soldiers did come.

"Get up! Come on, up!" they shouted. Corrie struggled out of bed. "Tell us, where are you hiding the Jews?"

"There aren't any Jews here," said Corrie. "Just me and my sister."

"Where's your secret room?"

The soldiers pushed her downstairs into the shop. Another soldier was guarding Betsie. Corrie saw that her lips were swollen and there was a dark bruise near her eye.

"If you don't tell us where the room is, we'll set a guard around the house until your Jews starve to death. Now, where are they?"

Corrie and Betsie still said nothing. They were taken away and put in separate prison cells in the Nazi headquarters in Holland. They knew nothing about what had happened to their friends in their hiding place.

Many weeks after they were put in prison, Corrie was allowed a visitor: her brother, Willem. A soldier stood guard, listening while they had a short conversation.

"I want you to know, Corrie," said Willem, "that all your watches are safe."

"What do I care about watches? Or the shop?"

"Corrie," said Willem, glancing at the guard, "I mean the 'watches' that were in the cupboard upstairs. . ."

"Oh!" said Corrie, realizing that he was really talking about her Jewish friends. "Oh dear Jesus, thank you. Thank you, Jesus."

Months later, Corrie was taken with many other prisoners to a railway yard. They were all herded toward a train. As they were pushed forward, Corrie suddenly saw Betsie. She pushed through the crowd until they were together again.

The train took them to Ravensbruck, a women's prison camp in Germany where many prisoners were put to death.

The days passed. The two sisters suffered from the cold, from beatings, and from hunger. One thing gave them hope. Corrie had been able to smuggle a small Bible with her into prison. At night, huddled around a tiny fire, Corrie and Betsie read from it aloud. In this way, they were able to encourage and help many of the other prisoners.

Later, they were moved into another building.

"Betsie!" screamed Corrie. "Look! Fleas! It's swarming with them. How can we live here?"

"The answer's in the Bible," said Betsie. "It says, 'Give thanks always.' Give thanks that we're still together. Give thanks that we've still got a Bible. And that it's crowded in here."

"Why should we be grateful it's crowded?"

"Because," said Betsie, "more prisoners will hear the Bible."

"But the fleas? I can't give thanks for them!"

"As long as there are fleas, the Nazis will keep away and we can say prayers without being disturbed."

Corrie ten Boom not only survived the war but went on to travel the world, telling people how Jesus had helped her forgive the atrocities the Nazis had committed against her and her sister.

Tomorrow the Churches Will Burn

Dietrich Bonhoeffer

SAINT'S DAY

Bonhoeffer is not officially a saint but is remembered on the anniversary of his death, 9 April.

WITH GOD BESIDE ME

Dietrich Bonhoeffer wrote these words from prison at New Year in 1945. He was to be hanged by the Nazis later that year.

With every power for good to stay and
*   guide me,*
Comforted and inspired beyond all fear,
I'll live these days with you in thought
*   beside me,*
And pass, with you, into the coming year.

HE WAS A CLERGYMAN, a man of peace and love. But he was prepared to be a spy and to plot against his own country. He was even prepared to kill the ruler of his country. How could that make Dietrich Bonhoeffer a holy person?

The answer is that he lived in Germany during World War II, when the ruler of that country was Adolf Hitler. Hitler was responsible for the deaths of millions of people (many of them Jews) in his terrible concentration camps—like the one at Ravensbruck where Betsie ten Boom died.

Adolf Hitler had come to power in 1933. He hated Jewish people. He didn't like the Christian religion either. Even so, many German Christians chose not to speak out against him. Sad to say, some Christians actually became Nazis. But not all did. A group of Protestant Christians who were against Hitler formed what they called the Confessing Church.

Dietrich Bonhoeffer became a member. Not only that, he began training its members to become teachers and preachers. When the Nazis found out, they closed the church down. Bonhoeffer was forbidden to teach and was banned from the city of Berlin.

Then came "Kristallnacht" or the "Night of Broken Glass." On that night, 9 November 1938, German troops led an attack on Jewish property. More than seven thousand Jewish shops were broken into and looted. Hundreds of synagogues were burned down.

Dietrich thought the Christians would be made to suffer next. He said, "When today the synagogues are set afire, tomorrow the churches will burn."

He began to speak out against the Nazis more and more. Friends he'd made while he was a student in America were worried that he'd be put in prison. They arranged for him to go to the United States in 1939 to give a series of talks.

When it became clear that war would soon break out, Dietrich decided to leave America where he was safe and go back home. "I must go and share the difficulty of this time with my people."

Back in Germany, he thought about joining some people who were plotting to free Germany and the world from Hitler by killing him. But he wondered if joining such a conspiracy as a Christian was the right thing to do. Before long, his sister and brother-in-law did persuade him to join a secret resistance movement. And he also became a double agent.

He did this by taking a job in the Nazi Military Intelligence Department. This allowed him to travel to Italy, Switzerland, and Sweden to visit churches there—as long as he brought back information that could help the Nazis. But he wasn't really working for the Nazis. He was working against them.

For example, he used one of these trips to help fourteen Jews escape from Germany to Switzerland.

In the end, the Nazis discovered he was a double agent, and he was put in a Berlin military prison. Even so, it was several months before they realized he'd also been involved in a plot to kill Hitler.

He was moved first to Buchenwald concentration camp and then to a Gestapo (or Secret Police) prison called Flossenburg. One Sunday in April 1945, he'd just finished holding a service of worship in that prison when two soldiers came in, saying, "Prisoner Bonhoeffer, make ready and come with us."

Dietrich knew that this was what the guards always said to a prisoner who was about to be put to death. As they took him away, he said to another prisoner, "This is the end—but for me it is also the beginning of life."

He was taken to be hanged the next day, just a few days before the end of the war. Among those who were taken with him were friends of his from the resistance movement. They were all ordered to remove their clothing and then led down some steps to the place of execution. Naked under the scaffold, Bonhoeffer knelt for the last time to pray. Within five minutes, his life was over.

Dietrich Bonhoeffer was a quiet and thoughtful clergyman, but he became a double agent in an attempt to hold back the evil done by the Nazis.

Martin Luther King Jr

Martin Luther King Jr is not officially a saint. He is remembered on Martin Luther King Jr Day: third Monday in January.

Martin Luther King Jr addresses a crowd about the importance of equal rights for all people, black and white.

O N THE EVENING OF 1 December 1955, Rosa Parks sat down on a seat near the front of the bus that would take her home. She was tired. When a white man got on, she refused to give up her seat for him. The law said that was what she should have done. In Montgomery, Alabama, the front seats of buses were reserved for white passengers. Black passengers had to sit at the back or stand. The bus driver had Rosa Parks arrested for breaking the law.

Because Rosa Parks was tired, she would not give up her seat. But she wasn't just tired from a long day at work. She was tired of all the laws that made black people like herself into second-class citizens.

By "sitting down" for what she believed in and by refusing to give up her seat, Mrs Parks made history. The following night, fifty leaders of the

black community met to discuss the matter. Among them was a young minister, Dr Martin Luther King Jr. With the others, he organized a boycott by black people of all the Montgomery buses. The boycott of the bus system lasted for 382 days. The bus company lost a huge amount of money.

Meanwhile, Rosa Parks was put on trial. Finally, the court ruled that "segregation" (which meant black people had to keep apart from whites in buses and other places) was illegal. That decision changed America forever. It also changed the life of Martin Luther King Jr.

He became convinced that the best way for blacks to win their proper rights was to do so by peaceful protests. In Atlanta and in Birmingham, he led "sit-ins" (a way of protesting by sitting in seats in an establishment) in what were supposed to be whites-only restaurants. He helped lead campaigns to allow black students to attend whites-only schools and universities. This was the beginning of the civil-rights movement.

Martin Luther King Jr and his followers gained a lot of support. In August 1963, they organized a public march in the capital of the United States, Washington, D.C. More than 200,000 people took part. It was after this very peaceful march that Martin Luther King Jr made his famous "I Have a Dream" speech. It inspired millions of people around the world to work for equal rights.

The next year, a civil-rights act was passed by the United States Congress. Other acts followed.

Then, in 1968, Dr King visited Memphis in Tennessee. He was supposed to lead a peaceful strike on behalf of underpaid rubbish collectors. The night before the demonstration, he went out onto the balcony of the Lorraine Motel in Memphis for a breath of fresh air. He was shot in the neck and chin by a sniper named James Earl Ray who fired from a passing car. Martin Luther King Jr died at once, and James Earl Ray was later arrested in England and returned to Memphis to stand trial. He was found guilty.

Martin Luther King Jr at the head of a civil-rights march.

Martin Luther King Jr died before his dream became true, but today all Americans, whatever their race, nationality, or religion, must be given equal treatment under the law.

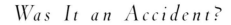

Was It an Accident?

Janani Luwum

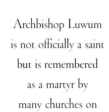

SAINT'S DAY

Archbishop Luwum is not officially a saint but is remembered as a martyr by many churches on 17 February.

Archbishop Janani Luwum.

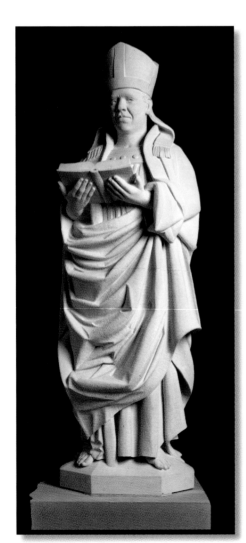

IDI AMIN WAS POWERFUL. His soldiers did whatever he said. People who made him angry were seized by these soldiers. They were either killed there and then, or they just "disappeared." No one knew what happened to them then. Perhaps they were tortured. Perhaps they were shot. No one ever knew the truth. Idi Amin was very powerful.

Idi Amin was president of the African country of Uganda from 1971 to 1979. Many Christians became his victims. But one person he left alone was the popular leader of the Church of Uganda, Archbishop Janani Luwum. Idi Amin hated the archbishop because he wasn't afraid to speak the truth. But he could hardly arrest such a popular man for that reason alone.

One night, Idi Amin's troops arrested a man named Ben Ongom. They tortured him for five days. They made him "confess" the names of anyone plotting against Idi Amin. They tortured him until he could think of no more names. He wanted the torture to end so he said the first name that came into his head: "The archbishop."

Just after one o'clock on a Saturday morning, there was a knock at the front door of the archbishop's house. He went to the door. Eight armed men were waiting for him. "Archbishop, show us the guns in the house," they shouted.

"What guns?" said the archbishop.

"There are guns in your house," they insisted, beginning a wild search. Of course they found nothing and eventually they left. But on Monday, it was announced on the state radio station that guns had been found near the archbishop's house.

Some days later, the archbishop and the other bishops were called to meet Idi Amin. They were made to wait in the hot sun from early morning until two o'clock in the afternoon. Army officers shouted all sorts of accusations at them.

When Idi Amin arrived, they were told to go home. "Except the archbishop," shouted a guard. "He's to see the president. Alone."

198 · *Saints and Holy People of the Modern Age*

The other bishops waited near the archbishop's car. Finally the soldiers ordered them to leave. "Get in that car and go!" They pointed their guns at the bishops.

The bishops drove off. At half past six, it was said on the radio that the archbishop had been arrested. The next morning it was announced that there had been an accident. The archbishop had been killed in a car crash. There were pictures of a crashed car in the newspapers. But it wasn't the archbishop's car. That evening the television news also showed pictures of the accident. These pictures were of yet another car.

The president would not let the bishops have the body. Instead, it was put in a sealed coffin and sent directly to Acoli (the village where he had been born) for burial. Against orders, the villagers opened the coffin. The body had gunshot wounds.

The next Sunday, thousands of people flocked to the cathedral in Kampala, the capital of Uganda. The city rang with the sound of their voices as they sang the Easter hymn in memory of their archbishop and to show their faith in God.

The following June, 25,000 Ugandans came to Kampala to celebrate a hundred years of Christianity in their country. Many of them had once been Christians but had given up their faith out of fear of Idi Amin. Now they returned to the faith after the martyrdom of Archbishop Luwum.

The cathedral in Kampala, where Ugandans gathered to demonstrate their faith in God after the brutal killing of their archbishop.

Mother Teresa is not
officially a saint. Days
on which she might
especially be remembered
are the anniversary of her
"Day of Decision,"
known in her order as
Inspiration Day
(10 September), or on the
anniversary of her death
in 1997 (5 September).

ONE BY ONE

Mother Teresa
dedicated her life to
helping individuals at their point
of need. She said this:

We can do no great things,
Only small things with great love.

A Home for the Dying

Teresa of Calcutta

ONE DAY, IN ONE OF the dirtiest and poorest streets of Calcutta in India, Sister Teresa came across a woman lying in the street, dying. This woman was so feeble that her body had been partly eaten away by rats and ants, even though she was still just alive. She'd been lying there for days but no one had taken any notice.

Sister Teresa had no trouble picking her up and carrying her to a nearby hospital. The people there said that the woman was too ill and too poor for them to care for her.

Sister Teresa didn't give up.

She took the old woman to another hospital. It was the same there. "We don't have any room for someone like that," they said. In the end, the old woman died.

Calcutta was full of people like that old woman. Sister Teresa knew she must help them. She got permission to use part of a building that had once been a Hindu temple but was now not used by anyone except a few thugs and beggars as a place for gambling and drinking. It would become her first "Home for the Dying."

But how did all this come about? At that time, Sister Teresa was a nun working as the head teacher of a school in Calcutta. Then, one day in 1946, she was on a train journey when she seemed to hear Jesus speaking to her. "I heard the call to give up everything and follow him into the slums, to serve him among the poorest of the poor. . . . It was an order, a duty." She would later call that day her "Day of Decision."

It took some time for her to get permission to leave the convent where she lived, but in 1948, she was allowed to leave. She stopped wearing the dark clothes worn by the other nuns and started wearing a sari, like an Indian woman—except that her sari was white with a blue border and had a cross on the shoulder. She went to a place called Patna to learn to be a nurse.

Back in Calcutta, she began working in the slums: helping the poor, washing their babies, and cleaning their wounds. The poor people were amazed. "Who is this European lady who wears a sari and speaks our language? Why does she do this for us?"

Soon, Sister Teresa got other people to help her, and they started a school for the very poorest children in Calcutta. In time, these helpers became a new order of nuns, the Sisters of Charity, and Teresa became their "mother."

Since then, the sisters have taken in thousands of dying, homeless people. They now have more than seven hundred shelters like that first one in India alone, and they have others in many countries around the world.

Mother Teresa once told how she picked a feeble little old woman out of some rubbish. The woman said her son had put her there to die. Mother Teresa said, "We took her home to our place and we helped her. After a few hours she died in great peace."

Even though that woman died, Mother Teresa was pleased to have been able to help her. "We have homes for the sick and dying and it is beautiful to see how these people, who have lived such difficult lives, die so peacefully." Mother Teresa called dying "going home" because she believed that people, when they die, go "home" to be with God.

Of course, many of the people that she helped got better. Some even became strong enough to work again. But what Mother Teresa wanted most was to let homeless, sick, and dying people know that there is someone who loves them and wants them.

Mother Teresa served the poor for many years before news of her work became famous. Then many photographs were taken of the slightly built and aging nun with remarkable inner strength.

An olive branch—a
traditional symbol
of peace.

Oscar Romero

SAINT'S DAY

Oscar Romero is not
officially a saint but is
remembered on 24 March.

IT WAS ABOUT HALF past six on a Monday evening. Archbishop Romero was about to celebrate a Eucharist, or Mass, in memory of his mother, who had recently died. He was in a little chapel that was part of San Salvador's Divine Providence Hospital, in which he'd made his home.

As he stood at the altar, four men entered the chapel and walked up the aisle. They were dressed quite ordinarily. Those already in the chapel were kneeling, saying their prayers. They didn't pay too much attention to these latecomers. Until, that is, they went right up to the altar.

The four of them put their hands in their pockets. Each took out a pistol and shot the archbishop several times in the chest and face. He died almost at once. Then the men escaped.

As the news spread through the city, traffic stopped. The whole city fell silent.

This happened on 24 March 1980, in San Salvador, the capital of El Salvador, the smallest and most densely populated country in Central America. It was ruled by the army, who were helped by many powerful, rich, and violent men. Death squads roamed the city. In the countryside, soldiers could kill whomever they wanted. Nobody asked any questions.

But the army didn't control everything. Also busy in El Salvador were men who called themselves "freedom fighters" and whom others called terrorists. They didn't have much power—but they did have guns, and they wanted a revolution.

In the middle of these two groups were the poor people of El Salvador, for whom life had become more and more miserable.

Oscar Romero had become archbishop in February 1977. He was probably chosen because it seemed that he wasn't on either side.

But a month after he became archbishop, a good friend of his was murdered by an army death squad. This man had been a priest, Father Rutilio Grande. His death made Oscar Romero think hard and speak out. He refused to attend any parades or ceremonies the army organized.

The army didn't like that. They weren't used to being criticized in public.

But Archbishop Romero went on speaking up on behalf of the poor. He made lists of people who had "disappeared"—which usually meant they had been murdered. He made lists of the times the government lied to the people. It was not surprising that attempts were made on his life. The newspapers, which were owned by the government, attacked him. A radio station that was owned by his church was bombed.

Even so, Archbishop Romero became more and more popular with the poor of El Salvador. His reports and speeches began to be heard in other countries. He nearly won the Nobel Peace prize. It was no wonder that the government of El Salvador wanted him silenced.

One Sunday, he spoke out again, pleading with the rulers of his country to change their ways. "In the name of God, in the name of these suffering people, I beg you, I beseech you, I order you to stop this cruelty! Do you realize, in this last week, one hundred and fifty people have died as a result of violence by both sides in this struggle?"

Oscar Romero was shot dead the next evening.

But that wasn't the end of it. A week later, during the archbishop's funeral, four bombs exploded. They killed twenty people, and two hundred more were injured—many by snipers. All this was probably the work of freedom fighters, who were angry at the archbishop's death and forgetful that he'd condemned violence by both sides.

Oscar Romero could have kept quiet and not spoken out against what he knew was wrong. But he didn't. He'd been prepared to risk his life. As he said when they blew up his radio station, "I cannot change, except to seek to follow the Gospel more closely."

Oscar Romero dared to speak out against the brutality of the government. As a result, he was murdered in a chapel as he was about to lead a church service.

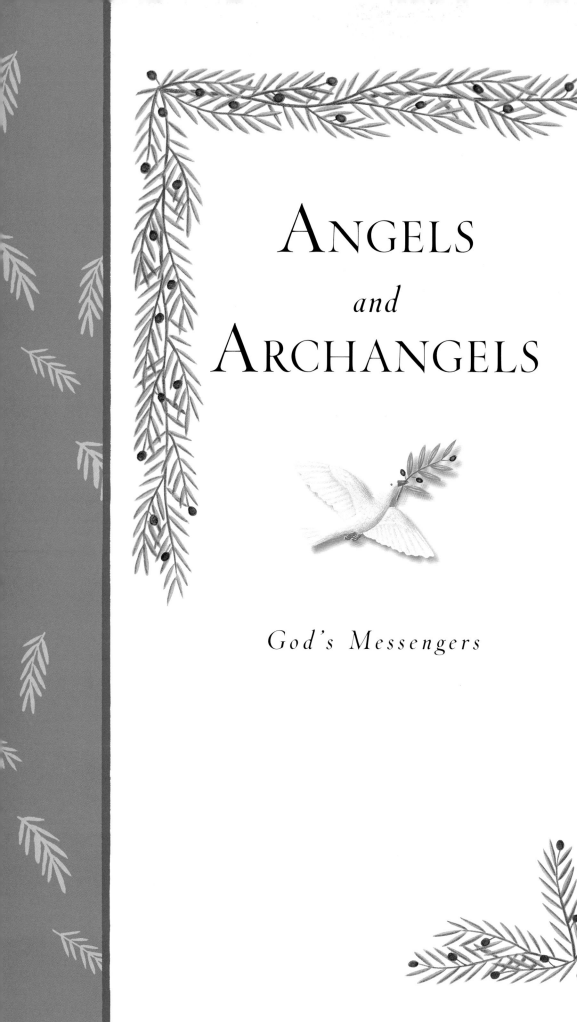

ANGELS
and
ARCHANGELS

God's Messengers

Gabriel and Raphael

God's Messengers

SAINTS' DAYS

24 MARCH
Gabriel

24 OCTOBER
Raphael

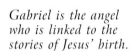

Gabriel is the angel who is linked to the stories of Jesus' birth.

ANGELS ARE GOD'S MESSENGERS. Many people believe they were created by God before humans and have greater powers and intelligence. Like humans, they are free to choose between doing good and doing wrong. Lucifer (also known as Satan, or the Devil) is said to have once been an angel. But he rebelled against God and so lost his place in heaven. He and his followers are called "fallen angels."

The other angels remained loyal to God.

Gabriel

Of all the angels, Gabriel in particular has been God's messenger. According to the Bible, he spoke twice to a man named Daniel when he was in prison and brought messages of hope.

It was Gabriel who told Zechariah that he was going to be the father of John the Baptist. Zechariah was working in the temple in Jerusalem, burning incense to make a sweet scent while people were praying there. As Zechariah did this, Gabriel appeared to him and told him what an important person John would be. He also told him that he must name him John. Because Zechariah didn't really believe Gabriel, Zechariah lost the ability to speak until his son was born. As soon as Zechariah wrote down the words "His name is John," he was able to speak again.

The most important message Gabriel ever brought to earth was the message he brought to Mary to tell her that she was to be the mother of Jesus. Because Gabriel brought this message, many people think it was also he who appeared to the shepherds and told them to go and worship Jesus in the manger at Bethlehem.

Gabriel is not just important to Jews and Christians. Muslims (who call him Gibrail) believe he dictated their holy book, the Qur'an, to the prophet Muhammad.

Raphael

The name Raphael means "God heals," and the archangel Raphael has always seemed to bring God's healing touch to this world.

Once, Raphael disguised himself as a human named Azarius. He joined a young man named Tobias on his journeys and they had many adventures together. One night, they rested by the River Tigris. Azarius ordered Tobias to go fishing, and he caught a large fish. Azarius told him to keep various parts of the fish.

Eventually, they reached home, and Tobias found that his father, Tobit, had become blind. Azarius told Tobias to take part of the fish's inside and to rub it on his father's eyes. Tobias did as he was told, and his father was able to see again.

This story comes from "The Book of Tobit," which is included in some Bibles.

The story of the pool of Bethesda is in every Bible. This pool was near one of the gates of the city of Jerusalem. Every day, a number of blind, lame, and paralyzed people came and sat around it. They waited for the water to bubble up or ripple, because it was said that every so often "the angel of the Lord went down into the pool and stirred up the water." Whoever was first into the water after it had moved was cured.

And the angel who stirred the water was said to be Raphael.

ANGELS ALL AROUND

*T*he Bible makes many references to angels who act as God's messengers. Sometimes they appear as ordinary people, and it is only the importance of the message that reveals who they are. At other times they are bright, shining creatures that inspire awe and fear. On the night Jesus was born, shepherds on the hillside saw a great company of angels singing and praising God.

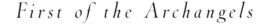

First of the Archangels

Michael

SAINT'S DAYS

29 SEPTEMBER
Michael

The archangels Gabriel, Raphael, and Michael are now often celebrated together on 29 September.

LIKE GABRIEL AND RAPHAEL, Michael is an angel—one of those beings who act as messengers between God and people in this world. In fact, Michael is said to be one of the most powerful of the angels and is one of the seven chief angels who are called archangels.

There is a story in the Bible that, long ago, the fallen angel Lucifer tried to overthrow God. Lucifer is said to have been a kind of dragon but Michael, the first of the archangels, was able to defeat him. This is how the Bible describes the battle between Michael and Lucifer:

ANGELS TO GUARD YOU

*J*esus once said that no one should look down on little children because their angels were always in God's presence, asking God to take care of the children. This statement has led to a popular belief among Christians that everyone has a guardian angel who takes special care of them. This traditional Celtic prayer asks Michael to act as a further guardian angel to all righteous people.

O Michael of the Angels
And the righteous in heaven,
Shield thou my soul
With the shade of thy wing;
Shield thou my soul
On earth and in heaven;

O Michael Militant,
Thou king of the angels,
Shield thy people
With the power of thy sword;
Shield thy people
With the power of thy sword.

Michael is traditionally shown as a warrior and a herald.

"And there was war in heaven. Michael and his angels fought against the dragon . . . And the great dragon was cast out, that old serpent called the Devil or Satan, who deceives everyone: he was cast out, and his followers were cast out with him."

Michael appeared to humans in Old Testament times. He spoke with Abraham and he appeared to Moses. The Jews regarded him as their special protector, helping them to win battles against their enemies. He is also important to Muslims and he is described in their holy book, the Qur'an, as having "wings of green emerald, covered with saffron hairs."

Christians think of him as the protector of the church. He is also said to guard high places, which is perhaps why there are hills called St. Michael's Mount in England, France, and Italy and why many churches built on hills are named after him.

Although Saint Michael is known as "the protector of all people," he is believed to look after people especially at the time of their death. Perhaps this is why his saint's day is at the end of September which, in the northern half of the world, marks the start of winter. At one time, people thought he took special care of the souls of people who had died by helping them to reach the new land of heaven. They imagined him taking them there by boat. This idea is remembered in the words of the song "Michael, Row the Boat Ashore."

Angels welcoming into heaven the souls of people who have died. At the end of all things, Christians believe they will be welcomed into God's presence, in the company of all the saints.

Biographies of the Saints and Holy People

These biographical notes are intended to be read with the relevant stories. Saints are traditionally indexed by their Christian name—so John Chrysostom appears under "J," not "C"; Thomas More under "T," not "M."

AIDAN FROM IONA *(page 114)* Details of Aidan's birth are uncertain, but he definitely became a monk on the island of Iona and King Oswald of Northumbria certainly sent for him to preach Christianity to his people. Aidan arrived in Northumbria in the year 635 and became bishop of Lindisfarne (which is another name for Holy Island). He made many journeys on the mainland, spreading Celtic Christianity through the north of England.

He died in the year 651.

ALEXANDER *(page 62)* No one knows for certain when Alexander was born, but we do know that it was in Cappadocia and that he later became bishop there. He was bishop of Jerusalem by the year 222 and died in prison in the year 251. We know too that by that time he was an old man.

ANDREW *(page 22)* Because Saint Andrew is the patron saint of Scotland, the flag of Scotland shows a white saltire, or Saint Andrew's cross, on a blue background. The blue is a reminder that Andrew spent much of his life near the sea.

Andrew is also the patron saint of Greece and of Russia but there is no proof that he ever visited Russia or Scotland in his lifetime.

ANNE *SEE JOACHIM AND ANNE*

ANTONY *(page 66)* Antony, who is also known as Antony of the Desert or Antony the Great of Egypt, was born about the year 250. In his story about Antony's life, Athanasius says he lived to the age of 105.

ANTONY OF PADUA *(page 144)* Antony was born in Lisbon, Portugal, in 1195 and was originally named Ferdinand. He became a follower of the teaching of Francis before he left Portugal for Morocco in North Africa.

He was made a saint just one year after his death in 1231, a sign that he was much loved and respected by Christians of his day.

ATHANASIUS *(page 66)* Athanasius was born about the year 296 and died in 373. In his books, he strongly states the Christian belief that Jesus was truly the Son of God.

AUGUSTINE OF CANTERBURY *(page 112)* Not to be confused with Augustine of Hippo, who lived 200 years earlier, this Augustine came from near Rome. Although there had been some Christians in England in Roman times, it was Augustine who established Christianity as the main religion in southern England. Some say he was rather bossy. Perhaps that is why he did not get on with the Christians in the west of the British Isles when he went to meet them at a place that later became known as Saint Augustine's Oak. Nor did he convert the northern part of the land of the Angles, called Deira.

He was however made bishop of the English (at Arles in France) and later became archbishop of Canterbury. We do not know in which year he was born, but he died in the same year as Gregory the Great, 604.

AUGUSTINE OF HIPPO *(page 92)* Augustine (who lived from 354 to the year 430) is one of the most important figures in Christian history. For more than a thousand years, his writings have influenced Christians. Nowadays many Christians disagree with some of what he wrote, such as his belief that babies who die before they are baptized will go to hell.

The city of Saint Augustine in Florida (the oldest city in America) is named to remember him because the Spanish first landed there on his saint's day.

BARNABAS *(page 50)* Barnabas is remembered as the man who first introduced Paul to the apostles of Jesus. He is also remembered as the founder of the church in Cyprus. One story, not in the Bible, suggests that Barnabas was killed in the year 61.

BASIL THE GREAT *(page 86)* Basil's family were all good Christians. He was born in the year 330, and his grandmother (Macrina), both his parents (Basil the elder and Emmelia), two of his brothers (Gregory of Nyssa and Peter of Sebaste), and his sister (Macrina the Younger) all became saints, each with their own saint's day!

We know a lot about his life from his own letters and sermons, many of which have survived. Both Basil and his friend, Gregory Nazianzen, became known as "fathers" or founders of the church in eastern Europe and their lives and teachings have inspired Christians there and in Russia throughout the centuries. Basil died in 379.

BEDE *(page 122)* Bede was born in 673 and wrote more than forty historical and scientific books, his most

famous being *Ecclesiastical History of the English People*. He wrote it in Latin, but it was translated into Anglo-Saxon, or Early English, by order of King Alfred. When it's printed as a modern paperback, it's 300 pages long.

Bede was especially clever at working out what had actually happened in the past and what was only legend or gossip. It is thanks to Bede that we know so much about such saints as Aidan, Cuthbert, Hilda, and Willibrord. He died in 735.

BENEDICT *(page 106)* Benedict was born in 480 in Nursia in what is now Italy. He went to Rome as a student, but he left to become a hermit when he was twenty. He then lived in a mountain cave near Subiaco, a place to the east of Rome. His holy way of living brought him many followers and he started a number of monasteries in the area. Some rich people sent their children to Subiaco to be taught by him.

These included two boys, Placid (who was seven) and Maurus (who was twelve). Like a teacher who always seems to know what is going on at the back of the class, Benedict always seemed to know what was happening to his pupils.

One day, Placid fell in a nearby lake. Benedict never looked up. "Maurus," he said, "the little one's fallen in the water." Maurus ran to the lake and pulled Placid safely out by his hair.

In the year 529, Benedict left Subiaco for Monte Cassino. He died in the year 550.

BERNADETTE SOUBIROUS *(page 180)* Marie Bernarde Soubirous (always known as Bernadette) was born in 1844, the first of six children of a miller. The family lived in great poverty. She was small for her age and asthmatic from the age of six. She also suffered from cholera. As a child, she was usually cheerful but was considered "backward."

It was in 1858, when she was fourteen, that she is said to have had her series of eighteen visions. She went to live in a convent, became a nun in 1866, and died in 1879 after a life of frequent illnesses.

BERNARD OF CLAIRVAUX *(page 136)* Bernard was born in 1090 and grew up in a castle near Dijon in southern France. He went to Cîteaux in 1113 and Clairvaux in 1115.

Sometimes his skills of persuasion were misplaced. In 1146 he toured Europe, persuading men to join the Second Crusade to fight the Turks in Palestine. Too many joined the vast army. There wasn't enough food for them all and thousands died of hunger and illness before reaching the Holy Land.

Bernard was, however, a great teacher and healer and much respected by all who met him. He died in 1153.

BONIFACE *(page 124)* He was originally christened Winifred. Later in life, the pope advised him to change his name. However, he then chose an equally odd one: Boniface.

He was born in 680 at Crediton in southwest England and entered a monastery in order to become a monk at the amazingly early age of five! He became a priest at the age of thirty and, soon after that, set out to continue the work begun by Willibrord of bringing Christianity to northern Europe.

Boniface took the Christian gospel to much of Germany, including Bavaria and Hesse, as well as to parts of France and the Low Countries. He founded many monasteries, nunneries, and schools, staffing them with English monks and nuns. One of them, at Fulda, is still a place where Christianity is very important. Boniface himself became archbishop of Mainz.

Along with fifty-two companions, he was murdered in 754 by a band of pagan Frieslanders (who obviously had not been made Christians by Willibrord) while he was journeying home to Crediton. His remains are buried at Fulda.

He stands alongside Saint Paul as one of the great missionaries of the church. Many of his letters survive. He also wrote the first Latin textbook to be used in English schools.

BRIGID *(page 104)* Brigid is also known as Bridget or Bride and the facts about her life are few, although it is thought she lived from about 450 until 523. However, many stories are told about her. Not all can be true. For example, she was unlikely to have been a friend of Saint Patrick as she was still a child when he died. They are both, however, patron saints of Ireland.

One of the legends told about her says that, one day, she came home after getting caught in a shower of rain. She threw her wet cloak over a beam of sunlight to dry, mistaking it for a wooden rail. The cloak stayed hanging in midair on the ray of sunlight, which did not move until long after the sun had set.

She is sometimes known as "the Mary of the Gael," or "the Mary of Ireland."

CAEDMON *(page 116)* Caedmon is remembered as the first poet to write in the English language. We do not know when he was born, but he died in the same year as Hilda of Whitby in 680.

CATHERINE OF ALEXANDRIA *(page 74)* Nothing can be proved about the life of Catherine, and there is real doubt about whether she ever lived. If she did exist, then she must have died in the year 306 or 307, which was when Maxentius was ruler of the Roman empire.

Despite these uncertainties, she was a most popular saint during the Middle Ages, but because many of the stories told about her are so unlikely, her name was removed from the official list of Roman Catholic saints in 1969.

CATHERINE OF SIENA *(page 152)* Catherine was born in 1347 and became a nun at the age of sixteen. She

gained her reputation for holiness because of her good work among the poor of Siena and because of her visions and the strict life she led. This kind of person is sometimes called a "mystic," and it was as a mystic that Catherine became respected by popes and other rulers.

After a prolonged agony of three months, she died at the age of just thirty-two. Her early death in 1380 was almost certainly the result of the long periods she spent fasting.

She never learned to write, but more than four hundred of the letters she dictated have survived.

CHRISTOPHER *(page 72)* There is little evidence to indicate when Christopher lived or even if he ever really existed, and as a result his name was removed from the official list of Roman Catholic saints in 1969.

Despite that, people still consider him to be the patron saint of those on journeys and (these days) of motorists. People often say the words "Saint Christopher protect" as a prayer before setting off on a journey. This is a reminder of the medieval belief: "If you see the image or picture of Saint Christopher on any morning, you will be protected all day from sudden death."

Saint Christopher is still much revered in the Eastern Church, where it is said that he was born in Toledo in Spain and lived in the first half of the third century.

His name in Greek, Christophoros, means "the one who carries Christ."

CLARE *(page 144)* Clare was born in 1194 and died in 1253. In 1958 she was named as the patron saint of television. She was chosen for this title because, at Christmas in the year 1252, while in her convent at Saint Damian, she "saw" in her mind a church service that was taking place at Assisi.

CLEMENT *(page 54)* Clement was the third man after Peter to be bishop of Rome. Because of the way that he was put to death (around the year 101) by being tied to an anchor and thrown into the sea, he is still respected for his connection with the sea. Seaside churches are sometimes named after him for this reason.

COLUMBA OF IONA *(page 110)* Columba (also known as Colm, Colum, Columbkill, or Columcille) was born in Donegal in 521, and one of his ancestors was a high king of Ireland. Columba became a monk and later a priest and founded many monasteries and churches in Ireland. He moved to Iona in 563. It was said of him in later years: "He had the face of an angel, he was of excellent nature, polished in speech, holy in deed . . . and loving unto all." By then he truly deserved to be known as Columba the Dove. He died in his little church on Iona. This happened exactly one week after Christianity was established at the opposite end of the British Isles when another saint, Augustine, baptized the king of Kent.

CONSTANTINE *(page 78)* The son of Constantius and Helena, Constantine was proclaimed emperor at York in England in the year 306. After gaining full control of the empire at the Battle of Milvian Bridge in 312, he rebuilt the ancient city of Byzantium (now Istanbul), which he renamed Constantinople.

In 321, he made Sunday a public holiday so Christians could worship on that day. Although he did much to help the Christian faith, he was not himself baptized until shortly before his death in 337.

He is so highly thought of in the Eastern Church that he is described there as the Thirteenth Apostle.

CORRIE TEN BOOM *(page 192)* Corrie (born in 1892) and her sister Betsie (who was two years older than Corrie) lived in the Dutch town of Haarlem. Because they were Christians, not Jews, they could have lived free of the Nazi threats their Jewish friends faced.

Betsie died in Ravensbruck, but toward the end of the war, Corrie was released. In 1968, she was acclaimed in Israel for her work in helping the Jewish people.

Corrie ten Boom is not officially a saint.

CUTHBERT *(page 118)* Cuthbert was born in either 634 or 635 and became a monk in about 651. He left the mainland for the life of a hermit on Inner Farne in 676. His boyhood friend's odd remark (that God had marked him out to teach grown-ups) came true in 684 when Cuthbert was persuaded to return to become bishop of Hexham. The following year, he "swapped" with another bishop to become bishop of Lindisfarne.

He died on Inner Farne in 687 and was first buried on Lindisfarne. But when the Vikings came raiding, his body was moved to other places, eventually being taken to Durham where it now rests in the cathedral.

CYRIL AND METHODIUS *(page 128)* The two brothers came from Thessalonika in northern Greece. Cyril (who was born in 827 and was also known as Constantine) became a teacher at the university in Constantinople while Methodius (born twelve years earlier in 815) was a magistrate. They then both became priests (and Methodius also became a monk), and in the year 861, they journeyed to Russia. Cyril is often credited with having invented the Russian, or Cyrillic, alphabet.

They were invited to Moravia in 863.

The younger brother, Cyril, died first in 869. Methodius did not die until 885. The two men are remembered as "the Apostles of the Slavs," and in 1980, Pope John Paul II proclaimed them patronal saints of Europe (along with Benedict). Despite their success in converting Moravia, that country eventually became part of the Western rather than the Eastern Church.

DAVID *(page 108)* David (or, in Welsh, Dewi) was the son of a Welsh prince. His mother's name was Non and

she too became a saint. David is thought to have been born in the year 520 near the present town of St. David's. The ruins of a small chapel dedicated to his mother can be seen near the cathedral that bears his name.

The story of his life was not written down until about five hundred years after his death in 601 and so we cannot rely on every detail being true. Even so, he was certainly a very holy man and is the only Welsh saint to be officially recognized in the Roman Catholic Church.

DIETRICH BONHOEFFER (*page 194*) Dietrich Bonhoeffer was born in Breslau in 1906 in what was then Prussia but is now part of Poland. He became a minister in the Lutheran Church, and after studying and working in Rome and New York, he became a lecturer at the University of Berlin in 1931.

He was imprisoned in Berlin in 1943. He used his time there to write several books, which were published after his death.

Dietrich Bonhoeffer is not officially a saint.

ELIZABETH *SEE* *ZECHARIAH AND ELIZABETH*

ELIZABETH ANN SETON (*page 174*) Elizabeth was born in 1774. After only nine years of marriage, she was widowed in 1803. After joining the Roman Catholic Church in 1805, she moved to Baltimore. In 1809, she made her vows and became known as Mother Seton. She opened several day schools and, with other teachers, moved to Emmitsburg. There they formed a community that became known as the Sisters of Charity of St. Joseph. Besides teaching, they cared for the poor and for orphaned children. She died in 1821 when she was forty-seven.

Elizabeth was the first native-born citizen of the United States of America to be made a saint.

ETHELBERT (*page 112*) King Ethelbert was born in 560 and was baptized as a Christian at the festival of Pentecost in 597. He believed that people should never be forced to become Christians, but many followed his example. He also gave much help to Augustine and his followers and arranged for the building of the first Saint Paul's Cathedral in London. He died in 616.

FRANCIS OF ASSISI (*page 140*) Francis was born in 1181 or 1182 and was originally named John. Francis (or, in Italian, Francesco, meaning "little Frenchman") was a nickname he was given because his father often went to France on business. The turning point of Francis's life came in 1206 when he left his family. In 1210, the pope allowed him to set up his new order of monks, or friars, and the Rule by which they lived was accepted by the pope in 1221 and, in a slightly different form, again in 1223. By this time, Francis was the leader of 5,000 friars. He died on 3 October 1226, and in 1979, he was declared the patron saint of ecologists, or environmentalists.

FRANCIS XAVIER (*page 164*) Francis was, like Ignatius Loyola, the son of a Spanish nobleman. He was born in 1506 in the castle of Xavier in the Basque country in northern Spain. After forming the Society of Jesus with Ignatius, he journeyed to Rome and then to Portugal. It was at the request of the king of Portugal that he went east to India.

In the ten very full years that he spent in the East, he is said to have personally baptized several hundred thousand people. He died, aged just forty-six, in 1552.

GABRIEL *SEE* *MICHAEL, GABRIEL, AND RAPHAEL*

GEORGE (*page 70*) Because the story of the dragon is only a legend and because many other fantastic tales are told about Saint George, some people say he never existed. However, in the year 495, the pope of those days named George among the saints of the church. The story of his battle with the dragon seems to have been first told many years after that. It is said to have happened either near Beirut in Lebanon or near the city of Silene in what is now Libya in North Africa. George is believed to have died around the year 300.

George's courage has always been highly regarded in the Eastern Church and in Palestine. When English soldiers were fighting there in battles known as the Crusades, they adopted this brave soldier as their protector, and in the year 1212, George became the patron saint of England. He is also a patron saint of Portugal and of many other places.

GERASIMUS (*page 96*) Gerasimus came from Lycia in Asia Minor (which is now Turkey) but spent most of his life in Palestine and Egypt. About 455 he founded a "laura" near Jericho. A laura was a colony of anchorites who lived in separate huts. Although they lived alone, they were under the rule of a senior monk known as an abbot. Gerasimus died sometime around the year 475.

The story of Gerasimus is sometimes (wrongly) told about another saint, Saint Jerome.

GREGORY (*page 112*) Gregory was born in Rome in 540 and grew up to become a monk. He journeyed to Constantinople but returned to Rome a few years later and in 590 reluctantly became the first monk to be made pope. But he proved to be a great organizer, sending missionaries to spread the Christian gospel throughout western Europe. Besides this, he did a lot to help the poor.

He loved music and encouraged a special kind of chanting in church services. This is now known as Gregorian chant or "plainsong." He also reorganized the calendar and wrote many books. Eight hundred of his letters and sermons have survived. Even in his lifetime, he was famous for his huge bald head. He died in 604.

GREGORY NAZIANZEN (*page 86*) Gregory was born in 329. His father was bishop of Nazianzus, a town a hundred miles southwest of Caesarea. After Gregory left Athens

(where he studied law), he became a priest, and in the year 372, his friend, Basil, bishop of Caesarea, arranged for him to become a bishop. He hated this, for he believed he was unworthy of such a position, and their friendship weakened. Even so, after Basil's death, Gregory preached a great sermon remembering their happy days together in "golden Athens." He himself died ten years after Basil, in 389. (See also Basil the Great.)

GREGORY (THE WONDER-WORKER) *(page 62)* Gregory was born in the district of Pontus in 213. When he died in 270, he was widely revered for his wisdom.

HELENA *(page 78)* Helena (or Helen) was born in Asia Minor (now Turkey) in 255 and, at the age of fifteen, became the wife of Emperor Constantius. After twenty years, but before he became emperor, Constantius divorced Helena.

When Helena was in her seventies, some years after her conversion to Christianity, she journeyed to the Holy Land and she died there in 330. It is said that while she was there, she discovered the cross on which Jesus died and also the robe he wore before his crucifixion.

There is also an English legend, which claims that she was not born in Asia but at Colchester in England. According to the legend her father was a fun-loving local king, a merry old soul, King Cole.

HILDA OF WHITBY *(page 116)* Hilda was born in 614, the grand-niece of a king. She became a nun when she was thirty-three. Aidan persuaded her to start the Hartlepool community in 649 and she moved to Whitby in 657. Five of her monks became bishops and, under her leadership, Whitby developed as an important place of study and learning.

She died in 680.

IGNATIUS OF ANTIOCH *(page 54)* Ignatius was born about the year 35, became bishop of Antioch in the year 60, and was put to death in about the year 101—probably in the arena in Rome known as the Colosseum.

IGNATIUS OF LOYOLA *(page 162)* Ignatius was born in the castle of Loyola in northeastern Spain in 1491. He was wounded when he was aged thirty and started his studies at university in the year 1526. In the summer of 1556, while in Rome, he suffered from fever. His doctors did not think it would have serious consequences, but Ignatius knew he was near death. On 30 July 1556, he asked for a last blessing, but he was told he was in no immediate danger. The next day he died.

JAMES CHALMERS *(page 182)* James Chalmers was born in a town named Ardishaig in Scotland in 1841 and attended the local Congregationalist Church. In time, he joined the London Missionary Society and trained at their college.

In 1865, he married and became a minister, and he left England the following year. He was moved to New Guinea in 1877. He introduced the gospel to the island and also established peace among the coastal peoples.

He was not only fearless, but also always tactful and cool. When asked what prompted one tribe to give up cannibalism, an old chief answered, "Tamate said, 'You must give up man-eating,' so we did."

James Chalmers and Oliver Tomkins were killed in 1901 and are not officially saints.

JANANI LUWUM *(page 198)* Janani Luwum was born in 1922. By 1948, he was a young schoolteacher and became a Christian. At once, he started teaching about the dangers of alcohol and tobacco. He became a priest in 1956 and later studied in both Canterbury and London. Back in Uganda, he quickly became an admired leader of its church. Just three years after his return, he was made bishop of northern Uganda.

Two years later, Idi Amin, then an army officer, seized power and began ruling Uganda by fear, violence, and corruption. In the midst of this, in 1974, Luwum was elected archbishop of Uganda, Rwanda, Burundi, and Boga-Zaire.

In February 1976, he protested to Amin against all acts of violence by the army and secret police. Luwum's life was in danger from that day on—until Amin finally had him killed in 1977.

Amin was overthrown by invading Tanzanian forces in 1979. He fled abroad and escaped justice.

Archbishop Luwum is not officially a saint but is remembered as a martyr by many churches.

JOACHIM AND ANNE *(page 14)* Joachim and Anne are not mentioned in the Gospels. Their stories are found in the Gospel of James, which is not in the Bible. It was written in the second century.

JOAN OF ARC *(page 154)* Joan of Arc (or Jeanne d'Arc, also known as "the Maid") was born in Domremy in the Lorraine about 1412 and became France's greatest heroine. It was in 1429 that she inspired the French army to recapture Orleans and persuaded the dauphin, Charles, to be crowned. She was captured by the Burgundians in 1430 who sold her to their English allies. She was tried and burned at the stake as a witch in Rouen on 30 May 1431. She was not yet nineteen.

In 1456, the pope decreed that her conviction was false and that she was a true "child of God." It took more than 450 years before the church decided she was indeed a saint. She was made a saint because of her holiness and faithfulness to God's word; not because of her bravery.

JOHN *(page 26)* John is mentioned many times in the Bible but these may be references to as many as three persons:

1 There was John the disciple Jesus loved. His story is told in the four Gospels.

2 There was John the Evangelist, who wrote the fourth Gospel, the Gospel according to John. It is possible that John the Evangelist also wrote all or most of the three letters known as the Epistles of John, which are part of the New Testament.

3 There was John the Divine. He wrote the last book of the Bible, Revelation, which is a vision of heaven. John the Divine was kept as a prisoner on a Mediterranean island named Patmos.

For many centuries, Christians believed that John the Disciple, John the Evangelist, and John the Divine were the same person. This is by no means impossible but it is more likely that they were different people.

JOHN BOSCO *(page 178)* John Bosco (who was born in 1815) eventually achieved his dream of creating an order. It was called the Salesian Order, or Society, (after a saint named Francis of Sales). By the time of John's death in 1888 there were 250 houses of the Salesian Society in all parts of the world. These contained 130,000 needy children, and from these 18,000 educated apprentices left every year. A similar order for girls was started in 1872.

Don Bosco never punished the boys. He said: "As far as possible avoid punishing. Try to gain love before inspiring fear."

JOHN CHRYSOSTOM *(page 90)* John Chrysostom was born in Antioch in about 347. After first training as a lawyer and then becoming a monk, he became a priest and preached his famous sermons in Antioch before becoming bishop of Constantinople in 397. When John was finally banished from Constantinople, he was made to leave on foot. He journeyed many days with the sun burning down on his bald head. He eventually died on that journey in the year 407, aged sixty.

JOHN MARK *(page 52)* It is thought that Mark died in about the year 68. In many paintings he is shown dressed as a bishop and with a pen in his hand.

JOHN THE BAPTIST *(page 18)* John was the son of a man named Zechariah and his wife, Elizabeth, who was the cousin of Mary, the mother of Jesus. John was born six months before Jesus, his birth having been announced by an angel in a way similar to how Jesus' birth was announced to Mary by Gabriel. When he grew up, John preached by the River Jordan. He is sometimes called "the forerunner of Jesus," the one who came before Jesus to prepare people to hear Jesus.

JOSEPH *(page 14)* All that is known for certain about Joseph is found in the Gospels. According to tradition he was an old man and may have been a widower when he married Mary, but there is no proof of this.

JOSEPH OF ARIMATHEA *(page 32)* The Bible says that Joseph asked for Jesus' body in order to give it a proper burial. There are many other stories told about Joseph but there is no proof that they are true. However, there is some evidence that Joseph did travel to other countries with Philip, another disciple, telling the story of Jesus. Some say Joseph visited Genoa in what is now Italy; others say he went to France with three of Jesus' followers who were all named Mary.

Another story suggests he journeyed as far as England, taking with him the cup that Jesus had used at his last supper with the disciples, a cup that is sometimes known as "the holy grail." It is said that he went to a place named Glastonbury and built the first Christian church in England there.

Yet another legend suggests that he was an uncle to Jesus and that, when Jesus was still a boy, Joseph took him to various places including Cornwall in southwest England.

LADY JULIAN OF NORWICH *(page 150)* The person we know as Julian was born in 1342. On 8 May 1373, when she was thirty, she received a series of sixteen "revelations" during a sudden and severe illness. She became an anchorite (like Gerasimus—see page 96), living permanently alone in a cell attached to Saint Julian's church in Norwich. She almost certainly took the name by which we know her from that church. For twenty years, she meditated on the visions she had been granted and wrote them down in *The Revelations of Divine Love*, the first book to be written by a woman in English.

We have evidence that Julian of Norwich was alive in the year 1413. We also know that in 1429, a Norwich man left her money in his will—by then she must have been eighty-seven—but we have no evidence that she was then still alive.

The Lady Julian is not officially regarded as a saint in the Roman Catholic Church.

KENTIGERN *(page 110)* Kentigern was born in Scotland in 518 and became a monk. Over the years, he was given the nickname "Mungo," meaning "darling." He died in 603.

LAWRENCE *(page 64)* Lawrence (sometimes spelled Laurence) came from Spain to Rome to serve Pope Sixtus. He was quick-witted and probably enjoyed a good joke. Although famous for the way in which it is reported that he died on the gridiron, he is much more likely to have been beheaded, according to the Roman law of the time. Even so, he is the patron saint of cooks!

However he died, he is remembered and respected in many countries and has given his name to a river in Canada, a cathedral in Spain, and to many churches around the world.

His death probably happened in about the year 258.

LUCIAN TAPIEDI *(page 190)* Lucian Tapiedi was born in 1921 in the village of Taupota, on the northern coast of

Papua. His father died when Lucian was still young. Lucian was taught at mission schools, and in 1939 he entered a local teacher training college. Here he became known as a hardworking and cheerful student who enjoyed sports and music. He became a teacher in 1941 and was killed the following year.

Although Lucian is not officially regarded as a saint himself, the New Guinea Martyrs are remembered on 2 September; Saints and Martyrs of Australia and the Pacific are remembered on 20 September.

LUKE *(page 52)* The Bible says that besides making the voyage to Rome with Paul, Luke had earlier joined Paul on parts of his second and third journeys. It is believed that Luke was one of the first non-Jewish followers of Jesus and that he died at the age of 84 some time before the end of the first century.

MARGARET CLITHEROW *(page 168)* Margaret Middleton was born in York in 1556. At the age of fifteen, she married a much older man, John Clitherow, and soon after (for reasons we do not know) became a Roman Catholic. Because of this she was imprisoned, but during her time in prison she learned to read and write. On her release, she began sheltering Catholic priests in her home, with her husband's knowledge. She was put to death in the year 1586.

She was made a saint in 1970, one of the "Forty Martyrs of England and Wales"—a group of people who gave their lives for their faith during the Reformation.

MARGARET OF SCOTLAND *(page 134)* Margaret was born in Hungary, probably in the year 1045, and was linked to two royal families. Her father was the son of an English king, Edmund Ironside; her mother was related to King (or Saint) Stephen of Hungary. Margaret arrived in England in 1057 and left for Scotland in 1067.

She did much to help link the Scottish church (which still clung to its old Celtic ways, despite the Synod of Whitby) with the wider church. She was the first to bring Benedictine monks to Scotland, and she re-established Iona as a holy place.

She died in 1093 and is one of comparatively few married women saints.

MARTIN LUTHER KING JR *(page 196)* Martin Luther King Jr was born in 1929. His father was the minister of a Baptist church in Atlanta, Georgia. Martin Luther King Jr went to college in Atlanta and was ordained when he was just nineteen. After graduating, he became pastor of a church in Montgomery.

The cost that he and his family paid for his work against segregation was great. They faced death threats, their home was bombed, and he suffered police harassment and imprisonment.

He was awarded the Nobel Peace prize in 1964 and was only thirty-nine years old when he was assassinated in 1968.

Martin Luther King Jr is not officially regarded as a saint.

MARTIN OF TOURS *(page 88)* Martin was born in around 316 in what is now Hungary and brought up in Italy, the son of an officer in the Roman army. While still a youth, he himself joined the army. After leaving the army, he became a Christian and (later) a monk. In either 370 or 371, by popular demand, he was made bishop of Tours in France—even though he was reluctant this should happen.

He could have lived in a bishop's palace. Instead, he shared his new wealth and lived simply, like a monk. He usually wore animal skins and was famous for never combing his hair. Until his death in 397, he used to travel throughout France, teaching the message of Jesus that people should love one another, help those in need and share what they have. He also preached against the death penalty.

MARY *(page 12)* Because she was given the unique privilege of being the mother of Jesus, Mary has always been considered extremely important among the saints. Some information about her life can be found in the Bible. For example, we know she was alive when Jesus was crucified. There are also many stories about her in other ancient sources—such as the belief that she was no more than a teenager when she gave birth to Jesus.

MARY OF MAGDALA *(page 34)* She was also known as Mary Magdalene or "the Magdalene" after her home-town. The Gospels show that she was one of the most loyal followers of Jesus. On the Sunday after Jesus was crucified, she went to the garden near the tomb where his body had been buried. There, in that garden, she became the first person to see the risen Jesus.

MARY THE EGYPTIAN *(page 98)* As a young woman, Mary was famous for her beauty—and for her sinfulness. After visiting Jerusalem she gave up all her old habits and went to live a life of great hardship in the desert. Her sacrifice is still remembered, especially in the Russian Church, on the fifth Sunday during Lent. Her dates are unknown, but she lived in the fifth century.

MARY, THE MOTHER OF JAMES AND JOHN *(page 34)* The Bible says that this Mary was present when Jesus was crucified and when he was buried and the great stone was rolled across the entrance to his grave.

MARY, THE MOTHER OF JOHN MARK *(page 34)* Although little is known about her for certain, it is clear from the Gospels that this Mary was certainly one of a number of women (not all of whom were named Mary!) who did so much to help Jesus and his followers, both during his life and in the months and years that followed.

MARY, WIFE OF CLEOPHAS *(page 34)* In the Bible she is also described as "the other Mary." She is remembered along with Mary of Magdala and Mary, the mother of James and John on the Festival of the Three Marys, 25 May.

MATTHEW *(page 24)* Matthew is most famous because one of the Gospels, the books in the Bible that describe the life of Jesus, bears his name. It is possible that he wrote it himself when he was a very old man, but it is much more likely that it was written by someone else. Most people now believe it was not written before the year 70 and might not have been written until the year 105. Also, whoever wrote Matthew's Gospel borrowed quite a bit from Mark's Gospel. If Matthew's Gospel was written by Matthew the taxman, he wouldn't have needed to do so because (as a close disciple) he would have known firsthand all that Jesus said and did.

MAXIMILIAN KOLBE *(page 188)* Born Raymond Kolbe in Poland in 1894, he became a Franciscan friar when he was only sixteen. He was sent to study in Rome, where he was ordained a priest in 1918. He was also a very clever scientist and mathematician.

Father Maximilian returned to Poland in 1919 and, with his fellow friars, began using modern printing methods to spread the Gospel. They published a daily newspaper and a monthly magazine. Maximilian also started a radio station and planned to build a film studio, believing these were important new ways to tell the world about Jesus.

Before the war, he worked for a time in Japan. He was executed in 1941.

METHODIUS *SEE CYRIL AND METHODIUS*

MICHAEL *(page 208)*, **GABRIEL AND RAPHAEL** *(page 206)* The Bible says there are seven archangels, or chief angels. Three of them are regarded as saints. They are the only non-human saints.

NICHOLAS *(page 84)* There are many stories told about this popular saint but very little is known about him for certain. It seems he was born into a Christian family and may well have been imprisoned during the Great Persecution when Diocletian was emperor of Rome. He died in 350 and was buried at Myra, but much later, in the year 1087, Italian sailors stole his remains and took them to Bari on the east coast of what is now Italy.

Because he once saved the lives of three boys and, on another occasion, the lives of some sailors, he is the patron saint of both children and sailors. He is also patron of Russia and of pawnbrokers. Pawnbrokers use as their sign three golden balls, a reminder of the three round bags of gold Nicholas gave the three young women of Myra.

NINO OF GEORGIA *(page 82)* A Christian girl, born in Cappadocia (in what is now Turkey), Nino was captured and taken as a slave to Georgia. She is considered responsible for introducing the faith to that country, one of the first outside the Roman empire to become fully Christian. She died in the year 340. In some places and at various times in history, she has also been known as Christiana.

OSCAR ROMERO *(page 202)* Oscar Arnulfo Romero y Galdames was born in 1917 in a town called Ciudad Barrios, high up in the mountains in the eastern part of the tiny country of El Salvador. Like most Christians in that country, he was a Roman Catholic. By the age of thirteen, he was sure he wanted to become a priest.

That happened in the year 1942, when he was twenty-five. He worked all his life in various parts of his country, becoming bishop in 1970 and archbishop in 1977. Despite the fact that he was loved by many of his own people, there were those who believed he was not popular with some church leaders in Rome. He has not officially been named as a saint.

OSWALD *(page 114)* Oswald was born in 604 and became king of Northumbria or the northern part of England. He did much to make his land a Christian country, with the help of Aidan, but King Oswald was killed in battle in 642 by Penda, the pagan king of Mercia which lay to the south of Northumbria. Aidan brought his body back to Bamburgh for burial.

PATRICK *(page 102)* Patrick's birthplace is unknown but it may have been in the west of England or Scotland. He was born around the year 390 and was probably part Welsh and part Roman.

For thirty years he spread the Christian faith throughout Ireland, the first country in the West outside the Roman empire to hear the Christian gospel. During those years, Patrick established many churches, monasteries and schools. He died when he was about 70.

PAUL *(page 44)* Paul was a Jew who came from Tarsus, which was then in Cilicia, an area that is now part of southern Turkey. He worked as a tent maker but was also known as a learned and wise student of the law.

He was a Pharisee and also the son of a Pharisee. The Pharisees were people who spent much time studying God's laws and who tried very hard to keep those laws in every detail. Many Pharisees were good and holy men but not all of them were as good as they pretended to be. At first they had agreed with Jesus' teaching, but some of them became jealous of his popularity and turned against him.

Besides being a Jew, Paul was also born a free "citizen" of the Roman empire. This was a rank that gave him legal protection and other rights.

He probably died between the years 64 and 67.

PAUL THE HERMIT *(page 60)* All that is known about Paul the Hermit comes from his life story, which was written by Saint Jerome. He was probably born around the year 230 and died in 342. Learned scholars have argued about how much of this story is true. Whatever the case, many have paid homage to him as the first Christian hermit.

PETER *(pages 28, 40)* We know that Peter was a fisherman named Simon before he met Jesus. He came from Bethsaida on the shore of Lake Galilee. His father was named Jonas. He had a brother named Andrew and was married. A brief remark in one of Paul's letters in the Bible suggests that, when Peter later went to other countries to spread the word of Jesus, his wife went with him. A legend (which is almost certainly untrue) suggests they had a daughter named Petronilla.

It is very likely that Peter helped Mark write his Gospel and he may have helped write part of the first letter of Peter, but it is unlikely that the Aramaic-speaking fisherman from Galilee actually wrote it himself since he probably would not have been able to write Greek.

It is almost certain that Peter died in the year 64.

POLYCARP *(page 58)* Polycarp was born in 70. As a boy, he was taught by John the Evangelist. By 107, he was bishop of Smyrna in Asia Minor, and he remained so until his death. He visited Rome shortly before the end of his life but was arrested on his return. The story of his martyrdom (the *Martyricum Polycarpi*) has survived and gives an account of his trial and death. His own Epistle to the Philippians has also survived.

RAPHAEL *SEE* **MICHAEL, GABRIEL,** *AND* **RAPHAEL**

ROSE OF LIMA *(page 170)* Rose was determined to give up much that life could offer and even to seek out suffering for herself as a way of saying sorry to God for all the sin and wrongdoing in the world. Today, the idea of somebody making him or herself a victim for other sinners seems very unusual. It is easy to forget that Jesus himself did exactly the same thing.

She was born in 1586, and it was at the age of twenty that Rose officially became a member of a religious order, though she continued to live in her garden shack. She died in 1617 and was made a saint in 1671, the first American to become a saint.

SEBASTIAN *(page 68)* Although Sebastian was born in France, then known as Gaul, his parents came from Milan in Italy and he was brought up in that city. The year of his birth is not known for certain, but he was put to death in about 288.

SERAPHIM OF SAROV *(page 172)* He was born in 1759 and his original name was Prokhor. His father was a builder at Kursk in Russia. When he became a monk at the age of nineteen, he took the name Seraphim. From 1794, he lived as a hermit in the woods near his abbey but later lived alone inside the abbey. At this time his "hero" (whom he tried to copy) was Saint Antony of Egypt.

From 1825, he welcomed visitors and was soon recognized as a *staretz*. This Russian word means "wise man," an older person who gives good advice. Seraphim is probably the most famous Russian *staretz* of the period.

Many people now visited him. Sometimes more than a hundred came in one day. It was said that he healed the sick and could answer questions before they were asked. He died in 1833.

SERGIUS OF RADONEZH *(page 148)* Sergius was born in 1314 in Rostov in Russia of devout Orthodox Christian parents. When he was baptized, he was named Bartholomew. He was fifteen when the family was forced to flee to Radonezh (fifty miles north of Moscow).

Sergius's group of monks grew to become known as the great Monastery of the Holy Trinity. Hundreds of years later, it was one of the last to remain open when the Communists came to power and opposed all religious activity.

Sergius is perhaps the best loved of the Russian saints and was a very gentle man. He never wrote anything, and he drew his knowledge less from reading and more from prayer. He died in 1392 and is the patron saint of Russia.

SIMEON THE STYLITE *(page 94)* Simeon was born in 390 in Sisan in what is now Turkey. Although it may seem unlikely that a man could live on top of a pillar for thirty-seven years, that is exactly what Simeon the Stylite did. There are several eyewitness accounts of his odd way of behaving. He was consulted by emperors and many people brought him their problems. He died in the year 459.

Other holy men imitated Simeon and they came to be known as the "pillar saints."

SIMON *SEE* **PETER**

SIMON OF CYRENE *(page 30)* Simon is remembered for his important role mentioned in the Gospels of helping Jesus to carry the cross when he was too weak to carry it himself. Cyrene is now named Shahhat and is in Libya.

SPIRIDION *(page 80)* Spiridion worked as a shepherd on his home island of Cyprus before becoming bishop of Tremithus on that island. He was present at the Council of Nicea and whatever the truth of the story about the mules, we know that Spiridion certainly took part in other church meetings around that time and that he died in about 348.

STANISLAUS KOSTKA *(page 166)* Stanislaus was born in 1550 at Rostkovo in Poland and died in Rome just before his eighteenth birthday in 1568. He is one of the most popular saints of Poland.

When the church held an investigation to see whether

Stanislaus should be considered a saint, both Paul and the tutor gave evidence, blaming each other for causing him to run away to Rome. Later, they both became Jesuits themselves.

STEPHEN *(page 42)* Stephen was the first follower of Jesus to lose his life because of what he believed. A person who dies for his or her beliefs is known as a martyr—so Stephen was the first Christian martyr. Because of this, his saint's day is the very first day after Jesus' own birthday.

STEPHEN OF HUNGARY *(page 132)* Born in 975, King Stephen holds a respected place in Hungarian history. His last years were saddened by ill health and by the fact that his only son, Emeric, died young and could not be king after him. Stephen died in 1038.

TERESA OF CALCUTTA *(page 200)* Agnes Gonxha Bojaxhiu was born of Albanian parents in Skopje (in Macedonia, formerly part of Yugoslavia) in 1910. While still at school, she heard of a group of nuns working in India. She joined their order (at first in Ireland) in 1928, at the age of eighteen, taking the name Teresa in memory of Thérèse of Lisieux.

The following year she was sent to work in India. In 1937, she took her final vows. In 1948, Sister Teresa was given permission to leave the convent to start, first, a school for the poorest children in Calcutta and, later, her Home for the Dying. In 1979, she won the Nobel prize. The nuns who continue her work are known as the Sisters of Charity.

Mother Teresa is not officially a saint.

THÉRÈSE OF LISIEUX *(page 184)* Thérèse (which is the original French spelling of Teresa) Martin was born in northern France in 1873. She was the daughter of a watchmaker (all five of whose daughters became nuns). She entered the Carmelite convent of Lisieux in Normandy in 1888. Her life there was uneventful and short. She died nine years later of tuberculosis in 1897.

THOMAS *(page 36)* Thomas was one of Jesus' twelve main disciples. One of the times he is mentioned in the Gospels is at the time of the Last Supper, just before Jesus was arrested. While Jesus was telling his disciples he was about to leave them, Thomas interrupted him, "Lord, we do not know where you are going." Jesus replied, "I am the way."

THOMAS AQUINAS *(page 146)* Thomas was born in 1225 and was educated by Benedictine monks before he joined the newly formed Dominicans. After finishing his studies, he taught in the universities of Paris, Orvieto, and Naples.

He was a patient, good-natured man and was genuinely humble.

Among the ideas he wrote about (and which are part of the teaching of the Roman Catholic Church) was his belief that contraception and abortion are wrong. He died in the year 1274.

THOMAS BECKET *(page 138)* Thomas was born in London in 1118. His parents were well-off and he was given a good education. He studied to become a lawyer, and then, in 1155, King Henry II made him royal chancellor. It was seven years later, in 1162, that the king made him archbishop of Canterbury. Their first quarrel happened in less than two years' time and Thomas's murder took place in 1170.

THOMAS MORE *(page 160)* Thomas More was born in 1478. After qualifying as a barrister, he entered Parliament in 1504 and married the same year. He had four children but was closest to his eldest daughter, Margaret. King Henry soon became aware of his skills and appointed him to several important jobs. In 1529, Thomas reluctantly accepted the post of lord chancellor, resigning when Henry divorced Catherine of Aragon. After Henry made himself head of the church in England, Thomas (who believed strongly in the unity of one church) would not deny his allegiance to the pope. In 1534, he was imprisoned and, a year later, executed.

TIKHON OF MOSCOW AND ALL RUSSIA *(page 186)* Vasily Ivanovich Belavin was born in 1865 in a Russian town called Toropets, where his father was the local priest. While studying to become a priest himself, Vasily was given his nickname "the Patriarch" by the other students,

He also became a monk and took the name Tikhon. In 1898, he was made a bishop in the Russian Orthodox Church—not in Russia, but in the United States of America, where he looked after that church in the Aleutian-Alaskan Diocese. Many Russians worked there as fur traders and fishermen.

For seven more years, he lived in America, first in San Francisco and then in New York. In 1907, he was appointed archbishop of Yaroslavl and Rostov, back home in Russia. Unlike some bishops of the time, he always lived very simply. When he was elected patriarch of Moscow and all Russia in 1917, "patriarch" was no longer just a nickname. He died in 1925.

TIMOTHY *(page 50)* Timothy was one of Paul's closest friends and most trusted followers. Although two of the books in the Bible are named Paul's epistles (or letters) to Timothy, it is unlikely that they were actually written by Paul himself. Timothy is said to have been martyred in the year 97 because he was a Christian.

TITUS *(page 50)* Titus died in the year 96 and was buried in a city named Gortyna, which was the capital of Crete in Roman times.

THE TWELVE DISCIPLES OF JESUS *(page 20)* Eleven of Jesus' twelve special disciples became known as saints.

Their names were:

Simon, later known as Peter, and his brother Andrew; James and his brother John, whose father's name was Zebedee; Matthew; Thomas; Philip; James, sometimes known as James the Less, the son of a man named Alphaeus; Bartholomew, also known as Nathaniel; Simon from Cana, also known as Simon the Zealot; Thaddeus, also known as Jude and said to be the brother of James the Less.

The twelfth disciple (who is not a saint) was Judas Iscariot, who betrayed Jesus.

VALENTINE *(page 68)* Little is known for certain about the two martyrs both known as Valentine, but their deaths probably happened in the year 269. The modern customs linked to Saint Valentine's Day began in England and France in the Middle Ages.

VERONICA *(page 30)* Veronica is not mentioned in the Bible. Despite the lack of historical information about her, Veronica has remained a popular saint. Because her name in Latin *vera icon* means "true image" perhaps she was only known as Veronica after meeting Jesus.

VLADIMIR THE GREAT *(page 130)* Prince Vladimir (also known as Grand Duke or Emperor) was born in 956, gained control of Russia in 980, and became a Christian in the year 988. The conversion of Russia is dated from this year. Some say he forced his subjects to become Christian. Even if that is so, this once harsh ruler became much more generous to the poor and kinder to wrongdoers after his own conversion. He died in 1015.

His name is pronounced Vla-dee-meer.

WILLIBRORD *(page 120)* Willibrord was born in Northumbria in about the year 658 and at the age of twenty went to study in Ireland. After twelve years there, he went with his eleven companions to Friesland in 690. He eventually became archbishop of Utrecht (in the Netherlands) and founded monasteries there and at Echternach, in what is now Luxembourg. He died in 739.

THE WISE MEN *(page 16)* Hundreds of years after the first century, when the Gospel story was written down, the wise men, or kings, were given names: Balthasar, Caspar, and Melchior. Balthasar means "the lord of treasures," Caspar—also known as Gaspar—means "the white one," while Melchior means "the king of light."

ZECHARIAH AND ELIZABETH *(page 14)* Nothing is known for certain about Zechariah and Elizabeth apart from what is found in Luke's Gospel. There is a tradition (which is far from certain) that Zechariah was later martyred.

ZOSIMUS *(page 98)* Surprisingly, there are at least ten saints named Zosimus! Little is known about this particular Zosimus apart from his meetings with Mary the Egyptian and the fact that he lived about four hundred years after Jesus.

 # Calendar of Saints' Days

Saints are usually remembered on the anniversary of their death. The Eastern and Western Churches do not always remember saints on the same dates. However, unless a separate Eastern date is listed, days shown are universal. Days of remembrance may also vary from one country or district to another. They may also be moved in certain years so they do not coincide with Easter or another major festival.

The Roman Catholic Church has removed some saints from its calendar but they are nevertheless shown here on their traditional dates.

JANUARY

1	Basil the Great *Eastern Church*
2	Basil the Great and Gregory Nazianzen
2	Seraphim of Sarov
4	Elizabeth Ann Seton
5	Simeon the Stylite
6	The Wise Men
7	Festival of John the Baptist *Eastern Church*
13	Kentigern (Mungo)
14	Nino of Georgia
15	Paul the Hermit
17	Antony the Great of Egypt
20	Sebastian
25	Gregory Nazianzen *Eastern Church*
25	Paul (Conversion)
26	Timothy
26	Titus
28	Thomas Aquinas
30	Festival of Basil, Gregory Nazianzen (or Gregory the Theologian as he is also known) and John Chrysostom *Eastern Church*
31	John Bosco

FEBRUARY

1	Brigid
2	Presentation of the Lord in the Temple
11	Caedmon
14	Cyril and Methodius
14	Valentine
23	Polycarp
24	Ethelbert

MARCH

1	David
5	Gerasimus
17	Joseph of Arimathea
17	Patrick of Ireland
18	Alexander
19	Joseph
20	Cuthbert
21	Benedict
24	Gabriel
25	Margaret Clitherow
25	Mary (The Annunciation)
25	Tikhon of Moscow *Eastern Church*
26	Festival of the Angel Gabriel *Eastern Church*

APRIL

1	Mary the Egyptian *Eastern Church*
4	Zosimus
6	Methodius
6	Cyril and Methodius *Eastern Church*
7	Tikhon of Moscow
9	Mary the Egyptian
9	Mary, Wife of Cleophas
16	Bernadette Soubirous
23	George
25	John Mark
29	Catherine of Siena

	30	James the Apostle (brother of John) *Eastern Church*	6	Thomas More *Anglican Churches*
MAY	1	Joseph the Worker	11	Benedict
	1	Philip and James the Less *Anglican Churches*	12	Veronica
	2	Athanasius	15	Vladimir the Great
	3	Philip and James the Less *Roman Catholic Church*	19	Seraphim of Sarov
	8	John the Evangelist *Eastern Church*	22	Mary of Magdala
	9	Christopher *Eastern Church*	23	The Wise Men
	9	Nicholas (translation of relics to Bari) *Eastern Church*	25	Christopher
	10	Simon the Apostle from Cana *Eastern Church*	25	James, son of Zebedee
	11	Cyril	26	Joachim and Anne
	21	Constantine the Great *(and, in the Eastern Church, also Helena)*	31	Ignatius of Loyola
	25	Bede	31	Joseph of Arimathea *Eastern Church*
	25	The Three Marys	AUGUST 5, 8, or 9	Oswald
	26	Augustine of Canterbury *Anglican Churches*	10	Lawrence
	27	Augustine of Canterbury	11	Clare
	30	Joan of Arc	14	Maximilian Kolbe
JUNE	5	Boniface	15	Mary (The Assumption)
	9	Columba of Iona	16	Stephen of Hungary *20 August in Hungary*
	10	Margaret of Scotland	18	Helena
	11	Barnabas	20	Bernard of Clairvaux
	11	Bartholomew (remembered with Barnabas) *Eastern Church*	23	Rose of Lima
	13	Antony of Padua	24	Bartholomew (Nathaniel)
	22	Thomas More *Roman Catholic Church*	28	Augustine of Hippo
	24	John the Baptist	29	John the Baptist (Beheading)
	29	Paul	30	Rose of Lima
	29	(Simon) Peter	31	Aidan from Iona
	29	Mary, Mother of John Mark	31	Joseph of Arimathea
	30	Festival of the Twelve Apostles (or disciples) *Eastern Church*	SEPTEMBER 1	Simeon the Stylite *Eastern Church*
JULY	3	Thomas	2	The New Guinea Martyrs
	5	Sergius of Radonezh (uncovering of the relics) *Eastern Church*	3	Gregory the Great
			4	Cuthbert
			8	Mary (Her Birthday)
			13	John Chrysostom
			20	Saints and Martyrs of Australia and the Pacific
			21	Matthew

25 Sergius of Radonezh

26 John the Evangelist (repose of)
    Eastern Church

29 Michael and All Angels

OCTOBER 1 Thérèse of Lisieux

4 Francis of Assisi

6 Thomas *Eastern Church*

9 James the Less *Eastern Church*

17 Ignatius of Antioch

18 Luke

21 Margaret Clitherow

22 Mary, the Mother of James
    and John

24 Raphael

25 The Forty Martyrs of England
    and Wales

28 Simon from Cana

28 Thaddeus (Jude)

NOVEMBER 5 Zechariah and Elizabeth

7 Willibrord

8 Festival of the Angels Gabriel,
    Michael, and Raphael
    Eastern Church

11 Martin of Tours

13 Stanislaus Kostka

13 John Chrysostom
    Eastern Church

14 Philip *Eastern Church*

16 Margaret of Scotland

16 Matthew *Eastern Church*

17 Gregory (the Wonder-Worker)

17 Hilda of Whitby

23 Clement

25 Catherine of Alexandria

30 Andrew

DECEMBER 3 Francis Xavier

6 Nicholas

8 Mary (Immaculate Conception)

12 Spiridion *Eastern Church*

14 Spiridion

15 Nino of Georgia

26 Stephen

27 John (Apostle and Evangelist)

27 Stephen *Eastern Church*

29 Thomas Becket

Acknowledgments

AKG-London: pp. 43, 97 (Scuola di San Giorgio degli Schiavoni, Venice), 114 (British Library), 120 (Kunsthistorisches Museum, Vienna), 125 (Univeritätsbibliotek, Göttingen), 131 (Tretjakov Gallery, Moscow), 149 (Univeritätsbibliotek, Göttingen), 155 (Bibliotheque Nationale, Paris), 161 (Musée Municipal, Blois), 165 (Jean-Louis Nou/Bom-Jesus Church, Old Goa, India), 167 (Museo Casa de Murillo, la Paz), 195.
Billy Graham Center Archives: p. 193.
Bodleian Library, University of Oxford: pp. 21 (ms. douce 293, fol. 11), 27 (ms. gough liturg. 2, fol. 28), 31 (ms. douce 223, fol. 7v), 35 (ms. douce 293, fol. 14v), 49 (ms. auct. t. inf. 1.10, fol. 312v), 52 (ms. e. d. clarke 10, fol. 51v), 99 (ms. rawl. d. 939, part 2, detail April), 109 top (ms. rawl. d. 939, part 2, detail), 111 (ms. gough liturg. 2, fol. 82), 123 (ms. tanner 10, fols. 57v–58r).
Bridgeman Art Library: pp. 7 top (*Saint Ignatius of Loyola* [1491–1556] [oil on canvas] by French School [17th century], Château de Versailles, France/Bridgeman Giraudon/Lauros), 141 (*St. Francis Preaching to the Birds* [1296–97] by Giotto di Bondone [c. 1266–1337], San Francesco, Upper Church, Assisi, Italy), 157 (Bibliotheque Nationale, Paris, France), 162 (*Saint Ignatius of Loyola* [1491–1556] [oil on canvas] by French School [17th century], Chateau de Versailles, France/Bridgeman Giraudon/Lauros), 174 (Victoria & Albert Museum, London, UK).
Collections: p. 168 (Michael Nicholson).
Corbis UK Ltd: pp. 7 middle (Bettmann), 36 and 62 (The State Russian Museum), 63 (Alexander Burkatowski), 67 (Francis G. Mayer), 80 (Jonathan Blair), 83 (Dean Conger), 105 bottom (Morton Beebe), 129 (Gianni Dagli Orti), 132 (Peter Wilson), 134 (Roger Tidman), 163 (Bettmann), 170 (Arte & Immagini srl), 172 (Archivo Iconografico, S.A.), 179 (Macduff Everton), 186 (Marc Garanger), 189 (Bettmann), 192 (Dave Bartruff), 196 and 197 (Flip Schulke), 201 and 203 (Bettmann).
Getty Images: p. 150 (Stone).
Amanda Hall: pp. 3, 104, 110 and borders throughout.
Hulton Archive: pp. 178, 187.
KNA–Bild: p. 199.
Keble College. By permission of the Warden and Fellows of Keble College, Oxford: pp. 89 (ms. 49, fol. 246), 137 (ms. 49, fol. 162), 139 (ms. 49, fol. 24).
Lion Publishing: pp. 48, 51; 32, 41, 74, 96 left, 98 (Dave Townsend); 13 bottom, 16, 18, 26, 30, 33 top, 42, 60, 66, 68, 73, 85, 87, 96, 105 top, 109 bottom, 118, 124 bottom, 166, 171, 180, 185, 188, 202 (John Williams).
Mary Evans Picture Library: pp. 55, 58, 183, 184.
© The National Gallery, London: pp. 17 (*The Adoration of the Kings* by Jacopo di Cione), 64 (*Saint Lawrence showing the Prefect the Treasures of the Church* by Master of the Legend of Saint Ursula), 70 (*Saint George and the Dragon* by Paolo Uccello), 75 (*Saint Catherine of Alexandria* by Carlo Crivelli), 93 (*A Bishop Saint* by Marco Zoppo),

106 (*Incidents in the Life of Saint Benedict* by Lorenzo Monaco), 144 (*A Group of Poor Clares* by Ambrogio Lorenzetti), 147 (*Saint Stephen and Saint Thomas Aquinas* by Carlo Crivelli), 152 (*The Marriage of Saint Catherine of Siena* by Lorenzo d'Alessandro da Sanseverino).
Rex Nichols: pp. 15, 22, 24, 28, 29 bottom, 44, 47, 54, 59.
Papua New Guinea Church Partnership: pp. 190, 191.
Nick Rous: p. 113.
Martin Sanders: p. 88.
Sonia Halliday Photographs: pp. 4, 5, 6, 7 bottom, 13 top, 14, 19, 20, 23, 25, 29 top, 33 bottom, 40, 45, 46, 50, 53, 61, 69, 72, 78, 79 top, 84, 86, 90, 95, 103 right, 108, 112, 115, 116, 122, 135, 138, 140, 141 top (birds), 142, 143, 145, 151, 181, 206, 207, 208, 209.
Ultimate Symbol Inc.: pp. 79, 103 left.
University College. By permission of the Master and Fellows of University College: p. 119 (ms. 165, fol. 35).
Westminster Abbey: p. 198.

Picture research courtesy of Lion Publishing plc, Zooid Pictures Limited and Sonia Halliday Photographs.

Extract on p. 194 by Dietrich Bonhoeffer from "Powers of Good" in *Letters and Papers from Prison*, 1971, used by permission of SCM Press (UK and world, excluding USA); reprinted with the permission of Scribner, an imprint of Simon & Schuster Adult Publishing Group, from *Letters and Papers from Prison, Revised, Enlarged Edition* by Dietrich Bonhoeffer. Copyright © 1953, 1967, 1971 by SCM Press, Ltd (USA).

Extract on p. 200 by Mother Teresa used by permission.